Pelican Books

Can Pakistan Survive?

Tel. 0272 561658.

Tariq Ali was born in Lahore in 1943. He was educated in Pakistan and came to Oxford in 1963 where he studied Politics, Philosophy and Economics, at Exeter College. He served as a member of the Bertrand Russell War Crimes Tribunal and visited Kampuchea and Vietnam in 1967. He was editor of the *Black Dwarf* and the *Red Mole* during the late sixties and early seventies. He has written on current affairs for the *New Statesman*, *New Left Review* and the *Guardian*, and is the author of a number of books. He was the first political analyst to predict the break-up of Pakistan in *Pakistan: Military Rule or People's Power* (1970). His most recent books include *1968 and After* (1978) and *Trotsky for Beginners* (1980).

Tariq Ali

Can Pakistan Survive?

The Death of a State

Penguin Books

Penguin Books Ltd, Harmondsworth, Middlesex, England
Penguin Books, 625 Madison Avenue, New York, New York 10022, U.S.A.
Penguin Books Australia Ltd, Ringwood, Victoria, Australia
Penguin Books Canada Ltd, 2801 John Street, Markham, Ontario, Canada L3R 1B4
Penguin Books (N.Z.) Ltd, 182–190 Wairau Road, Auckland 10, New Zealand

First published 1983

Made and printed in Great Britain by
Richard Clay (The Chaucer Press) Ltd,
Bungay, Suffolk
Set in Times

For Natasha
and her Grandparents

Contents

Preface · 9

Maps · 11

Statistical Tables · 13

1 · Origins · 15

2 · Post-Independence Realities:
   The First Decade 1947–58 · 41

3 · The Gun and the Hat:
   Military–Bureaucratic Dictatorship 1958–69 · 62

4 · The Break-Up of Pakistan 1969–71 · 83

5 · The Populist Experiment:
   Bhutto in Power 1971–7 · 99

6 · The Crisis of Legitimacy:
   Martial Law with an Islamic Face 1977–? · 133

7 · Between the Hammer and the Anvil:
   Geopolitics and the Super-Powers · 163

Appendixes:
   1 · Poem: For Dali, Who Dared to Struggle and Die · 199
   2 · Interview: Murad Khan · 200
   3 · How the Landlords Won in Sind · 210

Notes · 215

Index · 231

Preface

Pakistan has been in existence for thirty-five years. For half this period the country has been under the heel of the Pakistan Army, a mercenary force *par excellence*, whose major 'successes' have been politico-military campaigns against its own population. Since the distintegration of Pakistan and the establishment of Bangladesh in 1971–2, the ruling élites have been in search of a new identity. The collapse of populism and the execution of the country's first and last elected prime minister, Zulfiqar Ali Bhutto, has posed the question of survival. For the first time in Pakistan's chequered history, many ordinary citizens in the majority province of the Punjab and the minority provinces of Sind, Baluchistan and the North-West Frontier Province (NWFP) are questioning the birth of the new state.

The Pakistan army has been in power since 5 July 1977. It has attempted to utilize Islam in order to institutionalize a brutal dictatorship. On the external front, the army has mortgaged the country to the United States once again. In return, it has willingly agreed to help service and police the Gulf states. Everything is for sale in Pakistan: its labour force, its army, its women, its doctors and teachers are all leased to the oil-rich oligarchies in the Arab Gulf. Pakistan's uniformed mercenaries in Saudi Arabia are, in fact, strong enough to mount a coup in that country, should the need ever arise. Inside Pakistan itself, misery reigns supreme. The sense of demoralization and despair can be gauged by the fact that many people look eagerly to India and even the Soviet Union for salvation from this régime. In reality, relief will come only from within. The length of this third period of military rule is directly correlated with the level of mass struggle in the country. If there is a renewal of urban unrest, this régime will fall.

The problem, however, extends beyond the current dictatorship and its front-man. Ever since its inception, Pakistan has prevented its intelligentsia from discussing its own history. The poets (Faiz, Jalib, Fakhar Zaman, Ahmed Salim, Fehmida Riaz and many others) have occasionally managed to loosen this ideological straitjacket. Elsewhere silence has prevailed, sometimes broken by the whispers of Baluch insurgents or the loud explosions of the Bengalis. The question which now increasingly haunts the new generations in Pakistan is not simply whether the country can survive, but whether its existence was necessary in the first place.

This small book is an attempt to discuss hitherto taboo or undiscussed themes without inhibition. Some of the ideas contained here have never been publicly aired in Pakistan. The aim is to ensure that this material is read and discussed where it is most needed – and since ideas are notorious violaters of frontiers, one hopes that this book will reach its destination.

I would like to thank all those Pakistanis who gave me relevant factual information, on condition that their anonymity was preserved. I would like also to thank the O.J. Trust for the modest, but necessary, help they provided in 1980, to enable me to work on this project. Lastly, many thanks are due to my editor at Penguin Books, Neil Middleton, for all his help and encouragement.

Tariq Ali
London, 8 July 1982

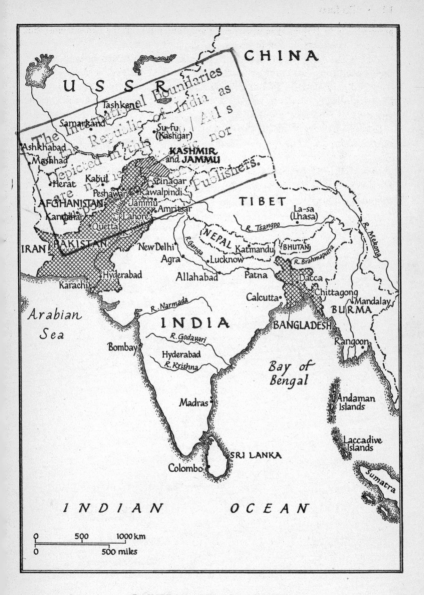

The International Boundaries of India as
Depicted in this map/Atlas
are neither correct nor
authentic. — Publishers.

PAKISTAN AND SOUTH ASIA

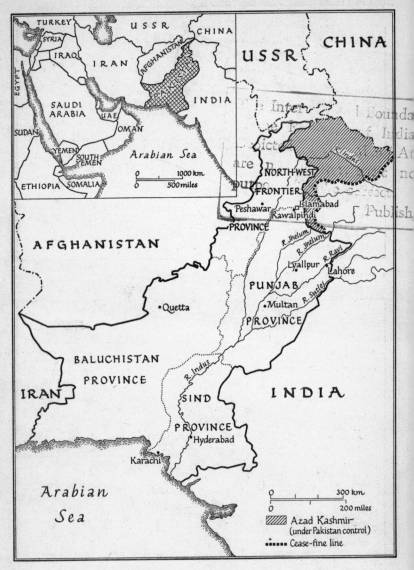

PAKISTAN: INTERNAL AND EXTERNAL FRONTIERS

Statistical Tables

(The 1965 figures do not include East Pakistan)

Demography, Culture and Armed Forces				
	Units	1965	1975	1980
Population	million	50.2	70.3	79.8
Density	Inhab. per sq. mile	161	225	256
Annual population growth	%	2.8[a]	3.0	4
Infant mortality	per 1,000 live births	142[b]	113	n.a.
Life expectancy	years	44[b]	50	52[c]
Urban population	%	22[b]	26	28
Illiteracy	%	85[b]	79	n.a.
Education:				
primary & secondary[e]	%	25	32	n.a.
higher	%	1.8	2.0	n.a.
TV receivers	‰	0.1	4	8[d]
Radio receivers[(L)]	‰	9	16	20[d]
Navy	'000	8	10	17
Air Force	'000	20	17	17
Army	'000	160	365	400
Military expenditure	% GDP	4.0	6.1	5.1

a. average 1960–70; b. 1960; c. 1978; d. 1977; e. 5–16 years.

External Trade				
	Units	1965	1975	1979
External trade[a]	% GDP	12.7	16.1	18.9
Total imports[b]	billion $	1.0	2.2	5.4
Food & agriculture	%	20.2	20.9[c]	19.9[d]
Raw materials	%	8.0	30.8[c]	29.6[d]
Manufactured goods	%	71.8	48.3[c]	50.4[d]
Total exports[b]	billion $	0.5	1.0	2.6
Food & agriculture	%	9.3	32.1[c]	30.2[d]
Raw materials	%	54.6	10.8	14.2[d]
Manufactured goods	%	36.1	57.0[c]	55.5[d]
Main suppliers	% imports			
United States		35.0	13.3	12.7[d]
Japan		9.8	12.9	12.6[d]
Kuwait		—	4.1	8.1[d]
Main customers	% exports			
Japan		4.5	6.8	8.2[d]
Hong Kong		3.6	11.1	6.9[d]
United Kingdom		—	6.2	6.3[d]

a. non-factor goods and services; b. manufactured goods; c. 1976; d. 1979.

Economy				
	Units	1965	1975	1979
Gross national product	billion $	4.3	11.3	21.0
Annual growth	%	7.2[a]	3.3	4.3
Per capita	$	85	160	260
Structure of GDP				
Agriculture	% ⎫	39.9	34.0	32
Industry	% ⎬ 100%	20.0[a]	22.6[b]	24[c]
Services	% ⎭	33.5[a]	43.3[b]	44[c]
Public external debt	billion $	n.a.	5.1	8.0
Rate of inflation	%	3.3[a]	14.6[d]	11.7[e]
Active population	million	n.a.	19.7	22.3[c]
Agriculture	% ⎫	61[f]	(55)	58[c]
Industry	% ⎬ 100%	18[f]	(18)	19[c]
Services	% ⎭	21[f]	(27)	23[c]
Public spending				
Education	million $	129[g]	120[h]	n.a.
Health	million $	23[g]	48[h]	n.a.
Defence	million $	483[g]	690[h]	n.a.
Energy production	MTCE	2.0[g]	6.8[i]	8.6[c]
Energy consumption	kg CE per head	61[g]	169[i]	172[c]

a. average 1960–70; b. average 1970–77; c. 1978; d. average 1970–78; e. 1980; f. 1960; g. figure does not deduct East Pakistan; h. 1974; i. 1973.
MTCE = millions of tonnes coal equivalent.

1 Origins

'We have not been elected or placed in power by the people, but we are here through our moral superiority, by the force of circumstances, by the will of Providence. This alone constitutes our charter to govern India. In doing the best we can for the people, we are bound by our conscience and not theirs.'

John Lawrence,
Viceroy of India, 1864-9

'I fired and continued to fire until the crowd dispersed, and I considered this as the least amount of firing which would produce the necessary moral and widespread effect it was my duty to produce if I was to justify my action. If more troops had been at hand, the casualties would have been greater in proportion. It was no longer a question of merely dispersing the crowd, but one of producing a sufficient moral effect from a military point of view not only on those who were present, but more especially throughout the Punjab.'

General Dyer, 1919, after ordering the massacre of
unarmed Indians attending a political rally at
Jallianwallah Bagh, Amritsar. Official figures were:
379 dead, 1,200 wounded. Unofficial estimates
were three times as high in both cases

If the British had not colonized and ruled India for nearly fifteen decades, the confessional state of Pakistan would not have come into existence on 14 August 1947. This is not to imply that *divide et impera* was the central tenet of the colonial state from its inception. It is probable that if India had been granted 'dominion status' on the Canadian and Australian model in the late nineteenth or early twentieth centuries, the entire pattern of political and economic development would have been strikingly different. The refusal of the British state to countenance such a solution aided the birth of Indian nationalism. In order to prevent the composite growth of such a movement, the strategists of the Raj sought to weaken the potential of their adversary at an early stage. They encouraged – both ideologically and through constitutional measures – the birth of communal politics throughout the subcontinent. Religious divisions, which prior to the British seizure of power had been of minor importance, were ruthlessly stimulated and utilized by successive consuls and pro-consuls to prevent the nationalist movement from feeling and acting upon its real strength. Communal historians in both India and Pakistan would no doubt challenge this view. For most of them, the concept of 'nation' is either shrouded in a mystique stretching back to Antiquity or the product of Muslim tactics under British rule. A dialogue could be useful, but the possibility of one is somewhat remote, since debate becomes difficult when one is compelled to dispute, not material facts, but the 'will of Providence'.

The growth of Islam in India was a direct consequence of the Mughal invasion in the third decade of the sixteenth century, and the ability of Babar and his successors to rule the country thereafter for nearly three hundred years. The bulk of India's Muslims were converts from Hinduism. They represented between 20 and 25 per cent of the population throughout India at the beginning of the twentieth century. It is worth remembering, however, that the vast bulk of the conversions to Islam were voluntary: an active protest in most cases against the grotesque inequality institutionalized by the caste system. Mughal rule was based on welding together a ruling class regardless of nationality or creed.

Akbar (1556–1605), the most gifted of the Mughal rulers, established an administrative network for the collection of revenue and a military apparatus for the maintenance of order that were not, and could not have been, based on the principle of religious loyalty. Akbar's military and political successes vindicated his secular approach. His attempt to promote a synthetic state religion which would unite Muslims and Hindus foundered on mass indifference. It was an audacious move, designed in reality to develop an ideology that would buttress the existing institutions of the Mughal state. Akbar's personal life symbolized his obsession with transcending all religious barriers: he married a Rajput princess. His successors maintained the framework he had established. The last major Mughal monarch, Aurungzeb (1658–1707), contrary to communalist mythology, did not qualitatively break with that tradition. He was a devout Muslim, but despite confessional excesses he preserved the basic composition of the ruling class. His generals were not chosen on the basis of religion and, as in the past, they defended the empire when ordered to do so. They fought with the same zeal to crush peasant *jacqueries* regardless of whether these were headed by Muslims or Hindus.

The Empire's collapse, as British rule was extended, did not come about because Akbar was a secularist or Aurungzeb an orthodox Muslim. It was the cumulative result of Mughal economic policies, which were unproductive and based on the extraction of revenue and taxes from a peasantry which obtained nothing in return. (It is true that the caste system helped to preserve rural docility, but the notion that the masses were passive throughout is over-simplified.) The real seeds of Mughal disintegration lay in the character of the Mughal state. Its parasitic character meant that it was bound sooner or later to antagonize those upon whom it relied for support. Provincial satraps with independent armies, but economically dependent on the central state, began to rebel against the system. The later Mughals could only respond militarily, when what was needed were economic reforms *from the top*. A state-sponsored feudalism could have delayed the decline and held the British at bay, but the empire was rotten-ripe. It fell.

The replacement of the Mughal state did lead to a recomposition of the old ruling classes. This did not affect Muslims alone, but also Hindus and Sikhs. It was this process that brought about the revolt of 1857 (the so-called 'Indian Mutiny'): a last inter-communal attempt by the old rulers to resist the new. The stated purpose of the rising was to expel the British from India and put the last nominal Mughal king, Bahadur Shah Zafar, on the throne. It was a doomed attempt, but had the effect of forcing the British to rule the country in name as well as in fact. The defeat of the old ruling classes was thus completed. Those who had relied on the old Court for employment – artisans as well as poets; retainers of every kind, including religious divines – all suffered. Those from the ruling classes who had fought against the British were punished and, in many cases, deprived of their rights to collect revenue or even their hereditary occupation of the land.

Muslims were held to be responsible for the rebellion by the ideologists of the Raj. This was factually incorrect and subsequently disappeared from propaganda pronouncements, but the Muslim gentry were now confronted by contradictory pressures. The *ulema* (Islamic clergy), for a combination of economic and religious reasons, were anti-British. Their most influential leaders proclaimed British India *dar ul harb* (enemy territory) and thus implied that a permanent *jihad* was mandatory for all Muslims. They encouraged Muslims to refrain from any collaboration with the new rulers.

Their most vociferous opponent was Sir Syed Ahmed, a petty official in the state bureaucracy. Ahmed combated obscurantism with great verve and vigour. He established a Scientific Society in 1864 with the declared aim of translating English books on political economy, history and philosophy. This was anathema to the theologians, but their criticisms merely goaded him further to outrage their sensibilities. He wrote:

> The old Muhammadan books and the tone of their writings do not teach the followers of Islam independence of thought, perspicacity and simplicity; nor do they enable them to arrive at the truth of matters in

general; on the contrary, they deceive and teach men to veil their meaning, to embellish their speech with fine words, to describe things wrongly and in irrelevant terms, to flatter with false praise . . . to puff themselves up with pride, haughtiness, vanity and self-conceit, to hate their fellow creatures, to have no sympathy with them, to speak with exaggeration, to leave the history of the past uncertain and to relate facts like tales and stories.[1]

The tradition which Ahmed attacked proved to have strong roots. One could use very similar language to describe the outpourings of communalist and chauvinist 'historians' in contemporary India and Pakistan. If Ahmed had restricted himself to a critique of obscurantism, he might have attracted very little attention. What made him a powerful figure in post-1857 India was that he combined his attacks on the *ulema* with a powerful plea for support to be given to the British take-over of the country. The title of two of his books – *The Causes of the Indian Mutiny* and *Loyal Mohammedans of India* – convey the flavour of the political project he had set himself, which was soon to receive material and political backing from the British administration.

The clash between Ahmed's pro-British modernism and the *ulema* continued for several decades. Ahmed was allowed to set up a college in Aligarh to educate Muslims in the virtues of science and loyalty to the empire. The *ulema* divided into competing seminaries, the most prominent of which, Deoband, developed a layer of divines who regularly preached rebellion against the Raj and, on occasion, attempted to carry it out. The majority of the *ulema* were to remain strongly opposed to Muslim separatism and argue for a unified struggle against Britain. The Jamiyyat al Ulema-i-Hind was to argue, in the first years of the twentieth century, that:

If non-Muslims occupy a Muslim land, which India was under the Mughals, it becomes the obligatory duty of Muslims of that land and of others to strive and retain independence. This *jihad* in India has to be non-violent and it can be fought only in alliance with the Hindus, who constitute the majority community. In independence thus gained Muslims and non-Muslims would be co-partners in creating a society and administration which, though not modelled entirely on the conception of an Islamic state, would comprise effective and influential elements in it.[2]

The tragedy of Indian Muslims and India was that no force existed that was capable of synthesizing Ahmed's rationalism and the anti-imperialist political thrust of the Deoband. There can be little doubt that such a movement would have been subjected to systematic harassment and repression, but it would none the less have represented an incalculable gain.

Ahmed and his successors advised Muslims to keep aloof from politics and serve the British. The formation of the Indian National Congress in 1885, as an organization which would pressurize London to grant reforms and some degree of self-rule, posed a few problems for loyalist Muslims. It could hardly be argued at this stage that the Congress was either dominated by Hindus or susceptible to 'extremism'. It had, indeed, been set up explicitly to ensure that nationalist-minded Indians would conduct their struggle within the framework laid down by the colonial state. But even the mild resolutions passed by the early Congress drew the wrath of Sir Syed and his coterie. They poured scorn on the whole project, putting forward the argument that any notion of a composite Indian nationalism was intolerable. This was now coupled with an ugly élitism (which bordered on racism as far as the Bengalis were concerned: some of Ahmed's utterances reflecting the official view of Bengalis as an 'infernal nuisance' and 'upstarts' could be certainly categorized as racist). In theory, Islam was an egalitarian religion which tolerated no caste distinction. All Muslims were equal before God. In one of his speeches opposing the elective principle, however, Ahmed revealed his prejudices extremely clearly:

> I ask you, would our aristocracy like that a man of low caste or insignificant origin, though he be a B.A. or an M.A. and have the requisite ability, should be in a position of authority above them and have power in making the laws that affect their lives and property? Never! Nobody would like it . . . The men of good family would never like to trust their lives and property to people of low ranks.

This was not an isolated statement. It reflected the views of a sizable section of the Muslim landed aristocracy. Keeping aloof from politics and trusting the Raj was, for this layer, not a question of sentiment, but the best possible way to safeguard their property. The growth of even 'moderate' nationalist sentiments was to meet with their strong disapproval.

As the Indian National Congress gathered new forces behind its banners, it was felt necessary by the Raj to encourage the formation of a Muslim party as a counterweight. There was not even any attempt to be subtle in bringing this about. The English Principal of the Aligarh College founded by Sir Syed, a Mr Archbold, acted as a broker between the Muslim gentry and the Viceroy. On 1 October 1906, Lord Minto received a deputation which described itself as: 'We the nobles, Jagirdars, Taluqdars, Zamindars, Lawyers and Merchants, subjects of His Majesty the King-Emperor in different parts of India.' It demanded separate electorates for Muslims and positive discrimination in state employment, highlighting their loyalty to the empire. Minto's reply stressed the 'representative character' of the deputation and agreed with its basic demands. He pledged that the partition of Bengal pushed through in 1905 by his predecessor Lord Curzon would be maintained, and that Muslim Bengalis would be rewarded suitably for their loyalty.

The Muslim League was founded with the blessings of the Viceroy. Its founding charter stated that one of its central objects was 'To foster a sense of loyalty to the British Empire among the Muslims of India'. The new League was to remain for long an alliance between Muslim landlords and British civil servants. There were some fears expressed that even a loyalist political party could become a conduit for more radical forces, but in the event the lawyers were held at bay. In 1910, the Governor of the United Provinces (UP) confided to his Viceroy:

> I have felt frightened lest the lawyer party, mainly consisting of young and irresponsible persons, would attain a predominant position in the League, and that they might at some time coalesce with the advanced Hindu politicians against the government on one or more questions and later on rue the fact that they had done so. I think the Aga Khan has put an effectual check to this, and that the League may be expected to be much more conservative and stable than it once promised to be.[3]

It would be far too simplistic to suggest that Muslim communalism was merely the result of British intrigue. Though it was only the colonial state that could institutionalize communalism, two other factors were equally important in engendering it: the growing impact of the changing economic pattern in the cities, and the peculiar ideology of the Congress, both served to strengthen separatism in parts of the subcontinent.

Despite the fact that the Congress was theoretically a secular organization and that its appeal was directed to all Indians regardless of class or creed, its practice tended to belie this approach. This became clearer as the Congress moved into a phase of mass campaigns. Anti-British agitation carried out by the Congress was, in fact, heavily overlaid with Hindu symbolism and mythology. During its 1905–11 campaign against the partition of Bengal, the Congress could have won the support of an overwhelming proportion of Muslim Bengalis. Apart from a small band of Muslim landlords and title-holders, few favoured the division Curzon had imposed on the subcontinent's most politically developed and cultured province. Yet the Congress leaders chose to conduct the movement by utilizing Hindu anthems and the worship of Hindu gods. Many Muslim nationalists were revolted by this imagery and withdrew from the movement.

The hostility to communal violence of Mohandas Gandhi, who rose to a dominant position in the Congress between 1915 and 1919, is beyond dispute; yet his entire political style was that of a Hindu leader. His speeches were full of mystical symbolism deriving from the past of Hinduism and designed to convince his followers that only a social-pacifist solution was possible in India. The links between the Congress and blatantly communal Hindu organizations have been well-documented in a number of studies. Membership of groups such as the reactionary Hindu Mahasabha was not incompatible with membership of the Congress. The pressure of Hindu communalism was directly responsible for the Congress discarding agreements with the Muslim parties on at least two important occasions. It was only in 1933 that the Hindu Mahasabha formally broke with the Congress and accused it of 'appeasing the Muslims'. Seven years prior to this rupture, the more extreme elements within the Hindu Mahasabha had initiated the formation of the Rashtriya Swayamsevak Sangh (RSS) – National Volunteer Corps – an organization designed to provide shock-troops for Hindu communalism. The RSS organized systematic attacks on Muslims and carried out acts of arson and sabotage designed to demoralize the minority community. They were denounced by Jawaharlal Nehru: 'Hindu communalism is the Indian version of fascism.' A more precise analogy would have been with the Orange Lodges and Loyalist communalism in the North of Ireland. Equally important was the tragic fact that the Congress leaders could not devise a strategy to defeat Hindu communalism within their own ranks.

It may be trite but is none the less true that this was the result of a refusal by the Congress leaders to acknowledge that the country for whose national independence they were struggling was also divided into social classes. The choice confronting the Congress was whether they should *base* their struggle for freedom on the support and mobilization of the oppressed masses in country and town, or instead *utilize* mass pressure to wring a series of escalating concessions from the administration. The character of the colonial state and the existence of an indigenous bourgeoisie pushed the predominantly middle-class and aristocratic Congress leaders in the second direction. This decision occasionally created serious rifts inside the Congress, but the towering personality of Gandhi was decisive in ensuring that unity was preserved.

British rule in India was a curious amalgam of conservatism and political intrigue. Karl Marx and the Utilitarians alike had placed great hopes on the modernizing impact which Britain would have on India. In a number of articles for the *New York Daily Tribune* in 1853 Marx had written that: 'England has to fulfil a double mission in India: one destructive, the other regenerating – the annihilation of old Asiatic society, and the laying of the material foundations of Western society in Asia ... modern industry, resulting from the railway system, will dissolve the hereditary divisions of labour, upon which rest the Indian castes, those decisive impediments to Indian progress and power.' Friedrich Engels had a more cautious estimate.

In a letter written to Marx while the above text was in preparation, Engels advised: 'An Oriental government never had more than three departments: finance (plunder at home), war (plunder at home and abroad), and public works (provision for reproduction). The British government in India has administered Nos. 1 and 2 in a rather narrow-minded spirit and dropped No. 3 entirely, so that Indian agriculture is now being ruined.' In fact, as Angus Maddison has convincingly demonstrated, the British administrators did not interfere a great deal with 'traditional' India.[4] There were a few, belated social reforms pushed through by Lord Bentinck, but the country-side (where 90 per cent of the population lived) was largely left intact.

The self-image of the British was modelled on the imperialism of ancient Rome, rather than on the Spanish Conquest in South America or even the French colonization of Indo-China. It was only a self-image. Britain's motives were conditioned by objective necessities. The most effective way to exploit India economically, while using it as a strategic military base to defend trade routes, defeat competitors and strengthen the empire, was to rely on one basic mechanism: the consent of the native ruling classes had to be obtained.[5] Where this was not possible, they were to be deprived of their power and new pliant ruling classes were to be created. Hence it was natural that the villages were left as they had been under the Mughal empire. The hereditary distinctions imposed by the caste system were crucial for consolidating the basis class structure and maintaining the status quo. To interfere with all this could well create a dangerous situation for the empire by unleashing new social forces. It was clearly best to leave things as they had been when the British arrived. (Dr Irfan Habib has indeed shown in some detail that there has been no basic change in the diet or consumption habits of the peasants in South Asia for the last four centuries.[6])

British strategy in India was thus to preserve caste, class and linguistic divisions – and soon to promote a new split on the basis of religious differences. In his notorious 1834 Minute on Education, Macaulay had explained that the bulk of the population could not be educated, since the priority was to create 'a class who may be interpreters between us and the millions we govern'. English was only to be permitted to a small élite who could help the British to administer the country. It was from this élite that the politicians of the Indian Congress and the Muslim League were drawn. Most of them were amply to satisfy Macaulay's hopes of creating people 'Indian in blood and colour, but English in taste, in opinions, in morals and in intellect'. Even if some of these were to study the wrong books (as many did), the fact that they were a minority of a minority meant that they could be contained. If the educational system had been extended to the entire population, on the other hand, Britain would have confronted a *national* upheaval much sooner.

Cultural élitism was coupled with the system of imperial tariffs, designed to protect British domestic industry against any competition from India. Until the 1870s, there were no laws impeding industrial development. Towards the end of the First World War, the total amount of Indian capital invested in Indian industry exceeded that of British capital. The cotton and subsequently the iron and steel industries were financed and dominated by Indian capitalists. Hindrances and restrictions became commonplace: whenever Indian products became competitive, discriminatory laws against Indian industry were immediately sanctioned by London. The first industries had been geared to aid the export of raw materials to foreign markets. It was when production for the domestic market accelerated that new tariffs were imposed to restrict indigenous industrialization. G. K. Shirokov has provided us with two instances of direct obstruction. The first involved a locomotive plant which had been constructed in 1924:

> The colonial authorities refused to purchase its output, redeemed the plant from its owners and had it dismantled. In the late 1930s the authorities refused to allow a group of entrepreneurs from Bombay to set up an automobile plant which they were planning to establish in collaboration with the American Chrysler Company.[7]

Despite colonial impediments, the Indian capitalists retained their footholds in the country's economy. They were not an insignificant force in the country and their links with Congress explained the economic nationalism of Gandhi, as well as his notorious hostility to militant trade-unionism and class conflict.

With this small but necessary detour concluded, we can better understand the restraints and the framework within which the Congress chose to operate. The Congress decided to evolve a strategy that would 'Indianize' rather than overthrow the colonial state. Such a political approach was a reflection of the social composition of the Congress leaders, on a national and provincial level. They represented upper and middle strata in town and country. Gandhi strongly favoured improving the conditions of the peasantry, but within very strictly defined limits. If his formula for the cities was to dissolve the antagonism between Capital and Labour through sermons on the virtues of harmony, in the countryside he was equally firm: 'Congressmen cannot, do not seek to injure the *zamindars*. We aim not at destruction of property. We aim only at its lawful use.' A political stance of this character made it extremely difficult for Congress effectively to confront Hindu communalism or to defeat politically its Muslim counterpart.

In order to dispel any notion that we are indulging here in abstract assertions or unfair generalizations, we shall briefly observe one particular uprising: the Moplah revolt of 1921. What is revealed is how rapidly the

Congress retreated whenever the masses were in motion, and how in this case a strategic political retreat *necessitated* a communalist rather than class view of an important peasant struggle.[8] The Moplahs were Muslim peasants in Malabar (now part of the state of Kerala) on India's west coast. In 1922 it had a population of 400,000, of which 163,328 were Hindus and 236,672 were Muslims. The Moplahs were amongst the most heavily exploited peasants in the entire subcontinent. Most of them worked as wage-labourers either on the land of others or on the rubber plantations. The landlords in the region were virtually all upper-caste Brahmin Hindus. In the century preceding 1921, there had been a total of fifty peasant uprisings. Of these, twenty-two had occurred within the space of seventeen years (1836–53). They were typically rural in character: the peasants had attacked and killed landlords, or burnt their houses, or done both. The cause of these revolts had been the notoriously unjust tenancy laws, which gave landlords the power of life or death over peasants. All the *jacqueries* had been ended brutally by state intervention. Hundreds of peasants had been killed.

The 1921 revolt was no different in content from previous movements. A tenants' movement had been organized and large peasant assemblies had called for rent strikes and a boycott of the landlords. Peasant unions had sprung up throughout Malabar. Attempts by the colonial bureaucracy to repress the meetings via the police had a counter-productive effect. On 8 August 1921 the authorities issued warrants for the arrest of the peasant leaders. A subsequent armed raid on a mosque where it was presumed the leaders were hiding acted as a spark for the revolt. Thirty thousand peasants armed with primitive weapons (such as hammers and scythes) descended on the area. The police opened fire and nine peasants were killed. In retaliation, the peasants killed a British civil servant who was supervising the operation, as well as the senior police and army officers accompanying him. The rest of the government forces retreated. The peasant rebels destroyed bridges, removed railway lines, dismantled telegraph wires and occupied railway stations. For ten days they reigned supreme. The British press portrayed the rising as a communal war of Muslim against Hindu. Yet, in the first phase, only landlords or their agents and government spies were executed. No Hindu was molested or killed because of his religion. There were some isolated incidents of looting of Hindu houses, but these were punished severely. Even this looting began only after Hindus began to give information to the police. In many places the poor Hindu peasants joined the revolt. Kunna Amed Haji, a peasant chief, sent a communication to the Madras daily *The Hindu*, rebutting charges of communalism and accusing government agents of attacking Hindu temples to try to sow division between the communities. The landlords sided with the government *en masse*, as did some rich Moplahs. The newspaper of the Malabar Brahmins,

Yogakshemam, explained the problem bluntly: 'Only the rich and the land-lords are suffering in the hands of the rebels, not the poor peasants.'

On 21 August 1921 the British authorities imposed martial law, but a guerrilla war lasted till the end of November. The rebellion was crushed by the army, with the use of Gurkhas and the Chinkan Chin regiment from Burma. Over 2,000 peasants were killed in the revolt and hundreds were hanged. A nephew of the Bengali poet-philosopher Rabindranath Tagore described the effects of martial law in a pamphlet, which was banned at the time:

> The atrocities perpetrated by the soldiers on the unarmed and defence-less men and women left behind in the Moplah villages were appalling. Women were insulted and outraged. Houses were looted and burnt. Men were mercilessly belaboured . . . In one particular case an old woman was assaulted and shot. Concentration camps were established where the Moplah women were held as hostages. It must be said in fairness that the charges of wanton brutality were mainly against the Chinkan Chin forces brought from Burma, but not against the British regiment. To strike terror in the hearts of the peasant masses, peasant rebels were hanged on wayside trees and left dangling there in order to create an 'impression' on the populace. Brutal terror was let loose on the peasantry by the army and police.[9]

There can be little doubt that the suppression of the Moplah uprising was a far more serious event even than the Jallianwallah Bagh massacre. Officialdom portrayed it as a sad case of communal frenzy. The Muslim communalists, fully aware that this was not a religious affair, remained silent or condemned the peasants. Gandhi prostrated himself before the Malabar landlords. In an article entitled 'The Meaning of the Moplah Uprising', which was written at a time when peasants were being massacred, he commented: 'The Moplah revolt is a test for Hindus and Muslims. Can Hindu friendship survive the strain put upon it? Can Muslims in the deepest recess of their hearts approve the conduct of the Moplahs? The Hindus must have the courage and the faith to feel that they can protect their religion in spite of such fanatical eruptions.' The leaders of the Congress in Malabar tried to stop the rebellion. A former leader of the tenants' move-ment, Narayan Menon, abandoned the peasants in the name of 'non-violence'. The British authorities, always pleased when their opponents became pacifists, issued Menon with a 'passport' which enabled him to travel through police and army lines to try to win the peasants to 'pacifism'. But he failed. The British withdrew their support and punished him for his failure: he was sentenced to twelve years in prison. Not a single leader of the Congress backed the rebels. There was no nation-wide campaign in defence of the Moplah peasants. The reason why the peasants fought for so long was that, in the liberated zones, their leaders abolished the payment of land revenue and rents for one year. The landlords had fled, but the peasants continued to till the land and harvest the crops, the surplus being used to provide rations for the peasant army.

Ironically, the Moplah revolt had coincided with a united nation-wide Congress–Muslim agitation on the question of the *Khalifat* (Caliphate). Turkey's defeat by Britain in the First World War meant that the *Khalifa* (Caliph), recognized by many Indian Muslims as their head, and who during the War had sought to rally all Muslims for a *jihad*, appeared bound to be dethroned. It was the occasion for a tremendous surge of anti-British radicalism amongst Indian Muslims. It was mainly the *ulema* who launched the movement (the modernists were implacably opposed to it). Since the objective was 'safe', Gandhi gave it his backing. A broader non-cooperation movement aimed at self-rule was launched at the end of 1920, and soon acquired mass support. However, within less than two years it had been brought to an end, for two reasons, one local and the other related to Turkey. In the first place, Gandhi was frightened by the militancy that had been aroused. The burning of a police station with policemen still inside it in 1922 led Gandhi to call a unilateral halt. The failure of Congress at this juncture to act as a conduit for mass discontent and pose a real challenge to British power was to have an important side-effect: the birth of terrorism in Bengal and the Punjab in the twenties was the result of despair on the part of young nationalists disgusted with what they saw as an act of betrayal. In the second place, the Kemalist national revolution came as a decisive blow for the Muslims. Ataturk declared Turkey a modern, secular republic and in early 1924 abolished the Caliphate.

While the *ulema* were thrown into confusion, a whole layer of Muslims now decided that the only force that could help them to defeat the British was the infant Soviet Republic of Lenin and Trotsky. Many left India and arrived in Afghanistan, where the anti-imperialist monarch Amanullah provided them with aid. Some went on to Tashkent and Moscow. The first two Indians to meet Lenin were Muslim agitators. Another, Mohammed Barakatullah, went to Moscow as a 'special envoy' of Amanullah. He stayed there for three years and wrote a lengthy text entitled: 'Bolshevism and the Islamic Nations.' In this he called on Muslims to understand and embrace the principles of Russian socialism. Impressed by the Soviet government's refusal to honour imperialist secret treaties, Barakatullah advised Central Asian Muslims to send their children to school to learn sciences, and ended one passage with the following appeal: 'Oh Muhammedans, listen to this divine cry. Respond to this call of liberty, equality and brotherhood which Comrade Lenin and the Soviet government of Russia are offering you.'[10]

Some of the first communists in India were Muslims, who rejected all forms of communalism and opted for its polar opposite.

The triumph of secularism in Turkey, and the abrupt halt of the nationalist struggle in India itself, marked the end of an important phase in Indian politics. In the period 1916–20 there had been a limited degree of Congress–Muslim League collaboration, but this had been ended by the Congress decision to launch its campaign of civil disobedience. The League's loyalism was strained and even the non-landlord layers were horrified. Their spokesman, Mohammed Ali Jinnah, who had been hailed as an ambassador of 'Hindu–Muslim unity', withdrew from politics for a period. Jinnah was a constitutionalist to the core. A brilliant lawyer, he felt most comfortable in a court or a legislative council. He could not grasp the fact that Gandhi's ultimate goal was fundamentally no different from his own. The contrast was one of style and tactics rather than political aims. Gandhi was an extremely clever politician. The ideology he implanted in the Congress enabled him to limit the scope of the mass movement and contain its militancy, while simultaneously using it as a lever to gain reforms from the colonial state. Jinnah, for his part, regarded civil disobedience with disgust. His élitist conception of national politics led him to view the very notion of street demonstrations with cold repugnance. This fact cannot be emphasized enough: Jinnah's break with Congress was not on a communal basis, but was the outcome of tactical differences. Separatism was still a decade away, though the path towards it was already being carefully prepared by the colonial state.

As London began to feel the pressure of agitation, it became clear that some form of self-rule was essential to forestall social upheavals and revolutionary outbreaks. In 1932, Sir Theodore Morrison, a former principal of the staunchly loyalist M.A.O. College in Aligarh, wrote an influential essay in support of separatism. He developed a mystical theme which was to become the leitmotif of Muslim communalism:

> The Hindus and Muslims were two distinct nations as different from each other as any two European nations; Muslim civilization could not survive under an 'alien' government – especially a democratic government which tended toward standardization of citizens; the Muslims should rest assured that they were not alone in their concern for the preservation of their characteristic civilization.[11]

The principle of separate electorates for Muslims had already been accepted and was to play a major role in institutionalizing communal politics in India; but the demand for Pakistan, a separate Muslim state, was only to become meaningful in 1944–6, both for the leaders of the Muslim League and for sections of the Muslim masses. Those who argue that the notion of

Pakistan was contained in the 'fact' that the Muslims were a 'distinct community' are simply re-writing history. If the question were posed: 'When did the Muslims become a distinct nation?', it would be impossible to elicit a common answer from the communal historians.[12] Can the Muslims of India be regarded as a 'distinct community' in any sense of the word? The overwhelming majority of Muslims in India were poor peasants. The languages they spoke were Bengali, Punjabi, Sindhi and Pushtu. What did they have in common with the Muslim aristocracy of the United Provinces, which conversed in Urdu and wrote poetry in Persian? Peasant struggles in these regions tended not to distinguish between Hindu and Muslim landlords.

In addition to linguistic and social differences, there were also rival interpretations of Islam. Apart from the Shi'a–Sunni divide, there were numerous other currents which defined themselves as reformers or defenders of orthodoxy. They disputed amongst themselves on questions of theology. They argued as to which political grouping should be supported inside India. Some theologians were in the pay of the British and wrote sermons on command. Others backed the Congress and declared in favour of a 'composite nationalism'. Others still argued for a universal Islamic republic and refused even to consider the notion of Islam in One Country. This was the view of Abul-Ala Maududi, who founded the Jamaat-i-Islami in 1941 to oppose the secular nationalism of his confessional rivals, the Deoband Group, and the aims of the Muslim League. Maududi accused Jinnah of being motivated 'by the worldly socio-economic interests of the Muslims' rather than by religion. He insisted that:

> Not a single leader of the Muslim League from Jinnah himself to the rank and file has an Islamic mentality or Islamic habits of thought, or looks at political and social problems from the Islamic viewpoint ... Their ignoble role is to safeguard the material interests of Indian Muslims by every possible manoeuvre or trickery.[13]

It should be stated that Maududi was right. Despite the demagogic Muslim League slogan of 'Islam is in danger', the League's leaders hardly presented a picture of Muslim respectability.

Were there any common characteristics shared by Indian Muslims, apart from the fact that they, like millions of other Muslims elsewhere, occasionally prostrated themselves in the direction of Mecca? Muslim historians searching for retrospective rationalizations were to claim that the Muslims of India were disproportionately 'backward'. This view had indeed gained currency amongst a certain layer of Muslims after the publication in 1871 of the Hunter Report. W. W. Hunter was an educationalist stationed in Bengal, a region where the Muslim peasantry was becoming increasingly militant. The Viceroy, Lord Mayo, was concerned lest the decaying Muslim gentry might link up with the peasants. Hunter's report, based on the conditions of the gentry in Bengal, argued that the colonial state should positively discriminate in their favour. (Hunter presumed that the situation of Muslims throughout India was similar, which was not the case.) The result of his recommendations was that by 1921 there was a higher degree of literacy among Muslims than among Hindus.[14] Similarly, the growing social and economic crisis in the country affected Hindus as well as Muslims. In fact, more Hindu families were dispossessed of land in Bengal than Muslims, since the latter had smaller landholdings in comparison.

Hunter's report, however, had been designed to wean Muslims away from rebellion. The Muslim landlords were only too eager to be wooed and won, and accepted with alacrity the special privileges which the state offered. The fact that jobs were reserved for Muslims meant that they would oppose the principle of competitive entry into the various public services. It was this opposition, engineered by concessions and argued by English principals of the Aligarh college, which was utilized on most occasions to obstruct moves towards equality on almost any level. The Muslim élite, whose property rights and social privileges rested on the state, were, over the decades, to demonstrate their loyalty in no uncertain fashion. The Muslim Defence Association of the UP, a notable preserve of this élite, stated: 'Any large measure of self-government, which might curtail the moderating and adjusting influence of the British government, would be nothing short of a cataclysm.' The leaders of the early Muslim League voiced similar sentiments. They were amply rewarded with titles (becoming knights, Nawabs, Khan Sahibs, etc.) and property. When the time came in the 1930s for them to dissociate themselves from the League – now dominated by the middle classes, not averse to a negotiated independence – the Nawabs and knights formed new groups and political associations. In some cases they adjusted to tactical changes in British policy with remarkable ease. In the Punjab, Muslim landlords set up an inter-communal Unionist Party, which brought together all landlords regardless of caste or creed.[15] In the United Provinces, they formed the staunchly servile National Agricultural Party; in Bengal, the United Muslim Party. It was only when they could no longer win seats that the landlords returned to the League. In the Punjab, this happened as late as 1946. Communal politics were, in many ways, a distorted reflection of class realities. The fact that they ultimately resulted in the creation of a separate state was by no means inevitable.

It was a combination of landlords and middle-class politicians which continued to run the Muslim League, but the latter dominated its politics. A turning-point was the Act of India passed by the British parliament in 1935. This was designed to provide a measure of self-rule, as a test-run in preparation for independence. The franchise was enlarged, and elections were to be held everywhere except in the 'princely states' (the rulers of these states were to be spared the ordeal of democracy, as a reward for their loyalty to the Raj). Electoral politics drew sections of the *ulema* into the Muslim League and the Congress. It also saw an increase of communal riots. The League drew its members now largely from the educated middle classes: lawyers, journalists, doctors and students joined it in growing numbers. Separate electorates for Muslims and Hindus meant (or so they thought) that some parliamentary representation was guaranteed. Careerism was not an unimportant motive for many middle-class Muslims joining the League. The economic crisis had created an imbalance which still exists in the subcontinent: the universities were producing more people with degrees than could be employed. The fact that certain places in public employment were reserved for Muslims meant very little so far as the unemployed graduates were concerned. These places were, in general, allocated on the basis of patronage by associations of landlords or by politicians in the landlords' pockets. While the economic crisis pushed Muslim students towards separatist politics, such politics could not satisfy their aspirations. Increasingly, the Muslim League was faced with a choice between moving left (in which case it could have become virtually indistinguishable from the Congress) or regressing in the direction of political mysticism. Opting for the latter course, it attempted a deal with sections of the *ulema*.

The Muslim intelligentsia was confronted with a parallel set of alternatives. For many Muslim intellectuals, the choice was not between a secular Muslim League and the *ulema*. It was between moving on from a nationalism transcending communal divisions to something even more radical (some form of Marxism) and making their peace with an Islamic tradition which sought to derive its ideas from medieval laws and philosophy. The poet Iqbal in some ways symbolized this dilemma. His early period produced poetry expressing a nationalist outlook. 'Anthem for India' (*Tarānah'-i-Hindī*) is still popular in India, but it was 'New Temple' (*Naya Shivala*) which was a more faithful reflection of the young Iqbal. This was all to be abandoned, when the poet decided to shift his loyalties. After a stay in Europe, he returned to India and explained how all social, political and philosophical problems could be solved by Islam. Europe had disgusted him. He rejected capitalism because it was based on profit and war. Socialism meant atheism: this he could not accept, though he accepted that many of the programmatic aims of socialism were not irreconcilable with his interpretation of the Koran. His political and philosophical beliefs became a *mélange* of East and West, jumbling together ethical socialism, Nietzsche and the *sufis*. The result, unsurprisingly, was confused. But it would be wrong to see Iqbal's system of thought as entailing a consistently negative political practice. His perception of reality remained acute.[16] In his more polemical moments, Iqbal could both call for destruction of the existing order and question the existence of a Creator who permitted so much suffering in the world. The poet's epigones do his memory a grave disservice when they identify him with the social, economic and political disasters that ensued from the communalist frenzy after 1947.

The supposition that Islam contained within its system the answers to all the problems of a strife-torn world was a view held not just by Iqbal or the *ulema*. Even anti-communalist Muslim scholars such as Maulana Azad (a major figure of the Congress) could argue that there was no need for Muslims to 'adopt a political or economic programme, when Islam gave *eternally valid* answers to these problems'. The combination of this ideology and the electoral reforms of the twenties could only accelerate the growth of communal politics. The Legislative Assembly and provincial legislative councils devolved some powers to the native population, but the franchise was limited (in favour of rural propertied interests) and separate electoral rolls were reserved for Muslims. The result was not totally unpredictable. Communal conflicts increased and there were Hindu–Muslim riots throughout the twenties. Hardy cites a report of the Indian Statutory Commission to assert that 'between 1923 and 1927 there were eighty-eight communal riots in the United Provinces, in which eighty-one people were killed and 2,301 injured'.

A number of attempts by Congress and Muslim leaders to reach agreement on a constitution for India foundered on mistrust. The Congress produced the Nehru report, which favoured separate electorates only in those provinces where Muslims were a minority. Jinnah was not hostile to the report, but preferred his own 'Fourteen Points'. The essence of these was to propose a federal constitution for India, provincial autonomy and separate electorates. Neither side was prepared to make the necessary concessions. In the face of this disaccord, the representatives of the British state retired to the drawing-board and produced the 1935 Act of India. The Muslim organizations had one agreement amongst themselves: they all favoured a weak Centre and strong provinces. It was this that gave them an all-India perspective for the first time and enabled the Muslim League to become the dominant political organization of the Muslim middle classes.

The 1935 Act was a crucial political intervention by the British, destined to shape the politics of South Asia for decades. Its timing was not unimportant. While the Muslim politicians and the Congress were failing to agree on a common platform for Independence, another struggle was taking place, however unevenly, at a different level altogether. Politics-from-above saw the division between Congress and the Muslim League dominate the stage with all its attendant paraphernalia: round-table conferences in

London, tea with the Viceroy, constitutional talks, press conferences, concentration on personalities, etc. Politics-from-below was hidden from the general view, but was beginning to penetrate the Congress: peasant struggles and strikes tended to transcend communalism.

In the mid-thirties, Jawaharlal Nehru dissociated himself from radical humanism and argued in favour of a socialism that would, of necessity, involve:

> vast and revolutionary changes in our political and social structure, the ending of vested interests in land and industry ... one can hardly have two contradictory and conflicting processes going on side by side. The choice must be made and for one who aims at socialism there can be only one choice.

Three years later, on 20 April 1936, Nehru stated:

> I am convinced that the only key to the solution of the world's problems and of India's problems lies in socialism ... I see no way of ending the poverty, the vast unemployment, the degradation and the subjection of the Indian people except through socialism.[17]

The Indian historian Bipan Chandra has argued convincingly that this was not empty rhetoric in the tradition of European social-democracy, but reflected a genuine radicalization of Nehru's thought. Chandra boldly asserts that 'he [Nehru] was during 1933–6 on the verge of becoming an anti-imperialist Marxist revolutionary'. It is not necessary to agree with this assessment *in toto* to understand that there was a deep division inside the Congress at this time. Nehru's speeches had greatly worried Indian capitalists, who began to attack him publicly. They were restrained by G. D. Birla, whom Chandra describes as 'the brilliant political leader and mentor of the Indian capitalist class, whose political acumen often bordered on genius'. Birla was convinced that Gandhi would tame Nehru's radical instincts.[18] The 1935 Act was to prove decisive in this regard. Nehru had demanded a fully-fledged Constituent Assembly to determine India's future. The Act offered partial self-government, and even that under the benign aegis of the colonial state. Nehru favoured outright rejection. Gandhi favoured acceptance. It was Nehru who capitulated in order to preserve the unity of the Congress. This unity was a decisive factor in ensuring a smooth transition from British rule to national independence. It also pushed the Muslim League to escalate its demands.

India's first general elections were held in 1937 (with the exclusion of the princely states). Of the total electorate of 30 million, only 54 per cent voted. Out of 1,585 seats in eleven provinces, the Congress won 711. In five provinces – Madras, UP, Central Provinces, Bihar and Orissa – it had an overall majority. It gained a majority in the North-West Frontier Province as well, where the population consisted essentially of Muslims. The Muslim League only won 109 out of 482 seats reserved for Muslims. Congress won 26 Muslim seats, the rest being divided amongst Muslims who were not in the League. The League offered to collaborate with Congress, stating that it favoured 'a full national self-government for the people of India'. It did not at this stage exclude 'unity and honourable settlement between Hindus and Muslims and other minorities'. However, it was effectively snubbed by the Congress high command.

On the outbreak of war in 1939, the Viceroy of India at once committed Britain's largest colony to the conflict. Enraged at not being consulted, the All-India Congress Committee instructed Congress ministers to resign. The war created another major divide in Indian politics. Congress opposed the war effort, the Muslim League declared its willingness to fight for the empire. As a result of its stance, a number of provincial ministries were made available to the League, which now grew in size, cementing an alliance with traders and wartime contractors; the League's weekly paper *Dawn* was given funds by the British administration to expand its audience. In August 1942, the Congress launched its 'Quit India' movement. The League refused to participate, winning it the support of social layers close to the colonial state.

The conjunctural character of the demand for the establishment of a 'Pakistan' can be judged by the fact that it not only meant different things to different groups, it meant different things at different times to the same person: Mohammed Ali Jinnah. In the period 1940–46, Jinnah had become undisputed leader of the League, but he was still not sure what bargain he would finally accept or reject. Jinnah did not totally discard a federal solution till 1946, which is somewhat odd for a politician who had since the thirties claimed that the Muslims of India constituted a 'nation'. Furthermore, even after the formation of a separate state had been accepted by the Congress and the British, Jinnah was undecided on the character of the new Muslim republic. He told an Associated Press correspondent in 1945 that 'Politically Pakistan would be a democracy'. Mr Jinnah said that he 'personally hoped that its major industrial and public services would be socialized'. A few *days* later he reassured a religious leader in the North-West Frontier Province: 'It is needless to emphasize that the Constituent Assembly, which would be predominantly Muslim in composition, would not be able to enact laws inconsistent with the Shariat [Islamic Code].'

The support for Muslim separatism was strongest in the UP, where Muslims were a minority and where competition for jobs between the Hindu and Muslim middle classes was most severe. In those areas where Muslims constituted a majority, the traditional governing élites were, till the very last, either openly hostile or luke-warm to the idea of Pakistan.[19] It is this dichotomy that explains Jinnah's reluctance to accept Nehru's call for a Constituent Assembly elected on the basis of universal adult franchise, *even with the guarantee of separate electorates for Muslims*. The League was not confident that it could win a majority of Muslim votes in an unrestricted communal election. The crucial consideration for the League by now was a political settlement, with the colonial state and the Congress, that would guarantee Pakistan. It could not demand that popular self-determination be the deciding factor, since in Punjab, Bengal and Sind this would undoubtedly have transcended communal barriers. The League's support came mainly from the middle and upper reaches of Muslim society. In Bengal it did win mass support, but this reflected a class polarization in the countryside between Muslim peasants and Hindu *jotedars* (small landlords).

The first act of civil disobedience called by the League was when it mobilized its supporters on Direct Action Day in 1946. The result was communal rioting: the carnage reached a peak in Calcutta, where Hindus and Muslims slaughtered each other and hundreds died. Not long after this outbreak of communal madness, the workers of Calcutta (both Hindu and Muslim) came out on strike and, in January 1947, unleashed a general strike. In February 1946, a naval mutiny had traumatized the British and the leaders of the Congress and the Muslim League alike. The rebellion began in Bombay and spread rapidly to Madras and Karachi. The sailors elected a Strike Committee and hoisted the red flag on the occupied ships with the slogan: Long Live Revolution! The British authorities were taken by surprise, but two factors helped them to restabilize the situation: repression, and support from the Congress and the League. Indian troops refused to open fire and British soldiers had to be used. On 21 February 1946, Admiral Godfrey threatened to destroy the whole navy unless the strike were called off. The Central Naval Strike Committee responded by calling on the workers in the cities to strike. The Congress leaders were opposed to such a course, but the Communist Party supported the call and Bombay, the financial capital of India, was paralysed by a general strike on 22 February. The British authorities, confident of nationalist support, decided to shoot the workers. Over 500 people were killed. The following day the Congress and League leaders, perturbed by this display of class unity, advised the naval ratings to surrender. Feeling isolated, the Strike Committee called off the action and accepted defeat. Within two days the leaders were arrested. They were never to be employed again in the defence services, not even by independent India.

The wave of strikes was not restricted to either the navy or Bombay. In the same month 300 sepoys mutinied in Jabalpur, and on 18 March there was an unheard-of development: Gurkha soldiers rebelled at Dehradun, where a top military academy was stationed. In April, nearly 10,000 police-men refused to work in Bihar.[20] At the same time there was a wave of peasant struggles in the Punjab, where Muslim peasants fought against the illegal practices of their landlords, most of whom had by this time switched their loyalties to the Muslim League. Gandhi was as worried as the Viceroy. In his newspaper *Harijan* he wrote on 7 April 1946 that to accept this 'unholy combination' (of Hindus and Muslims indulging in strikes) would mean 'delivering India over to the rabble. I would not wish to live up to 125 to witness that consummation. I would rather perish in flames.'

Throughout 1946 India hovered on the brink of a pre-revolutionary crisis. It was this objective situation that inexorably pushed the Congress, the Muslim League and the British towards each other. Nehru explained the problem in a letter to a Congress colleague: 'the situation is volcanic and definite choices have to be made . . . [even though] the choice is often a very difficult one.' Not to be outdone, Jinnah too expressed his fear of inter-communal solidarity. At the height of the naval strike (one of whose key leaders, M. S. Khan, was a Muslim), the League leader released a press statement to the Bombay *Free Press Journal*. After the usual banalities concerning the grievances of the men, he made a direct communal appeal:

> I appeal to all RIN [Royal Indian Navy] men not to play into the hands of those who want to create trouble and exploit those on strike for their own ends. I urge upon them to restore normal conditions and let us handle the situation . . . I, therefore, appeal to the ratings of the RIN to call off the strike and to the public in general not to add to the difficulties of the situation. Particularly, *I call upon the Muslims to stop* and create no further trouble until we are in a position to handle this very serious situation.[21]

It was the acclivity of class tensions which sealed the fate of the subcontinent: partition and the creation of a confessional state were the tragic outcome.

The Congress and the League had, for different reasons, become the two major political parties in the country. But they were not able to exercise a total monopoly of politics. The Communist Party of India (CPI), although numerically small, was not politically impotent in its formative phase. Nor was it without influence within the nationalist movement. Its potential was recognized by the colonial state which, for its part, ensured that communist activists were the targets of almost continuous repression. Hundreds of communists were imprisoned in the late twenties and thirties. Most of them were convicted on the basis of planted informers, fake testimony and blatant forgeries. The CPI cadres were instrumental in the formation of trade unions in parts of Bengal and the Bombay region; they also played an important role in helping to organize poor peasants in some of the most backward areas of the country.

The courage and dedication of thousands of communist militants was, however, continually squandered by the strategic misconceptions of the party leaders and the Communist International. In the early twenties, the tiny groups of Indian communists were encouraged to initiate a military struggle for liberation long before the preconditions for such a struggle were present. The Comintern under Lenin and Trotsky did not grasp the specific nature of the Indian social formation, nor did it correctly assess the role of bourgeois nationalism.[22] For instance, it insistently maintained that the Congress would not undertake *any* struggle against British rule. This error was further compounded in the infamous Third Period of the Comintern with Stalin at the helm. Congress was now denounced as a vulgar instrument of British imperialism. The turn towards Popular Fronts inaugurated by the Seventh and final Congress of the Comintern was to help the CPI to develop as a nationally organized force. Its membership grew from a few hundreds to over 5,000. This was due largely to the party's decision to work with Congress in the anti-imperialist struggle. In Bengal in the north and Kerala in the south, the CPI acquired a mass influence during this period which it has managed to retain to the present day.

The crucial test for the CPI came during the Second World War. At the outbreak of the war, the Indian communists opposed any support for Britain and France and argued that India's freedom should not be compromised by any deals with the occupying power. Their opposition to the war led to widespread arrests of party leaders on a national, provincial and local level, but it also brought them closer to the left wing of the Congress. The German invasion of the Soviet Union created dissension in the party ranks. A minority of party leaders, among them K. Damodaran of Kerala, opposed the thesis developed by Moscow that the war had now been transformed into a 'People's War', and accordingly the duty of communists everywhere was to support the Allied war effort. The CPI fell into line and became a virtual recruiting agent for the British authorities, but those communists who opposed the new line were not released till much later.

In August 1942, when Congress launched its 'Quit India' movement, the Viceroy responded by unleashing a new wave of repressive measures.[23] Congress leaders and activists now entered prison cells which had only recently been emptied of CPI inmates. Many decades later, Damodaran revealed in an interview how damaging the consequences of the CPI's servile compliance with Stalin's dictates had been:

There is a view developed by some of the apologists for the 'People's War' line which argues that the CPI gained a lot of support as a consequence of 'swimming against the stream'. I do not subscribe to this view.

Of course the party took advantage of legality granted to it by British imperialism to gain new members and increase its trade-union strength, but the point is that it was swimming against the stream of the mass movement and was to all intents and purposes considered an ally of British imperialism. It became respectable to be a communist. Many young communists joined the British army to go and 'defend the Soviet Union' in Italy and North Africa. Some of them rapidly shed their 'communism' and stayed in the army even after the war – and not to do clandestine work! It is true that the membership of the party increased from about 4,500 in July 1942 to well over 15,500 in May 1943 at the time of the First Party Congress . . . But most of these new members had no experience of any militant mass struggle or police repression but only the peaceful campaigns conducted by the party to 'grow more food', 'increase production', 'release national leaders', 'form a national government' and 'defend the Motherland' from a Japanese invasion which never came. Strikes were denounced as sabotage . . . On the other side, the growth of the Congress and its influence after the 'Quit India' struggle of August 1942 was phenomenal. Millions of men and women, especially the youth, were attracted and radicalized by the struggle, which was considered as a revolution against imperialism . . . we branded the Congress Socialists, Bose's followers and other radicals who braved arrests and police repression, as fifth columnists and saboteurs . . . In reality the CPI was isolated from the mainstream of the nationalist movement for the second time within a decade. In my view the party's policy virtually delivered the entire anti-imperialist movement to the Congress and the Indian bourgeoisie on a platter. At the time, if the CPI had adopted a correct position the possibility existed of winning over a sizable and influential section of the Congress to communism . . . On my release from prison I experienced the wrath of the left-wing nationalists who used to chant 'Down with supporters of British imperialism' at our meetings. So swimming against the stream when the stream was flowing in the right direction resulted in drowning the possibility of genuine independence and a socialist transformation. We were outmanoeuvred and outflanked by the Indian bourgeoisie.[24]

One of the essential criteria for evaluating a political line is to examine the extent to which it is based on a correct or false analysis of reality. The CPI's position during the war was untenable on all counts. It created a sharp divide between party activists and the base of the nationalist movement; it misconstrued the reality of Indian politics; and its misplaced notion of loyalty to the Soviet Union meant that it was incapable, even in practice, of breaking with the ideology of Stalinism. The CPI theses on the war brought it closer to the Muslim League, which likewise remained loyal during the war and saw an increase in its political influence and standing.

It was the League's growth that was to provide an opportunity for the CPI to make another major strategic error. Instead of providing its supporters with a trenchant critical analysis of all brands of communal politics and offering an alternative, the CPI, in the words of its theorist Adikhari, 'began to see that the so-called communal problem, especially the Hindu–Muslim problem, was really a problem of growing nationalities'. It was during the 'People's War' years (1942–5) that the CPI, forced into the same political camp as the Muslim League, first discovered the intricacies of the national question. A resolution, 'Pakistan and National Unity', was passed by the Enlarged Plenum of the Central Committee in September 1942 and approved by the Party congress seven months later; it was a *mélange* of opportunist politics and theoretical confusion. It took as its starting-point Stalin's insufficient definition of a 'nation', went on to develop a completely false analogy between India and Tsarist Russia and drew the conclusion that the Muslims constituted a *national* minority which should be granted the right of self-determination.[25]

The CPI leaders failed even to refer to the classical definition of a nation within the Marxist tradition. To have done so would merely have revealed the political distance they had travelled over the years. For Marx and Lenin alike, neither a common language nor a common culture constituted the basis of a bourgeois nation. The latter was a synonym for the modern state. Religion merely expressed the separation of an individual from the community as a whole, and could not constitute the basis for a community. It was the Austro-Marxist tradition which had de-materialized the discussion on nationalism by introducing mystical notions such as 'national character'. The initial development of capitalism was regarded as progressive by Marx and Engels precisely because of its role as a leveller of nationalities. It was the centralizing dynamic of modern capitalism which would create a proletariat united by its relationship to the means of production rather than by religion or caste. The only other basis for nationalities developing into nations was a situation where they were oppressed by a dominant nationality. In Tsarist (and one might add, Stalinist) Russia, the Great Russians were the overwhelmingly dominant nationality. Hence Lenin's insistence that the right to secede be written into the constitution of the infant Soviet Republic.

But comparisons between India and Russia were largely futile. It could hardly be argued that the British colonial state oppressed Sindhis and Bengalis more or less than Punjabis or Pathans. In fact, a common subjection to British rule had unified India economically and politically as never before. The native bourgeoisie was a shining example of cosmopolitanism!

It was not dominated by any particular religious or caste grouping.[26] In fact Jinnah, realizing that this was an obstacle so far as his project for a separate state was concerned, pushed through in 1944 the formation of a separate Muslim Chamber of Commerce (many of the businessmen who joined this body were later to be amply rewarded with a captive market in Pakistan).

This was a time when the CPI should have swum against the stream of Muslim communalism; but their approach of 'national unity in the holy defence of our Motherland' against 'pitiless and powerful enemies' (the Japanese) made any application of Marxist politics impossible. The politics being effectively applied became *ipso facto* the only possible politics. It was only after the conclusion of the war that the CPI altered its position, this time on the urging of R. Palme Dutt, a leader of the British Communist Party. Dutt argued in 1946 that Pakistan was based on religion and not nationality. The CPI obligingly changed its position and denounced Pakistan as a plot between British imperialism and 'Muslim bourgeois feudal vested interests'. Many Muslim communists, however, were slow to catch up with the change in line and found themselves in 1947 still members of the Muslim League, which they had been instructed to enter in order to help the 'progressive' elements against the landlords.

After a set of complicated negotiations Jinnah, on behalf of the Muslim League, had accepted a divided Punjab, a divided Bengal and the provinces of Sind, NWFP and Baluchistan.[27] The logic of communalist politics had never been totally understood by Jinnah. He had imagined that the new Pakistan would contain a substantial minority of Sikhs and Hindus, and for that reason had insisted that it would be a modern, secular state with no distinctions of caste or creed. Heartbroken at the partitioning of Bengal and the Punjab, he was shattered at the communal violence accompanying the mass migrations which followed the announcement of a British withdrawal. Lord Mountbatten, the last Viceroy, expressed Jinnah's dilemma well in the course of an address to the Royal Empire Society in London on 6 October 1948:

> He [Jinnah] produced the strongest arguments why these provinces should not be partitioned. He said they had national characteristics and that partition would be disastrous. I agreed, but I said how much more must I now feel that the same considerations applied to the partitioning of the whole of India . . . Finally he realized that either he could have a united India with an unpartitioned Punjab and Bengal or a divided India with a partitioned Punjab and Bengal and he finally accepted the latter solution.

It was, of course, in the character of the League's politics (and to a lesser extent those of the Congress) that decisions were made by 'the Leader'. Consulting the masses was not seen as necessary: they were merely informed of the decisions that had been taken.

It was a supreme irony that, in the last months preceding British withdrawal, the only people who could walk the streets secure in the knowledge that they would not be harmed were British officers, civil servants and their families. Hindus and Sikhs slaughtered Muslims and vice versa. The most fitting statement on the carnage and suffering that ordinary people were inflicting on each other was expressed by a teenage Sikh girl, Amrita Pritam, who wrote a poignant poem appealing to the rationalism of the Punjab's most famous Sufi poet, Warith Shah:

> I call on Warith Shah today:
> O speak up from your grave
> And from the Book of Love unfurl
> A new and different page.
>
> When *one* daughter of the Punjab did weep,
> You wrote countless verses.
> Today, millions of daughters are in tears
> With this message for you:
> 'Arise, you healer of inner pain,
> And look now at your Punjab;
> The forests are littered with corpses
> And blood flows down the Chenab.'[28]

2 Post-Independence Realities:
The First Decade 1947–58

Contradictions of the New State

The departure of the British left a political vacuum in the territories which now comprised Pakistan. India proper had, since the last decade of the nineteenth century, been permitted to construct a political party (Congress), which by 1947, when Independence was achieved, had won the backing of India's powerful capitalist class. The Congress was a unique political instrument: backed by capitalism, supported by the rural and urban petty bourgeoisie and with a limited following inside the working class, it had no equal in the rest of the colonial world. Pakistan, by contrast, had the Muslim League, an organization with a limited mass base, but strong in the countryside because of the grip which landlords and religious mystagogues (*pirs*) exercised over the peasantry. Politics began at the top and was marked by a distinctly feudal approach to problems. Individual landlords could make or break parties by utilizing the 'parcellized sovereignty' they enjoyed over their lands and their tenants.

The areas which formed West and East Pakistan were predominantly agrarian. The mass exodus of Hindus and Sikhs from West Punjab, Sind and Bahawalpur and their replacement by Muslim refugees from India had created a dislocation on the political, economic and social levels. The new state was, inevitably, confronted by a whole set of contradictions that had not been visualized either by Jinnah or by his leading political lieutenants from the United Provinces. None of them were familiar with the problems of Bengalis, Punjabis, Sindhis, Pathans or Baluch. Neither Jinnah (as Governor-General) nor Liaquat Ali Khan (as his prime minister) spoke any of the languages of the country's provinces. Liaquat spoke Urdu, but Jinnah's first language was English.

On the political front, two sets of interrelated dilemmas had to be solved. The first and most important was the geographical division of the country. West and East Pakistan were separated by 1,000 miles of Indian territory. 60 per cent of the population was Bengali and lived in the Eastern wing, while political power was concentrated in the West. Nothing could have exposed the irrationality of the 1947 partition as much as this single fact, which was to dominate Pakistani politics for three decades. The second problem was the absence of political unity. The Punjabi landlords had, until recently, been extremely hostile to the League and were both ultra-reactionary and extremely unreliable.[1] Baluchs had hardly heard of the Muslim League and had, in any event, never been asked whether or not they wished to be part of the new state. Their ruler had signed the accession documents without consulting any segment of the population.[2] In the Frontier province, the League was a novelty, its support coming from petty-bourgeois layers in the city of Peshawar (*nouveaux riches* contractors who had done well out of the war, shopkeepers, civil servants, traders); in the Pathan countryside, the *Khudai Khidmatgars* of Khan Abdul Ghaffar Khan, with a militant, anti-imperialist record, retained their following among the peasants. In Sind, the League had grown but was split between the landlords and their opponents.

Jinnah favoured the creation of a bourgeois-democratic state, but the theoretical inconsistencies of the advocates of the 'two-nation' theory now made themselves felt in the practice of fashioning the new republic. A state of the Indian type was excluded by the contradictions inherent in the structure of Pakistan. The weakness of the League in West Pakistan meant that the only 'political party' Jinnah could rely on was the civil service of Pakistan, born out of the Indian civil service and conceived by the British imperial administration. Jinnah clearly viewed Pakistan as a constitutional social democracy. His first address to the Constituent Assembly in Karachi, on 11 August 1947, explicitly dissociated itself from interpretations which stressed the confessional character of the new state:

> You are free; you are free to go to your temples, you are free to go to your mosques or to any other place of worship in this State of Pakistan. You may belong to any religion or caste or creed – that has nothing to do with the business of the State ... We are starting with this fundamental principle that we are all citizens and equal citizens of one State. Now I think we should keep that in front of us as our ideal and you will find that in course of time Hindus would cease to be Hindus and Muslims would cease to be Muslims, not in the religious sense, because that is the personal faith of each individual, but in the political sense as citizens of the State.

This speech has been strongly criticized (usually in private, since Jinnah is above public criticism in Pakistan) by religious divines, confessional sects and right-wing political parties because of its opposition to the creation of an 'Islamic state'. The criticisms are not without logic. If Pakistan was the culmination of the struggle for a 'Muslim nation', then clearly secularism was a somewhat inappropriate ideology for it. A 'Muslim nation' should have a 'Muslim constitution'. An additional point could also be made regarding the speech: if its aspirations could be implemented in Pakistan, then surely they could equally have been put into practice in a united India. In reality, if the subcontinent had not been divided on a religious basis, the Muslims would actually have been a stronger force.[3] Jinnah's addiction to constitutionalism was creditable, but it merely brought to the fore the confused character of the campaign which had preceded the formation of the new state. Soon after Partition, Jinnah seriously considered the possibility of declaring the Muslim League a secular party and changing its name to the Pakistan National League. His intention, however, was prematurely revealed by the then left-wing daily, the *Pakistan Times*, and the resulting hue and cry from reactionary elements compelled him to shelve the proposal. Jinnah's death in 1948 and Liaquat Ali Khan's assassination in 1951 left the civil service in total command. The blatant manipulation of the country's political life by civil servants has been well documented elsewhere.[4] We can merely indicate the size of the impediments that lay across their path.

The political intricacies have already been mentioned. The economic situation was not much better. The agrarian character of the new state was highlighted by the fact that agriculture accounted for 60 per cent of total output and 70 per cent of total employment. The comparable figures for industry were 6 per cent for output and 10 per cent for employment. Service sectors made up the remainder. Large-scale production was non-existent: 41 per cent of all industrial enterprises were devoted to the processing of agricultural raw material and were in seasonal operation. Pakistan had inherited a total of 1,414 factories. Of these, only 314 were situated in East Pakistan. The little that did exist was controlled by the leading captains of Indian industry (the houses of Messrs Tata, Birla and Dalmia) and by British capital.[5] British control of trade and credit enabled it to determine the pattern of Pakistan's growth. The country was seen as a producer of raw materials tied to Britain by a whole network of economic and political links. The latter were mediated via the Commonwealth.

It was in the countryside that the situation was worst. In Pakistan as a whole, 6,000 landlords owned more land than 3.5 million peasant households. Many of these were also political and/or religious leaders in their regions. Their adherence in large numbers to the League, on the eve of and following Pakistan's creation, meant that the country's major political party was paralysed from birth. The landlords were the largest single grouping on the Muslim League National Council (the supreme authority of the party). Following Jinnah's death, the landlords (in league with civil servants) prevented any basic reforms in the country's social structure. All attempts to implement even the most elementary changes were branded as 'un-Islamic'.

The Sindhi leader G. M. Sayed spoke for many when he expressed his disgust with the League leadership:

> Do not forget also that Islamic society actually in existence is that in which the religious head is an ignorant Mullah, the spiritual head an immoral Pir, the political guide a power-intoxicated feudal landlord ... their cry of 'Islam is in Danger' became a cloak for dark deeds and reactionary moves, complacency and tyranny. Such is the extent to which mockery can be made of Islam in these days of capitalist subterfuge and commercialized politics.[6]

The weakness of civil society meant that the state was all-powerful. The two instruments at the service of the state, the army and the civil service, were both direct descendants of their British forebears. An attempt was made to create a cohesive ruling class, a stable ruling party and a permanent constitution; but all these attempts failed, and the decades that followed exacerbated the 'crisis of identity' that had consistently confounded the ideologists of the new state.

The specific characteristics of the Pakistani state were a reflection of the particular political contradictions which dominated it from the very beginning and acquired a more explosive character with the passage of time. The single most important amongst these was the impossibility for the rulers of Pakistan to implement the universal principles of a bourgeois democratic state: adult franchise, regular general elections, political liberties, creation of a national market, etc. The army and the civil service were based in West Pakistan (largely the Punjab). The political capital of the new country was Karachi and economic capital tended to gravitate towards the centres of real power. The handful of entrepreneurs who had left Bombay to try their luck with the backing of a new state opted to settle in West rather than East Pakistan. Regional disparities are, of course, not unknown even in the advanced capitalist countries: there are examples of 'underdeveloped' regions in every major capitalist state. Pakistan, however, systematically developed such disparities on political and racial grounds. The question of democracy was explosive from the very beginning, since an unrestricted franchise would have meant a tension between the majority of the population in the Bengali East and the majority of the ruling class and the state apparatus based in West Pakistan.

The contradiction was first highlighted by the language question. It was decided by Jinnah and approved by the League's high command that Urdu would be the national language of the country. The Bengalis argued that there should be two state languages, Urdu *and* Bengali. The suggestion was a constructive one, since Bengali was spoken by 56 per cent of the population, Punjabi by 37 per cent, while the remainder spoke Pushtu, Sindhi,

Baluchi and Urdu. On his first and only visit to East Pakistan, Jinnah was confronted by a predominantly student committee of action. Since February 1948, the language issue (in itself a reflection of the national divide) had dominated Bengali politics. On 11 March there were student strikes and demonstrations throughout the province. Bengali members of the Constituent Assembly had not been allowed to speak in their mother tongue. Liaquat Ali Khan, the prime minister, replying to protests had stated: 'Pakistan is a Muslim state and it must have as its *lingua franca* the language of the Muslim nation . . . It is necessary for a nation to have one language and that language can only be Urdu and no other language.' Bengal rose in anger against this display of philistinism and was answered by state repression. When Jinnah finally arrived in Dacca, he was greeted by a sullen populace. When he refused to compromise on the language issue (largely, it should be stated, on the advice of recalcitrant and arrogant Punjabi civil servants), students tore down his portraits in schools and colleges. In his convocation address at Dacca University, Jinnah (speaking in English) reaffirmed his support for Urdu. He was greeted with large-scale heckling, walk-outs and chaos. He could not finish his speech. A subsequent discussion with the leaders of the action committee ended in a similar stalemate.[7] Jinnah's obstinacy made no impact on the students, who were in no mood for compromise. The struggle was to recur in different guises until 1971.

The weakness of the Muslim League as a political party soon led to splits and the formation of new political groupings. Once again the West–East divide determined the character of the new formations. The most crippling blow suffered by the League was in East Pakistan. The Bengali leader H. S. Suhrawardy had initially favoured a united Bengal as part of a broad Indian federation. Opposed to the 1947 Partition, he decided to leave Calcutta (the capital of West Bengal) and come to Pakistan only in 1949. He linked up with the veteran peasant leader Maulana Bhashani, and together they decided to form the Awami (People's) League in opposition to the Muslim League. The new party became the conduit of middle-class opposition on the language issue, and immediately identified itself with the demand for provincial elections on the basis of adult franchise in East Pakistan.

Large-scale arrests of oppositionists and curtailment of civil liberties coincided with a worsening economic situation. Pakistan's refusal to devalue the rupee during the Korean war had resulted in a temporary boom, but with the end of the war there was a sharp drop in the prices of agricultural raw materials. The Eastern province was the world's largest producer of raw jute, which earned the bulk of the country's foreign exchange. The Central government destroyed 'surplus' jute and restricted the sowing process. This was coupled in 1952–3 with a massive food shortage and a famine, cruelly exploited by West Pakistani merchants and speculators in league with the bureaucracy. The Muslim League proved incompetent to deal with either the black market in food or the economic crisis.

Policies were, in any case, determined by the Central government, whose general attitude to East Pakistan and its citizenry was a parody of English colonialism. The economic exploitation of East Pakistan began almost immediately after Partition (see Tables 1 and 2 on pp. 85–6). By 1956, economists worked out that at least 300 million rupees were being extracted annually. East Pakistan's resources were utilized to develop parts of West Pakistan. Between 1948 and 1951, a sum of 130 million rupees was sanctioned for development. Of this only 22.1 per cent went to East Pakistan. Three years later the gap had increased further. The industrial enterprises set up in East Pakistan were, in the main, controlled by non-Bengali businessmen and financed by West Pakistani capital. It was a classic colonial situation: raw materials from the East brought in foreign exchange, which was used to develop Karachi and the Punjab. The goods produced in the West were off-loaded in the East. Between 1948 and 1953, exports from West Pakistan to the East exceeded imports from East to West by 909 million rupees. Bengalis found themselves prisoners of the new state, and their part of the country a captive market.

In order to prevent the Bengali population from feeling its own strength and occupying a leading position in the politics of Pakistan, the new ruling class institutionalized a form of ethnic discrimination (see Table 3 on p. 87). Bengalis were not welcomed into the ranks of the bureaucracy or the army. It was Punjabi civil servants, moulded by the Raj, who determined political developments in the country. The Muslim League was a creature of the state bureaucracy. Its isolation was revealed in stark fashion following the provincial elections of 1954. The elections had been preceded by a fresh outbreak of mass struggles on the thorny issue of language. On 21 February 1952 a large student demonstration had been 'dispersed' by the police in time-honoured fashion: it had fired on the crowd, killing twenty-six and wounding 400 others. The response to the killings developed on two levels: opposition parties formed a United Front in 1952, with a twenty-one point platform; and a defensive bureaucracy agreed that elections would take place in the province on 16 February 1954.

The Twenty-One Points were the first charter of a disenfranchised middle class. The central demands were for equality among the provinces at the federal level, and for provincial autonomy for East Bengal. The overall thrust of the demands was to push through a process which would clear the path for capitalist development in the East, coupled with agrarian reforms, nationalization of the jute trade and the ending of discrimination against Bengalis in the armed forces. To achieve the latter task, it was suggested that the naval headquarters be transferred to East Pakistan. Unable to counter the arguments, the Muslim League encouraged the mullahs to tour the countryside and denounce the United Front as an agency for communists and Hindus.

As the date for the elections approached the bureaucracy was in a state of panic. It postponed them for a fortnight in order to silence the left. Twelve hundred communists and trade-unionists were arrested within the space of forty-eight hours. When the voting was finally allowed – from 8 March till 12 March 1954 – the Bengalis showed how isolated the Muslim League was from the mainstream of political consciousness in the province. Out of 309 seats, the League won only ten. Neither the League chief minister nor any member of his cabinet succeeded in retaining their seats.[8] The Communist Party won four of the ten seats it contested, and interestingly enough it was communists of Hindu origin who were elected rather than their Muslim comrades – a revealing footnote to illustrate the outrageous character of the 1947 division!

The electoral victory of the United Front marked the first major defeat to be inflicted on the bureaucracy and its favoured coterie of politicians. After a series of vulgar provocations, the Central government dissolved the newly elected Assembly only two months after the elections and proclaimed Governor's rule under Section 92A of the Constitution. The Governor, ex-Major-General Iskander Mirza, was a shrewd, reactionary time-server. He was a bureaucrat with a military record. The latter consisted of services provided to the British in crushing recalcitrant tribesmen in the North-West Frontier Province. Mirza's military-bureaucratic status was ideal for the job that he had been assigned: the United Front leaders were arrested, as were thousands of their supporters. The Communist Party was banned and employers were instructed to dismiss communist workers or face the wrath of the administration. While repression was used to demobilize the left, the right wing of the United Front was offered a number of inducements. After a year of bargaining, the provincial Assembly was restored and Governor's rule ended. Political prisoners were released. A right-wing Bengali leader moaned in the Constituent Assembly:

> Sir, I actually started yesterday and said that the attitude of the Muslim League here was of contempt towards East Bengal, towards its culture, its language, its literature and everything concerning East Bengal . . . In fact, Sir, I tell you that far from considering East Bengal as an equal partner, the leaders of the Muslim League thought that we were a subject race and they belonged to a race of conquerors.[9]

The 'race of conquerors', however, was also worried about West Pakistan. As it continued to suffer defeats in successive by-elections, it became clear that if free elections were permitted the Muslim League would lose three provinces. The bureaucracy was petrified. Its recurring nightmare was a combination of Bengal and the non-Punjabi provinces in West Pakistan, which would represent a large majority in any national or federal legislative assembly. The scheme of 'One Unit' was conceived to prevent any such development. This entailed the abolition of provinces in the Western part of the country, and the formation of a party which could unite the landed gentry of all regions. It was imagined that a 'united' West Pakistan would be better able to combat the demands of East Bengal. However, the plan ran into a whole series of problems. For a start, it split the Muslim League. The League's parliamentary caucus opposed One Unit, and when the matter was discussed in the Constituent Assembly the result was a defeat for the bureaucracy: the Assembly accepted a plan which was diametrically opposed to One Unit, favouring a re-organization of West Pakistan into six provinces.

Differences between the bureaucracy and non-Punjabi Muslim League politicians also reflected differing approaches to the problem of international alliances. The Governor-General, Ghulam Mohammed, was a foul-mouthed bureaucrat closely in league with the Dulles brothers in the United States. The country's prime minister, Mohammed Ali Bogra, was himself a favoured protégé of John Foster Dulles, US secretary of state. Together with the commander-in-chief of the army, General Ayub Khan, Bogra was dispatched by Ghulam Mohammed to the United States to negotiate a long-term military and economic aid pact and obtain authority to run the country.[10] On their return to Karachi they went straight to the Governor-General's residence, where the decision was taken to dissolve the Constituent Assembly and proclaim a 'state of emergency' – the first of many to be inflicted on the country. Ayub was subsequently to describe the scene in his memoirs: 'The Governor-General was lying in his bedroom upstairs . . . He was bursting with rage, emitting volleys of abuse . . . I was about to step out of the room when the nurse attending the Governor-General tugged at my coat. He then beckoned me with a peculiar glee in his eye . . . He then pulled out two documents from his pillow . . .'[11] According to Ayub, these documents offered him the power to take over the country with the army and produce a new Constitution. He refused, probably because the plan did not have the backing of the United States.

Following the dissolution of the Constituent Assembly, the country was governed by the civil service. The symbolism behind the fact that the Governor-General was virtually insane did not bother the bureaucracy. A new cabinet was formed which brought in the army chief as defence minister and included H. S. Suhrawardy, the Awami League boss from East Bengal, in the government. It was Suhrawardy, an ardent exponent of provincial autonomy in the East, who was to become the extinguisher of provincial rights in the West. The One Unit plan was forced through by the Central government and provincial assemblies were ordered to vote in its favour. In Sind, even Suhrawardy later acknowledged that 'terror' had been used to force members to vote. The provincial assemblies then elected a new Constituent Assembly, and the One Unit Act was passed. On 14 October 1955 the new 'province' of West Pakistan came into existence. A short-sighted bureaucracy, desperate to balance East with West, had thus injected the national question into the heart of West Pakistani politics.

Ghulam Mohammed's resignation in August 1955 saw him replaced by Mirza. Another bureaucrat, Chaudhri Mohammed Ali, was appointed prime minister and the two new bosses succeeded in pushing a new Constitution through the Assembly. On 23 March 1956, Pakistan became an Islamic Republic. Mirza became president. The main function of the new Constitution was to institutionalize political discrimination against the Bengalis, by denying them the weight they should have had as a majority of the population. The president was given wide-ranging powers, and the Central government was to be so powerful that provincial autonomy was reduced to a farcical status.

The sole dissenting voice on a national level was the country's largest daily, the *Pakistan Times* (owned by West Pakistan's leading left-wing politician, Mian Iftikhar-ud-Din):

> It seems strange indeed that nine years after independence it should still be necessary to explain that freedom is a good thing and that democracy is neither dangerous nor undesirable. The phenomenon is easily understood, however, in the context of the direction, or rather misdirection, of our political life since independence. On the one hand, the core of our ruling class have steadily moved themselves further and further away from the danger of political contamination by contact with the masses ... and, in consequence, have almost completely divorced State policies domestic and foreign from national sentiment and the wishes of the people ... these policies are the brain-children of bureaucratic scribblers in the Secretariat, of foreign experts, of big and small fry in the Government and not a codification of popular desires. On the other hand, the bulk of the intelligentsia and the politically conscious elements, at least, in West Pakistan, have either given up the fight or have become more and more resigned to the inevitability of a long period of waiting before better days come round again. And the people have been left out in the cold by both sides.[12]

A bureaucrat is characterized by, among other things, a total contempt for the ability of the people to decide their future or anything else for themselves. In the best of cases, the result is a benevolent but firm paternalism. In the worst, it leads to grotesque manipulation and repression of any real opposition. Mirza belonged to the latter category of bureaucrat. He genuinely believed that a deal 'at the top' with the senior Bengali leader would solve the constitutional contradictions of the Pakistani state. Accordingly, H. S. Suhrawardy was bribed with the premiership in September 1956. He accepted, and Mirza hurriedly organized the necessary parliamentary support. Suhrawardy was a talented politician. He was a proficient lawyer, an artful manipulator, a glib conversationalist and an extremely able intriguer. He was undoubtedly head and shoulders above most of his political equivalents in the country. His ultimate ambition, however, was typically unrealistic. He wanted to transform the Awami League into a national electoral machine, ignoring the realities of the new state: it was class and not geography that was the driving force behind the bureaucracy.

Mirza had been irritated by the antics of the Muslim League in opposing One Unit. He needed a totally pliant pawn. He now, therefore, split the League and brought the Republican Party into existence. The landlords had shifted allegiances once again. The new party had a one-vote majority in the West Pakistan Assembly. Suhrawardy presided over an Awami League–Republican coalition. Such an association excluded any possibility of a rational solution to the national question. The formation of the new government failed to stabilize the political situation even temporarily. Politics from the top was failing to deliver anything. The purchase of legislators by rival parties became a national scandal. Suhrawardy was only to last a year in office.

Foreign Policy

Jinnah, in a number of press statements, had indicated that the foreign policy of the Pakistani state would be non-aligned. This proved to be yet another unfulfilled hope. The post-war world saw the emergence of the United States as the dominant Western power. The decline of British imperialism reflected the precarious condition of the world's first major industrial power. The changes brought about by the war had also resulted in the division of Europe into 'spheres of influence': in the Western sector, it was the Marshall Plan that resuscitated a badly damaged capitalist system; in the East, it was the Soviet Union that influenced developments and carried out social upheavals 'from the top' (with the exceptions of Yugoslavia and Albania). The continuing upheavals in China, Indo-China and the Korean peninsula threatened the 'spirit of Yalta'. What these processes revealed was that genuine mass movements pushing in the direction of social revolutions (under the leadership of communist parties) could not be impeded by the United States or manipulated by the Stalinist bureaucracy in the Kremlin. It was the revolutionary wind in Asia (as much as the struggles in Greece) which transformed the wartime alliance of the USSR and the

Western states into a 'cold war'. The success of the Chinese revolution in 1949 led to a 'hot war' in Korea and a massive escalation in Indo-China. The defeat of the French at Dienbienphu in 1954 helped to inspire the Algerian *maquis* to step up their resistance to France.

It was in these global conditions that Pakistan's first prime minister, Liaquat Ali Khan, rejected an invitation to visit Moscow and, instead, boarded a plane for Washington. His successors formally cemented the alliance. Ghulam Mohammed and Iskander Mirza, the two bureaucrats who effectively ran the country as heads of state in the fifties, needed the alliance with the United States to shore up their position at home. American aid had already started in 1951. In 1953, an artificially induced wheat crisis led to large-scale hoarding and price increases. The United States announced a fresh offer of aid (which was to arrive a year later) and the bureaucracy installed a new prime minister (a former ambassador to the United States). John Foster Dulles acclaimed Pakistan as 'a bulwark of freedom in Asia'. Any idea that the aid came without any attached strings was brutally dispelled by an official US document which laid down the guidelines:

> Technical Assistance is not something to be done, as a Government enterprise, for its own sake or for the sake of others. The US Government is not a charitable institution, nor is it an appropriate outlet for the charitable spirit of the American people. That spirit finds its proper instrumentality in the numerous private philanthropic and religious institutions which have done so much good work abroad. Technical Assistance is only one of a number of instruments available to the US to carry out its foreign policy and to promote its national interests abroad ... these tools of foreign policy include economic aid, military assistance, security treaties, overseas information programmes, participation in the UN and other international organizations, the exchange of persons programmes, tariff and trade policies, surplus agricultural commodities disposal policies and the traditional processes of diplomatic representation.[13]

In a world situation characterized by a cold-war stalemate in Europe and a developing colonial revolution in Asia and North Africa, American policymakers viewed all talk of 'neutrality' with unconcealed hostility. India's prime minister Nehru, one of the main initiators of the non-aligned movement, encouraged a policy of hostility to imperialist adventures in the third world. The refusal of India or Afghanistan to become part of the Western alliance gave Pakistan a certain geopolitical importance. The army and bureaucracy agreed to make the country an American base. In the autumn of 1953 the Pakistani army chief, General Ayub, negotiated military aid for Pakistan and accepted the conditions laid down by the United States. In

April 1954 a Pakistan–Turkey alliance was signed in Karachi: its aim was to extend the American sphere of influence along the Soviet frontiers and to isolate India. A month later the United States and Pakistan signed the Mutual (*sic*) Aid and Security Agreement in Karachi; this marked the virtual displacement of the British and their replacement by US personnel in terms of access to the Pakistan army.

In September 1954, the South East Asia Defence Organization (SEATO) was created. Its Asian members were not merely acting as clients, they were actually in a minority within the organization, whose members were the USA, Britain, France, Australia, New Zealand, Pakistan, Thailand and the Philippines. SEATO's main aim (which appears somewhat ironic today) was to 'contain Chinese aggression': every advance of social revolution in Asia was seen as a result of Chinese 'intervention'. Exactly a year later the United States orchestrated a new arrangement: Britain, Iran, Iraq, Turkey and Pakistan signed the Baghdad Pact, whose main aim was to prevent any new Nasserite/radical nationalist developments in the Middle and Near East which might threaten imperialist investments in the region. Only a few months after the signatures were completed, a radical army coup overthrew the monarchy in Iraq and withdrew the country from the Pact; a somewhat embarrassed Foreign Office in London rapidly renamed the bloc CENTO (Central Treaty Organization). All these pacts involved utilizing Pakistan as a base of operations against any new social upheavals in the area. Senior American policy-makers made it clear that the pacts would not be operative in the event of an Indo-Pakistan conflict.

The most important result of US military and economic aid, however, was internal rather than external. Aid of this sort produces a shift in the domestic relationship of political and social forces in favour of reactionary and conservative parties and institutions. The United States is strongly conscious of this; it admits that 'from a political viewpoint US military aid has strengthened Pakistan's armed services, *the greatest single stabilizing force in the country*, and has encouraged Pakistan to participate in collective defence agreements'.[14] At the same time, Pakistan's foreign policy became a faithful reflection of the needs of the State Department. Pakistan recognized the American client régimes of South Korea and South Vietnam, and backed the Anglo-American alliance wholeheartedly.

Opposition to the pro-American policy began to develop rapidly. It was foreign-policy issues which were to lead to the formation of new parties in both parts of the country. The climax was reached when Pakistan justified the Anglo-French-Israeli invasion of Egypt in October 1956. The Western powers had not been able to adjust themselves to the changing realities of the post-colonial world. The overthrow of the pro-British monarch Farouk and the rise to power of Nasser in Egypt marked a turning point for

Middle-East politics. Arab nationalism was in the ascendant. On 26 July 1956, Nasser reacted to the refusal of the West to finance the building of the Aswan Dam by nationalizing the Suez Canal. The imperialists could, he stated, 'choke in their rage'. Nasser's defiance of the British evoked a responsive chord in other former colonies. India welcomed the nationalization and Nehru defended Nasser at home and abroad. When the invasion came, it was India which emerged as the strongest backer of Arab nationalism. Pakistan backed the West. The prime minister at the time was H. S. Suhrawardy. He was greeted with protests throughout the country and a wave of anger spread through Pakistan. Suhrawardy subsequently modified his position, but only *after* the United States had opposed the adventure and pressured the British and French to withdraw.

Suhrawardy's pro-Western policy split his party. Maulana Bhashani attacked his former colleague in language laced with vitriol. In early 1957 Bhashani visited West Pakistan, where he conferred with left-wing leaders and decided to convene an All-Pakistan conference of progressive organizations. This was held in Dacca on 25 and 26 July 1957, and resulted in the creation of the National Awami Party. The social composition of the party varied from province to province, but overall it was a united front of the communist and non-communist left throughout the country. Its stated aims were a combination of radical nationalism and social democracy. It was committed to ending feudalism through a drastic agrarian reform; breaking with the pro-Western alliances; speeding up industrialization; holding immediate general elections; ending One Unit in West Pakistan and simultaneously guaranteeing regional autonomy in East Bengal. It is likely that such a formation would have come into existence in any event, but hostility to Karachi's foreign policy undoubtedly speeded up the process.[15]

The Pakistani Left

Partition resulted in a severe dislocation of the left. The effects of this were especially felt in West Pakistan, where the communist movement had never acquired a mass following, as it had in Bengal, Bombay and parts of southern India. The Punjab was to be the largest and most powerful province in the Pakistani state. At its peak, the CPI had had a membership of only some 3,000 in a united Punjab: since the majority of these were of Hindu or Sikh origin, their departure from the Western portion of Punjab to India upon Partition further depleted the strength of the party. The NWFP, Sind and Baluchistan meanwhile had a handful of members at best.

The reasons for the weakness of the communist movement in the Punjab could be summarized in the following way.[16] The lack of large-scale industrial enterprises meant that the areas which made up West Pakistan were either predominantly agrarian or tribal in character. Moreover, the Punjab was developed as a granary for the entire subcontinent, and the colonial authorities invested in an irrigation system to enlarge the amount of land available for cash crops such as wheat and cotton. This was determined not simply by economic necessities, but also by political imperatives. The Punjab was regarded as the 'sword arm of India'. The bulk of the colonial army was recruited from the Punjabi countryside. Availability of land was essential to bribe ex-servicemen and their dependants, in order to inoculate them against the nationalist infection. Not content with material incentives, the British administration in the thirties had devoted a lot of time and energy to launching the Unionist Party as a rival to the Muslim League and Congress in the Punjab. As we have already indicated, this was an inter-communal bloc of landed gentry which maintained a strong grip on the countryside. It did so not simply by exercising the traditional mechanisms utilized by landlords, but also by agitation against city-dwellers and equating the nationalist movement with the hated money-lenders, curse of the Indian peasantry.

Unionist hegemony was not total. A radical Muslim congressman, Mian Iftikhar-ud-Din, succeeded in defeating a prominent Unionist in the 1937 elections, when a total of twenty Congress candidates were also elected. This was an undoubted advance, though the Unionists still held 102 out of a total of 175 seats. A limited peasant agitation was organized by the left, and areas like Lyallpur, Montgomery (now Sahiwal), Multan, Khanewal and Jullundur saw a number of peasant strikes and peasant–landlord clashes. The Punjab premier and Unionist leader, Sir Sikandar Hyat, used a combination of repression and concessions to end the agitation. He stated that the Unionist Party would 'steadily pursue its policy of relieving the agricultural and labouring classes of their burden of debt'. The money-lenders were curbed, but peasant demands for a reduction of land revenue and water rates were ignored.

The Punjab student movement had had a strong inter-communal, left-nationalist component, but developing communal divisions now resulted in many Muslim students moving towards the Muslim League. On this front, too, the bulk of communist activists were Hindus and Sikhs. The satirical poet Akbar Allahabadi (1846–1921) had bitterly attacked those Muslims who wished to ally with the British and who celebrated every reversal suffered by the nationalists as *their* victory. Akbar had insisted that it was the organ-grinder and not the monkey who was the real victor, and had ridiculed separatist illusions:

> The fish has swallowed the bait
> And merrily pulls the line;
> The angler lets it run,
> He knows the catch is fine.

This is not to suggest that Muslim students who became standard-bearers of the League were conscious agents of imperialism. Their actions reflected a deformed and twisted nationalism, and they were utterly hostile to the pro-British Unionist government. But they ultimately became the victims of their own irrationality.

As we pointed out in the preceding chapter, the CPI during the war years appointed itself as an honest broker between the Muslim League and Congress. The League was non-existent in the Punjab in 1937, before the Muslim Unionist notables led by Sikandar Hyat joined its ranks. Hyat stated that 'in provincial matters he was a Unionist, but in all-India affairs a Muslim Leaguer'. The CPI theoretician Sajjad Zaheer explained this as a contradiction between pro-imperialist landlords and patriotic Muslims. The Muslim League was designated as an anti-imperialist patriotic party. The logic of such a view was spelt out by Zaheer as follows:

> The task of every patriot is to welcome and help this democratic growth which at long last is now taking place among the Muslims of the Punjab. The last stronghold of the imperialist bureaucracy in India is invaded by the League. Let us all help the people of Punjab to capture it.[17]

A whole group of communists and fellow-travellers of Muslim origin now linked arms with their old enemies. They went into the Muslim League to help its 'progressive wing'. A number of these who left after Partition never managed to get rid of the taste for political intrigue and opportunism they had acquired while in the League. At the time of Partition, most communists were still associating with the League. Mian Iftikhar-ud-Din was appointed minister for refugees and rehabilitation in the post-Partition Punjab government. When the League refused to accept his radical demands for resettling the refugees, he resigned his ministry and organized the Azad (Free) Pakistan Party, a body which in effect provided the left with a safe, constitutional cover.

The Communist Party of Pakistan (CPP) was set up by decision of the CPI in 1948, and the latter obligingly sent a number of Muslim communists to lead the new organization. Thus the CPP was no exception to the general rule that categorized all Pakistan's political parties: they were established from above. The first general secretary of the CPP was Sajjad Zaheer, a resident of the United Provinces and scion of a landed family, who held a commanding position as a critic in the realm of Urdu literature. In the field of aesthetic discourse he was a master. His organizing abilities, however, did not match his literary skills. Organizing a party committed to fundamental social change is somewhat more arduous than arranging a dinner party. In the conditions of West Pakistan, building a mass communist party could not but be a very long haul. The membership of the CPP in West Pakistan was less than two hundred. With committed cadres (and they did exist) a party could have been developed and an influential trade-union network established. The CPP was fortunate in that it possessed in Mirza Ibrahim a dynamic working-class leader and in Ferozedin 'Dada' Mansur an experienced veteran with detailed knowledge of the countryside. However, the skills and talents which existed were not put to their proper use, and the CPP leadership was constantly engaged in a search for short-cuts.

The left – CPP and Azad Pakistan Party – were to receive an added bonus. Mian Iftikhar-ud-Din decided that his speeches in parliament in favour of the oppressed were not sufficient to form public opinion. He decided to launch a series of daily papers. Progressive Papers Limited, formed in 1947, provided the left with a chain of extremely radical newspapers: the *Pakistan Times* became the largest circulation English daily in the country, and *Imroze* pioneered new techniques in Urdu journalism and became extremely popular. The newspapers employed radical journalists, and soon emerged as the most influential public voice of the left. During the Suez crisis, it was the progressive newspapers which spearheaded the movement against the Suhrawardy régime, and they became the ideological vanguard of the Pakistani left. Yet, despite this press support, the latter could never build a popular base.

In 1951, the Rawalpindi Conspiracy Case exploded on an unsuspecting country. The mastermind of this attempted putsch was Major-General Akbar Khan, chief of staff of the Pakistan army and widely regarded as an audacious and relatively progressive officer. The officers who supported him were a mixed bag of radical nationalists, outright chauvinists and religious freaks. The infant CPP became embroiled in the plan when Sajjad Zaheer met General Akbar at a cocktail party. The general broached the subject of the intended coup, and requested help in drafting manifestos and hit-lists. The CPP leadership approved of the enterprise and participated in various meetings with army officers. It was decided that the plan be shelved for a period, but one of the military conspirators, fearing that the truth might come out, turned informer and unveiled the whole affair. The plotters were arrested. General Ayub, commander-in-chief of the armed forces, was shocked to learn that he was to be shot. The amateurishness of the plot ensured that those involved received light sentences. Sajjad Zaheer returned to India after his release. The CPP virtually dissolved itself after being banned, and many of its cadres joined the Azad Pakistan Party. This débâcle was to leave a lasting impact on the demoralized remnants of the party, which was never again to emerge as a national, independent force. Its politics were instead to be submerged in successive multi-class formations of one variety or another.

The situation in East Pakistan was radically different. Many non-Muslim communists had left after the province was divided in 1947, but many others had remained. Nine million Hindus had decided not to leave their homes and become refugees, but to remain in East Pakistan. The dislocation was thus less severe and the Communist Party maintained its strength. Unlike in the West, the CP had an influence among sections of the peasantry and the urban intelligentsia. Its closest links, however, were with the CPI in neighbouring West Bengal, rather than with the CPI leadership based in West Pakistan.[18] Even ideological links with the latter were lacking, since Progressive Papers Ltd, presumably for reasons of convenience, had not given serious consideration to producing a Bengali daily as part of their chain.

The decision of the CPI to embark on an ultra-left course, following Zhdanov's injunctions from Moscow in his famous report to the founding conference of the Cominform in September 1947, led to disastrous consequences. The CPI leader B. T. Ranadive elaborated a set of theses which denounced independence as a mockery and instructed the party to move towards armed struggle and insurrection. The result was to isolate the party's cadres from the masses. The East Pakistan CP loyally implemented the line. The districts of Rangpur, Dinajpur, Mymensingh and Jessore were chosen as the areas to launch a struggle. CP activists raided local police stations and seized arms, but were rapidly isolated and crushed. Local militants, in most cases of Hindu origin, were uprooted and dispersed. Between 1948 and 1954 there were over 3,000 political prisoners in the gaols of East Bengal, most of them communists.

Among these communist prisoners was the former leader of the Mymensingh peasants, Moni Singh. He came from a landlord family, and because of his radicalism all the family lands were confiscated. Mymensingh had been the venue of an important peasant struggle known as the Tebhaga movement in 1945–6. The peasants had demanded that the share of the landlord be reduced from a half to a third of the crop. The movement had resulted from the Bengal famine of 1943, during the course of which three million peasants had starved to death. Many share-croppers had drifted to the cities and did not return. The Tebhaga militancy was encouraged by the shortage of labour in the countryside. A national peasants' conference held in Mymensingh in 1946 on Moni Singh's initiative had been attended by 200,000 peasants. The East Pakistani communists were officially banned in 1954, but by that time they had already declined in strength and large numbers of Hindu communists had left for India. Moni Singh (after his release) and Sukhendu Dastidar, however, remained in East Pakistan as leaders of the underground communist movement.

In April 1950 a leading Indian communist, Ajoy Ghosh, wrote an open letter to members of his party from a prison cell in South India, where he had been held after the party's 'left turn'. Ghosh attacked the 'left deviation' and called for a return to the party's traditional policy of alliances. He argued that India needed a bourgeois revolution and this could only be accomplished in collaboration with the political instruments of the national bourgeoisie. The Ghosh letter created chaos in the top ranks of the party. It was finally agreed to seek 'international advice', and accordingly three leaders of the CPI representing different currents went to meet Stalin in Moscow. Stalin approved the Ghosh line. The leadership of the Indian and East Bengali parties was, as a result, changed. The Ghosh line posed some sharp problems for East Bengali communists. They were mainly in prisons from which it was difficult to pursue an active policy of class collaboration.

There were two sets of communist prisoners, in Dacca and Rajshahi gaols respectively. The Rajshahi communists produced a set of theses arguing that the East Bengal Communist Party should work openly as a legal party and not through other bourgeois or petty-bourgeois organizations. This was their response to a suggestion from Dacca prison that they should enter the Awami Muslim League (the split-off from the Muslim League, led by Suhrawardy and Bhashani, described on p. 45 above). Rajshahi objected that, since many of their members were Hindus, they could not work through a party that restricted membership to Muslims. The matter was resolved by a note published in the Cominform journal *For a Lasting Peace, For a People's Democracy*, which suggested that progressive forces in East Pakistan were working through the Awami League. This authoritative source also maintained that the Awami League was responsible for 'unleashing a struggle against feudalism and colonial domination'. The dispute between Rajshahi and Dacca started afresh, with the former arguing that the party should continue to maintain an independent existence and build itself a base in the trade unions and the peasantry. The weight of Stalinist orthodoxy, however, was with Dacca, and the official line was finally accepted. 'Muslim comrades' went into the Awami League, while 'non-Muslim comrades' were asked to work in the trade unions and peasant committees.

Bengali communists also established the Youth League, whose aim was to organize broad support on a 'minimum programme of secularism, anti-imperialism, anti-feudalism, world peace, unfettered democracy . . .'. It was the Youth League which launched the Bengali language agitation in 1952. In March 1952 70 per cent of the Youth League's leaders were in prison. The remainder dissolved the League and organized the East Pakistan Students Union (EPSU) in April. Following the communist entry into the

Awami Muslim League, the party dropped 'Muslim' from its title in 1953 and moved towards secularism. The 1954 election triumph of the anti-Muslim-League forces gave Bengali communists their biggest success. They won four seats as communists, and eighteen 'entryists' in the Awami League were also elected: the party thus had twenty-two members of the East Pakistan provincial assembly.

With the formation of the National Awami Party (NAP) in 1957, East Bengali communists found a new home for another decade. The NAP had a ready-made parliamentary force of twenty-two in the East Bengali assembly, which was large enough to hold the balance between rival Bengali factions represented by the Awami League and the Krishak Samik party. The formation of NAP was greeted with uncontrolled hysteria by the right-wing parties and the pro-government press. The Awami League, ignoring the vilification it had itself suffered a few months earlier, joined in the anti-communist campaign. Indeed, it went further and organized gangs of hood-lums to disrupt meetings. The organizer of this violence was Suhrawardy's protégé, Sheikh Mujibur Rehman. A leading member of the East Pakistan cabinet, Mahmud Ali, resigned in protest against this gangsterism. It was acts of hooliganism spearheaded by the Awami League that were to provide the pretext for the military coup which was being prepared in the wings.

The NAP was the first national attempt to organize the country's fledg-ling opposition. It was the most radical party in Pakistan, although not a socialist organization. Its political development was a consequence of the triune influence of provincial Autonomists, populism and mass hostility to the pro-American foreign policy of successive governments. The NAP was a remarkable entity: despite the occasional intrigue in West Pakistan, it was the only political party in the country that did not succumb to the lure of cabinet posts. The NAP communists in East Bengal began to organize a Peasant Association and a trade-union federation. The influence of the latter grew rapidly in the docks, jute mills and tea plantations. Excited by these successes, communists in both East and West became NAP func-tionaries, or office-holders in peasant and trade-union bodies. They virtually abandoned the task of building an independent political force to represent the toilers in town and countryside.

The political and economic situation deteriorated simultaneously in 1958. Since Partition ten years before, the bureaucracy had creamed off the agri-cultural surplus and handed it over to traders (mainly immigrants from India) to finance Pakistan's industrial development. There had been a limited industrialization in West Pakistan, as domestic industry proceeded to construct import-substitution industries under the protection of the state, which became the sole dispenser of import and export licences. Patronage resulted in corruption on a very high level within the ranks of the bureaucracy. A decline of agriculture followed, and in 1958 agricultural output decreased by 4.2 per cent: rural production and consumption went down as less land was cultivated. An economic recession in the United States led to an increase in the price of essential foods. This coincided with a crop failure in East Pakistan. Instead of taking the crisis seriously and implementing measures to counter its effects, the bureaucracy made matters worse. It decreased the amount of money allocated for social services (low enough as it was) in the spring 1958 budget, increased outlays on military spending and abolished price controls. The cost of living in the towns registered a phenomenal rise: an average of 8.2 per cent.

The result was increasing agitation in town and countryside. Strikes became commonplace and were crushed by private armies in the pay of the employers or state repression. The NAP-sponsored Peasant Association began agitating for an abolition of landlordism. In Lahore, capital of West Pakistan, hundreds of thousands of peasants marched through the streets to demand that: (a) eviction of tenants be outlawed; (b) landlordism be abolished; and (c) all uncultivated land be given to landless tenants. Peasant leaders were victimized by gangs of thugs in the pay of the landlords. On 8 May 1958, in one of numerous episodes, the police attacked peasants in the village of Lundo in the heart of the province of Sind. They attacked the *haris* (poor peasants), seized their harvest, ransacked their homes, raped the women and arrested seventy peasants. The local landlords provided valuable aid by burning *hari* dwellings.[19] The entire pattern of rural life made such actions possible. On 20 June 1958, workers attempted to occupy a strike-bound factory in Lyallpur in protest against the imprisonment of a union leader. The police opened fire, killing six workers and seriously injuring another twenty-one.

The country's first ever general election was scheduled to be held in March 1959. The bureaucracy was extremely worried, and with good reason. There was every likelihood that the left would make gains on a provincial and national level. There was also a real possibility that the mere holding of a general election could trigger off a mass upsurge which might overflow electoral channels. In the provincial legislatures of West and East Pakistan, there was continual chaos generated by the desire to obtain ministerial posts. Fist-fights between members dominated the West Pakistan assembly in March 1958, while East Pakistan saw the murder of the deputy speaker by angry members. The bureaucracy, in ten years, had failed to build a stable bourgeois political party. Its alliance with the landlords had reduced the politics of the country to a complete mess. It was obvious that the bureaucracy's pet creation, the Republican Party, would be ignominiously defeated in any free election. A left-wing daily commented perceptively in an editorial:

Feudal lords and their retainers, old bureaucrats and their satellites, business sharks and soldiers of fortune, men who have never lost a day's rest or a night's sleep in the cause of freedom, democracy, or people's rights, have little use for rights, conventions and institutions won after centuries of suffering and struggle. They are only interested in the benefit which the trappings and stage-properties of democracy may help them to grab ... [All this] provides an argument against democracy and people's rights to those who would prefer to have even the trappings and stage-properties out of the way.[20]

Until 1958, the bureaucracy had been the senior partner in the bureau-cratic-military alliance dominating the state apparatus. On 7 October 1958, eleven years after Pakistan was created, its political structures lay in shambles and the army took political power through a coup d'état. The attempt to construct a bourgeois–democratic state on the Indian model had ended in disaster. A Western observer had commented in the year preceding the coup: 'The civil service and the army have shown no desire to back any potential dictator.' The same observer had reflected at length on the fact that democracy was the only serious alternative in the country, and that 'no serious totalitarian groups have yet emerged in Pakistan'. History recorded its own sombre verdict on this shallow analysis.[21]

3 The Gun and the Hat:

Military–Bureaucratic Dictatorship

1958–69

Nature of the New Régime

The military coup of October 1958 was a direct result of the bureaucracy's failure to construct a viable ruling-class party in Pakistan. The collapse of the Muslim League and the emergence of the radical National Awami Party had coincided with a growth of peasant militancy and working-class unrest in the cities. The future was uncertain. The bureaucrats, the military officers and their American advisers considered that a general election based on adult franchise was far too risky an enterprise, given the peculiar characteristics of the state of Pakistan. President Mirza formally asked the C.-in-C., General Ayub, to take over political power. The general obliged and then asked the president to resign and leave the country. It was a gentlemanly affair.

The new régime was an undisguised dictatorship of the bureaucratic–military élite.[1] It lasted for a decade and was marked by two distinct phases. The first period (1958–62) was dominated by the army: the generals were the senior partners in the dictatorship, ably backed by the civil service. The years that followed (1962–9), however, saw the bureaucracy re-asserting its dominant role in the country's politics: it was now senior civil servants rather than Ayub's tame band of sycophantic politicians who determined policy. The coup should have provided the country's intelligentsia with an opportunity for serious reflection. Now was the time for a sober reappraisal of the arguments that had preceded the establishment of Pakistan. Once Jinnah, in a noteworthy address to the country's Constituent Assembly in 1947, had implied that history would be the ultimate judge of the wisdom or otherwise of Partition.[2] The coup, in its own way, revealed the flimsy basis of the state. The 'mass base' of the Muslim League seemed to have disappeared without trace. The League had become merely a clutch of corrupt and quarrelsome caciques. The fact that a majority of the country's population were Muslims had resolved neither the tortuous 'crisis of identity' nor any of the material problems which confronted the new state.

The Pakistani state, from being a vulgar and hurriedly modelled replica of neighbouring India, now embarked on a fresh course. It was hoped in Washington that the new régime might provide a model for other developing countries. General Ayub's own reflections on the post-colonial state ('Democracy cannot work in a hot climate. To have democracy we must have a cold climate as in Britain') were treated seriously by State Department policy-makers and their satraps elsewhere in the world. Eleven years after Independence, the Pakistani state had discarded all attempts to create a democratic polity. It had, instead, returned to the rule of gun and hat – the form of government that had prevailed in India during the decades of British colonial occupation. The two dominant institutions, the army and the bureaucracy were the direct descendants of the colonial state.

The importance of these institutions in maintaining colonial rule cannot be underestimated. The small size of the British presence had, in fact, been a remarkable feature of the Raj. Angus Maddison has pointed out that:

> There were only 31,000 British in India in 1805 (of which 22,000 were in the army and 2,000 in civil government). The number increased substantially after the 1857 mutiny, but thereafter remained steady. In 1911 there were 164,000 British (106,000 employed, of which 66,000 were in the army and police and 4,000 in civil government). In 1931, there were 168,000 (90,000 employed, 60,000 in the army and police and 4,000 in civil government) . . . never more than 0.5 per cent of the population.[3]

The conclusion is obvious. British rule in India, with its many-millioned masses, could not have been defended adequately simply by the British. The Indian social formation was more advanced than anything the British ever encountered, for instance, in Africa. To maintain British hegemony, it was essential to develop alliances and create structures which could integrate a sizable section of the indigenous populace.

The post-1857 British army in India established a tradition which persists in the subcontinent to this day. A new recruitment policy, designed to exclude South Indians and 'volatile' Bengalis, was initiated. The major conurbations, more susceptible to nationalist agitation, were also ruled out. It was the politically backward rural hinterlands of the Punjab and the North-West Frontier which were to be the catchment area for the new-style army. A novel 'theory' was elaborated to rationalize this policy, encapsulated in the title of Sir George MacMunn's book, *The Martial Races of India*. The author stated:

> The staunch old Indian yeoman who came into the Indian commissioned ranks via the rank and file, or the young Indian landowner, made the Indian officer as we know him . . . The clever young men of the Universities were quite unfitted for military work . . . the army officers had long realized that the Indian intelligentsia would never make officers.[4]

The British Indian army was established on the principle of British officers and Indian foot soldiers. The first Indians were to get their commissions only when the empire was threatened or at war. The rigid hierarchy was strongly defended by excluding any possibility of promotion from the ranks. The 'staunch old Indian yeoman' could never rise above the ranks. The competitive spirit was to be sustained by creating a new layer of NCOs, subordinate to the officer caste and in effect little more than glorified flunkeys. The soldiers and NCOs were expected to regard themselves as superior to their fellow-citizens and encouraged to believe that they enjoyed a special relationship with their British superiors. This was not pure idealism: soldiers and their dependants were allotted special plots of land in newly irrigated zones – at once ensuring their loyalty and separating them from their fellow-peasants.

Officers enjoyed other and more substantial privileges. Sandhurst was opened up to Indians in 1918, those selected to become officers being drawn exclusively from landed families. Their political reliability was never in doubt. For the first few decades after Independence, the blatant class dichotomy was maintained in the Indian and Pakistani armies alike. The ratio of country to town in terms of selecting officers was carefully preserved: 70 to 30 in favour of the rural gentry, many of them from traditional 'military families'. The division between officers and men was jealously guarded by the former: life in the officers' mess could not have been more different from leisure hours in the barracks. In the mess, the evening would be taken up with billiards, bridge or poker, helped along by a generous consumption of whisky, gimlets (gin and lime), rum and beer. Barracks life had none of this. Class differentials were extended to the sports field. Officers played polo, tennis and golf: soldiers and NCOs hockey, football and basketball. The British Indian army was created on the model of the British army. Native officers, once they were allowed to exist, aped and mimicked their British superiors. This was an indispensable part of their training at Sandhurst – and subsequently at Dehradun and Kakul Military Academies, in India and Pakistan respectively.

The British Raj was prepared to negotiate with nationalists and agree to concessions on many different levels, but the army always had to remain untouched. The reason was expressed succinctly by the C.-in-C., Field Marshal Sir W. Birdwood, in 1921:

> The Army in India is one link in the Imperial chain of defence of the Empire and naturally, therefore, no alterations in its organization, which might in any way affect its efficiency, can be taken without the fullest consideration of His Majesty's Government, which is ultimately responsible for Imperial security.

The Simon Commission of 1930 backed Lord Birdwood's view unequivocally. It was meant to be considering a form of self-government for India, but it warned that in one field the empire must not be challenged:

> India and Britain are so related that Indian Defence cannot, now or in any future which is within sight, be regarded as a matter of purely Indian concern. The control and direction of such an army must rest in the hands of agents of the Imperial Government.

British fears were perfectly comprehensible. The Indian army was a vital component of the empire. It was useful not merely as cannon fodder in the trenches, as in 1914–18; its strength and discipline were equally important in defeating uprisings of colonial peoples elsewhere. Indian troops were used to quell mass upheavals in China, Malaya, Burma and Iran. In 1945 (two years before Indian independence), it was Indian troops under the command of General Gracey who occupied the major cities of southern Vietnam and paved the way for a reoccupation by the French. When a former Pakistani general, writing on the role of Muslim Indian officers in the service of the British, states that: 'They fought and died not as hirelings of a mercenary army, but as loyal soldiers conscious of their worth and proud of the splendid part they were playing in defending their own country, their own culture and faith', he is distorting the truth.[5] In fact the officers at least were precisely mercenaries in the service of the empire. In most cases they did their job well; professional pride, however, must not be allowed to obscure their objective role. The fact that both the Indian and Pakistani armies were led by British generals in the years immediately following Partition is not insignificant. It indicates a continuity which was not merely sentimental.

The Pakistan army after Independence was thus a product of the imperialist past. It continued to be largely recruited from those sections of the Punjab peasantry that had traditionally provided artillery fodder for the British. The generals, brigadiers and colonels who comprised its select élite had been carefully screened: their class background and political outlook was considered impeccable. They were scions of the landed aristocracy and kulak gentry of the Punjab and Frontier provinces. Partition and the mass migrations had provided them with a sprinkling of wealthy immigrants (with similar social credentials) from Uttar Pradesh and Hyderabad. All had been trained at British-staffed military academies. Bengalis were effectively excluded. The quasi-fascist concept of 'martial races', a vital component of British military ideology, survived as the conventional wisdom of the Pakistani officers at the head of the new army.[6] The racial myths they propagated contained the same admixture of prejudice and paternalism: Bengalis were short and dark; they could not fight well; they were nature's cowards, because of their relatively recent conversion from Hinduism. The British had applied these crude generalizations for a specific purpose, namely, to isolate Bengal from the northern part of the subcontinent. The political vanguard of India was to be placed in quarantine. The army, in particular, could not be contaminated with the nationalist disease. The lynchpin of the Pakistani state apparatus thus came to be a military–bureaucratic élite in which Bengalis – a majority of the country's population – were hardly represented. This contradiction was a political time-bomb threatening the very foundations of Pakistan from its inception. The top leaders of the army and bureaucracy, however, were blind to this reality. The smugness and complacency of the military were complemented by the bureaucracy's myopic self-interest.

A contrast with the Egyptian army of the same period is extremely instructive, revealing the crucial role played by the class background of the Pakistani officer caste in ensuring that it remained conservative in politics and outlook. The bulk of Egypt's young officers in the forties and fifties were not the offspring of rural autocrats, but were recruited from the cities, mainly from petty-bourgeois backgrounds. The entire leading nucleus of twenty officers who constituted the effective leadership of the 'Free Officers' were university graduates (most having studied at Cairo University). They had imbibed the main urban influences of the time: Islamic revivalism as preached by the Muslim Brotherhood, and socialism as advocated by the Egyptian left. While Anwar el Saadat had been an activist of the Muslim Brotherhood, Gamal Abdel Nasser, Khalid Mohieddine and Gamal Salem were all associated with the left. During his period as a cadet and later an officer, Nasser for his part had read Voltaire, Garibaldi, Ataturk, Napoleon and Clausewitz. The Free Officers combined radical nationalism (anti-imperialism) with a programme of agrarian reforms that dented the authority of rural oppressors. Externally, the impact of Nasserism on the entire Middle East was dramatic.[7]

The Pakistani generals were a totally different breed. Created, nurtured and trained by the British, their vision of the world was somewhat jaundiced. Their politics was formed by Partition, which transmuted Sandhurst jingoism into a new indigenous form. Generals Ayub, Azam, Sheikh and Burki were bland and insipid figures, whose view of the world came from the pages of *Reader's Digest*, *Time* and the *Royal United Services Journal* produced in London. (Occasionally they might glance at the *National Geographic* magazine, to admire the photographs.) British influence was gradually displaced after Independence by that of the United States, a reflection of changing political realities on a world scale. In February 1954, USMAAG (United States Military Assistance Advisory Group) was set up in the army GHQ in Rawalpindi; as Pakistan's domestic and external policies had by then become largely subservient to US interests, few politicians were bothered by the fact that there was now a direct link between the army chiefs and the Pentagon. There can be little doubt that the relevant authorities in the United States were fully aware in the late fifties that the Pakistani army was planning a coup d'état: some years later, Ayub's brother, Sardar Bahadur, was to allege that the CIA had been fully involved in the military take-over.

After October 1958, the military chiefs and their civil-service collaborators argued that the coup had been essential in order to save Pakistan from the politicians. It is perfectly true that Pakistani politics was notoriously unstable and the country's parliamentary institutions were new and extremely weak. These were, however, not the real reasons for the army action. The Pakistani state was not a viable entity. Its ruling class was weak. The possibilities of radical advance and mass explosion were built into the very structure of the new state. So the army, with guidance from abroad, decided to circumvent the whole process of obtaining mass consent, substituting itself for a homogeneous ruling class and a strong ruling political party alike. It was aided and abetted by the civil service.

The first phase of the Ayub dictatorship saw the régime attempting a 'cleaning-up' operation. Politicians were prosecuted and barred from political activity for several years. Trade unions and peasant organizations were banned, and students were warned against initiating or participating in any form of political activity. The Progressive chain of newspapers owned by the veteran leftist Mian Iftikhar-ud-Din was taken over by the state, on the grounds that Mian was a 'foreign agent'. This was the sharpest blow against the left, at a stroke depriving it of its voice and providing the new régime with newspapers under its direct control.[8] At the same time, the military attempted to modernize the country, setting up commissions to prepare recommendations on land reform, education, marriage and family law, pay and services, and a number of other subjects. With the exception of the Family Laws Ordinance (which placed serious restrictions on polygamy and allowed women to sue for divorce), none of the other commissions resulted in any serious reforms. The Pay and Services Commission report did propose a drastic overhauling of the country's civil service, which would have challenged the traditional élitism inherited from the Raj; but this report was conveniently shelved.

The Land Reforms Commission proved to be the biggest disappointment. The reforms proposed and subsequently implemented were designed to preserve the status quo (after making a few cosmetic adjustments). In sharp contrast to the Nasserite reforms in Egypt or the Cardenas agrarian measures in Mexico, the land reforms in Pakistan were actually welcomed by the country's main landlords. Though the ownership ceiling was placed at 500 acres of irrigated and 1,000 acres of unirrigated land, orchards and cattle-farms were exempted, as were landlords who had gifted some of their land to their heirs or dependants. A leading Sindhi landlord, Mir Ghulam Ali Talpur, declared that the reforms were exceedingly generous 'because of the big heart of the President'. In reality, the reforms evaded the central issue in the countryside: the separation of ownership and cultivation. The only equality embodied in the reforms was equality between landlords. Even though limited areas of the excess land made available through the reforms were offered to tenants, the latter did not possess the money to make an offer. Since the departure of the Hindu money-lenders, the peasants had had no access to ready cash, since landlords had taken over the functions of the money-lenders. The government did not set up rural credit institutions to aid poor peasants.

At the time of the land reforms, 6,000 landlords owned 7.5 million acres of land in estates of 500 acres and over; 2.2 million peasant families owned an average of less than 5 acres per family; 2.5 million peasants owned no land and worked as share-croppers or seasonal workers. This situation was not qualitatively altered by the reforms. As the *Pakistan Times* pointed out, a few months before it was seized by the army: 'Even a conservative body like the Muslim League Land Reform Committee recommended an upper limit of 150 acres of irrigated land.'[9] The total land surrendered by the landlords was only 6 per cent of the total area under cultivation, and it was also the worst land. General Ayub strongly condemned absentee landlords. As a result, many landlords evicted weak tenants and put their retainers or heirs in charge of direct cultivation. The dispossessed tenants joined the growing army of landless labourers.

The new régime thus did not alter the basic structure of class relations that prevailed in the countryside. It did, however, begin to inject government subsidies to raise agricultural output. Capitalist farming was encouraged and the area under cultivation grew. But small farmers were virtually ignored. The main beneficiaries of the 'green revolution' were the large landlords. They were the major recipients of subsidies and loans, and were not required to pay income-tax. Hardly any money was made available to build village schools or rural hospitals and dispensaries; to improve sanitation facilities; or to carry out other welfare measures. The rural poor who comprised the overwhelming majority of the population received few benefits from the 'green revolution'.

'Dramatic' economic developments, however, were to take place in the cities. The military régime made Pakistan a haven for capital investment by removing cumbersome restrictions: in particular, by suppressing trade unions. Pakistan had not possessed a capitalist class in 1947. The north-western areas of the subcontinent had not been particularly hospitable to the industrial entrepreneur. It was Bohra and Ismaili Khoja traders from Bombay who were destined to become the agency of Pakistan's limited industrialization. Together with their Chinioti counterparts from the Punjab, the traders became the clients of a powerful civil service. It was the latter, acting on behalf of the new Pakistani state, that put into effect a series of measures designed to aid capital formation. Government aid involved supplying cheap machinery, raw materials and interest-free loans, while turning a blind eye to large-scale tax evasion.

The state had decided to create and strengthen private capitalism in Pakistan, but it ensured that the new bourgeoisie would be tied to the coat-tails of the bureaucracy. There thus developed a close and mutually profitable relationship between bureaucrats and businessmen. After the 1958 coup, the army top brass too entered the relationship, and corruption increased tenfold. While the army and bureaucracy exercised political power, the capitalists exercised economic power. Profits increased, but real wages in manufacturing industry declined drastically, as the working class grew in size in the industrial centres of Karachi, Lyallpur, Lahore and Rawalpindi.

Pakistan's growth was to become a reference-point for US economists 'advising' other neo-colonial régimes, a 'model' for the rest of the third world and a shining example of free enterprise. Yet, as we have shown, there was nothing free about this enterprise. It was state subsidies and protection which enabled capitalism to establish itself, and where this was insufficient the state established factories (through bodies such as the Pakistan Industrial Development Corporation) and subsequently offered them to private capitalists at 'reasonable prices'. This process was labelled a major gain of the 'free market economy' by Gustav Papanek, boss of Harvard's Development Advisory Service. Papanek affectionately referred to Pakistan's fledgling bourgeoisie as 'robber barons', and defended the growing exploitation which accompanied their progress. In what might seem an unconscious parody of Lewis Carroll, Papanek acknowledged the rising inequalities in his Wonderland, but wrote: 'Inequalities in income contribute to the growth of the economy which makes possible a real improvement for the lower income groups.'[10] The social explosions which ended Ayub's rule were to prove Professor Papanek wrong. The Harvard advisers gravely underestimated the damage being done to Pakistani agriculture in the same period that funds were pouring into industry. Moreover, two-thirds of capital investment in West Pakistan came from outside the country, as a stable military régime induced foreign investors to help the growth of indigenous capital.

The policies of the military régime led to an incredible concentration of wealth in the country. Yet as the country's economists began to assemble in

1964 to discuss a third five-year plan, they were gripped by the realization that Papanek's plaudits could not conceal the stagnation of real income so far as the bulk of the population was concerned. Dr Mahbubul Haq, chief economist of the Planning Commission, revealed a set of figures which startled the country. He stated that 66 per cent of the country's industrial capital was in the hands of twenty families: Dawood, Adamjee, Saigols, Valika, Bhimjee, Dinshaw, Fancy, Marker, Ispahani and Habib were the most prominent. At the same time, the draft outlines of the third plan showed that the real condition of the economy did not give much reason for optimism. Growth of the national income and economic expansion had gone side by side with a deterioration in the living standards of the mass of the population, whose food consumption had actually declined over the preceding five years. In the towns, the army and bureaucracy had helped to create a monstrous millionaire élite on the basis of intensive and large-scale exploitation. In the countryside, they had similarly concentrated on promoting the interests of landlords and capitalist farmers, at the expense of peasants and landless labourers.

Any attempt by the people to challenge this state of affairs was met by repression. In the urban areas, all trade-union activity was kept firmly under control. There were a number of reasons for the slow growth of trade-unionism. Acceptance by many workers who had only recently entered the factories of a tenant–landlord model on the shop-floor was one factor. Also significant were official cooptation and repression. The creation of company unions was encouraged by the state, while local bureaucrats aided factory-owners in victimizing those who tried to organize representative unions. During the Ayub years, all strikes were outlawed and many union leaders were put on the régime's payroll. But there is also an important objective reason for the weakness of trade-unionism in Pakistan. The existence of a very large pool of unemployed labour does not facilitate strong unions. In the countryside, meanwhile, the combined powers of the bureaucracy and the landlords, ensured the passivity of the tenants.

On the development front, the régime's much vaunted 'tube-well revolution' benefited only the rural rich. Instead of being geared to planned investment in rural infrastructure, social welfare and producer technologies, the Pakistan economy was geared to the consumption habits of the urban upper classes, which lay behind the country's topsy-turvy imports policy. On a mass level, cheap import substitutes (symbolized by the numerous companies producing imitation Coca-Cola) encouraged unnecessary consumption rather than saving. The economic mess and the role of US advisers was summed up rather well in a pamphlet produced by a group of Harvard students in 1969:

A succession of capitalist governments, operating with DAS [Development Advisory Service] advice, have done nothing for the people of Pakistan. Income inequality, between classes and between East and West, shows no signs of decreasing. Repression and corruption are as common today as when Harvard first intervened in the 1950s. Capitalism in Pakistan is not an independent, developing system, but a very dependent client of the major capitalist powers, unable to finance its investment plans without massive foreign aid.

Its ideological orientation prevents the DAS from offering advice which can help the Pakistani people change their society . . . The success of which DAS boasts, an apparently temporary period of rising income per capita, means little as long as it occurs within the capitalist framework of inequality, repression and dependence on foreign benevolence. The DAS cannot change that framework; at its best, it can provide technical improvements in transportation, agriculture, planning methods. Such improvements, far from leading to basic change, can only serve to stabilize an illegitimate military government.[11]

Industrial growth had two major consequences for Pakistan. It highlighted the differences between East and West, and it led to a rapid increase in the size of the working class in the cities. In the years following Partition, the bureaucracy and army had premised their entire strategy on denying East Pakistan its political rights. The failure of this crude, anti-democratic project had led to a direct military take-over. With the coercive powers of the armed forces now at their disposal, the bureaucratic–bourgeois alliance sought to exploit the resources of East Pakistan in order to aid economic development in the West. The combination of political and economic deprivation led to the growth of a Bengali national consciousness in the Eastern wing of the country. The West Pakistani ruling class was so busy congratulating itself that it was blind to political developments which would soon threaten the entire fabric of the State.

Foreign Policy

The first years of the military–bureaucratic régime saw a continuation of the staunchly pro-Western foreign policy. The central issue in Pakistan's external affairs, however, was the series of disputes with neighbouring India. Of these, the vexed problem of Kashmir constituted the principal bone of contention between the two countries. Kashmir had been a princely state in pro-Independence days. Its ruling family was Hindu, but 80 per cent of the population was Muslim (the bulk of it supporting the non-communal nationalists led by Sheikh Abdullah, while a minority backed the Muslim

League). Partition of the subcontinent led to both sides manoeuvring to ensure the accession of Kashmir to their respective states. The Hindu ruler signed accession papers and declared for India. Pakistan sent in a number of army units and irregulars (mainly tribesmen from the Frontier province), but these were so busy looting and raping that they failed to capture the airport of the capital Srinagar – the only way Indian troops could get to Kashmir. The result was that the Indians landed in force and threw back the Pakistani attack. A fully fledged war fought by two armies commanded by British generals would undoubtedly have been a unique – and highly unwelcome – occurrence in the annals of the empire: accordingly, British pressure prevented it from taking place.

The cease-fire enshrined a division of Kashmir, with the richest and most populous areas under Indian control and the remainder under Pakistani suzerainty. In the early years, successive Indian leaders pledged that the Kashmiri people would be permitted to determine their own future. It was, however, obvious that in any referendum Kashmir would opt either for Pakistan or for independence – with its neutrality and security guaranteed by both states. The Indian state soon discarded all notions of the Kashmiri people exercising their right to choose. The Pakistani state, meanwhile, essentially utilized the Kashmir issue as a safety-valve within Pakistan: during periods of economic and political crisis, it was a convenient subject with which to divert people's attention from domestic events. The single factor that could have brought about a genuine resolution would have been a mass uprising in the valley itself; but, despite widespread unrest, popular discontent never approached insurrectionary proportions.

The military dictatorship in Pakistan saw itself as the most loyal defender of US interests in the region.[12] In September 1959, Ayub approached the Indian prime minister Nehru with an old American proposal: joint defence of India and Pakistan against outside aggression. The Indian leader rebuffed the Pakistani dictator with the remark: 'Joint defence against whom?' The Sino-Indian conflict of 1962 did not change Nehru's views on this question, despite Ayub's anti-Chinese positions. At the time, in response to a direct plea for closer relations with India from American president John F. Kennedy, Ayub penned the following reply:

We believe that [the present situation on the subcontinent] is the direct outcome of distorted and fallacious thinking on the part of Mr Nehru and his associates . . . It is based on the following factors:
    (a) bend over backwards to appease Communism;
    (b) hoist the white flag of neutralism to appease Communism and get other wavering nations to join India in order to be able to create a world nuisance-value for themselves;

(c) intimidate and threaten Pakistan in order to politically isolate it and economically weaken it; and

(d) abuse the West, and especially the USA in season and out of season.[13]

The naïvety of such an approach did not please the United States, which was busy wooing India in the aftermath of the Sino-Indian border war. While the Pakistani press and academic community dubbed Ayub a 'soldier-statesman', his US paymasters were unimpressed. Unable to understand that, from the point of view of the United States, it was India which was the key to the situation in South Asia, the Pakistani rulers dispatched a delegation to China. The Chinese were preoccupied by one key question at the time: they were desperate to breach the wall of encirclement constructed around them by the USA, especially given their increasingly fraught relations with the USSR. Pakistan offered a first opportunity. The Chinese leaders concluded a border treaty with Pakistan whereby the latter gained 750 square miles of territory.

This foreign-policy success, however, was not sufficient to quieten the masses at home. So in 1962 martial law was formally ended and a new Constitution promulgated. This was designed to end political conflict: the franchise was restricted and a strong president given unlimited powers. The bureaucracy advised Ayub to form his own political party; accordingly, the Convention Muslim League was born. It was essentially a collection of unprincipled careerists, many of whom were ruthlessly corrupt and acted as mediators between the criminal underworld and bureaucratic politics. This element was especially strong in East Pakistan, while in the West it was our old friends the landowners of the former Unionist party who provided a rural base for Ayub.

The opposition parties now combined under a single political umbrella (Combined Opposition Parties – COP), and found a candidate to oppose Ayub in Miss Fatima Jinnah, the ageing sister of Mohammed Ali Jinnah. During the tail-end of martial law, the students had already opened a breach. When the Congolese leader Patrice Lumumba was murdered by the CIA in 1961, students in Lahore had defied martial law and demonstrated on the streets chanting anti-US slogans.[14] Within weeks, students throughout the country had joined the protests, which had often taken on an anti-dictatorship character. Miss Jinnah's candidature united all the anti-dictatorship forces. What became known as 'the General's election' was held in 1965, and though the franchise was restricted to 'basic democrats' – elected local councillors on a rural and urban level – Miss Jinnah was only defeated thanks to repression, large-scale rigging and the failure of pro-Chinese sections of the left in East Pakistan to give whole-hearted backing.

The mood following the 1965 elections was one of frustration and anger. Senior cabinet ministers (who included Z. A. Bhutto) recognized that the régime was even more isolated than before. So it was decided to focus attention once again on Kashmir. The valley had been experiencing some unrest, and it was thought that infiltrating Pakistani soldiers disguised as civilian volunteers might trigger off a general uprising. It was assumed that the armed conflict this would precipitate would give the Pakistan army an opportunity to score an easy victory and 'liberate' Kashmir. The army high command assumed that the war would remain confined to the Kashmir area. The Pakistani infiltrators were soon spotted by Indian military authorities and clashes ensued.[15] The Pakistan commanders sent in units to engage in direct combat. It should be emphasized that no general strike took place in the Kashmir valley. The expected mass mobilizations did not materialize. Indian troops suffered some initial reverses, but counter-attacked rapidly and crossed the international border, threatening the West Pakistani capital of Lahore. The Indians deliberately chose not to take the city, but it was clear that they had turned the tide. Ayub had not foreseen that the war might spread and was in a state of panic. According to Bhutto, he was 'shitting in his pants and desperately ringing the American ambassador every few hours and pleading with him to intervene and arrange a cease-fire'. Ironically enough, it was a Chinese threat to enter the war that forced the USA and USSR to stop the conflict. The vulnerability of East Pakistan was another factor which impelled Karachi to come to terms (and the fact that the province was totally unprotected helped to fuel the nationalist cause there).

A cease-fire was finally signed in Tashkent, under the benign supervision of Soviet premier Kosygin and with the backing of the United States. The Chinese regarded the Tashkent conference as yet another attempt by US imperialism, backed by the USSR, to encircle China. The conference discussed everything except the right to self-determination of the Kashmiri people. Many Kashmiris were now convinced that national liberation or independence could only be achieved by their own efforts, not by the action of foreign armies. The reaction of the masses in the Western wing of the country to Tashkent was anger. The subsequent removal of Bhutto as foreign minister, coupled with his denunciation of Tashkent once he was no longer in office, boosted his standing in the Punjab – a stronghold of national chauvinism and the area from which most of the country's soldiers were recruited.

China's support for Pakistan was to produce a remarkable shift in Pakistani politics. Its ultimate consequences were to prove disastrous for the left, but it did achieve one goal. It led to a mass revulsion against US policies and a massive growth of support for the struggle of the Vietnamese.

China's policies, however, went far beyond the requirements of diplomacy. Chinese leaders praised the Ayub dictatorship, stated that the system of 'basic democracies' had something in common with Chinese 'people's communes', ignored the struggle of the masses in Pakistan, falsified Pakistan's history and proclaimed the ludicrous Indo-Pak conflict as a 'people's war'. Marshal Chen Yi, the Chinese foreign minister, on a visit to Lahore after the Tashkent Agreement, issued a statement which summed up the Chinese position:

> Under the leadership of President Mohammed Ayub Khan, the Pakistani people united as one and filled with a common hatred towards the enemy, triumphed over the enemy . . . and finally repulsed the aggressor in safeguarding the independence and sovereignty of their country.[16]

China's fulsome support provided only a temporary respite for the beleaguered régime of Ayub Khan. A visit to the United States by the Pakistani president was widely construed as a pilgrimage, in the course of which Ayub would apologize to the American president for the débâcle of the recent war. Once he had repaired the breach with the United States, Ayub became confident once more that he was firmly in control of the country. The band of sycophantic civil servants and politicians who surrounded him cocooned him off from every section of the masses. The press and radio sang his praises, while tame intellectuals on the payroll of the Ministry of Information abased themselves before him in every possible fashion. The Secretary of the Writers' Guild, for instance, welcomed the dictator to a Guild meeting with the following remarks:

> It is you, the greatest component of this era, the central power of all this activity, who promised freedom of expression to writers in the days when they suffered from nothing but doubts about their destiny. Under you we have enjoyed complete freedom of expression, and we are proud of the fact that we have not misused it.[17]

Pakistan presented a dismal picture in the years 1965–8. It was beset by a host of internal problems, none of which could be solved without a process of radical social change. The concentration of wealth had produced grotesque inequalities. The upper classes led an existence which bore no relationship to that of the rest of society. While workers on strike were being shot dead on the orders of bureaucrats and capitalists, the latter's wives were attending expensive fashion parades at luxurious international hotels, applauding new creations entitled 'Hello Officer', 'Rajah's Ransom' and the like. In a country of 100 million, only 18.9 per cent of the population was literate, and of these only 3 per cent were women. As the régime sealed itself off, corruption increased tenfold. The dictator's eldest son, Gohar

Ayub, became a millionaire industrialist one day and a leading politician the next. Opposition politicians were imprisoned. The revolutionary poet Habib Jalib, whose ditties were extremely popular with the poor, claimed that he was in and out of prison so often that he always gave two addresses to admirers who asked him where he lived. The spreading economic and intellectual oppression combined to produce a situation in which an explosion of mass anger was clearly visible on the horizon. The régime decided to celebrate, in the autumn of 1968, a 'Decade of Development'. The press produced special supplements under the direction of the Ministry of Information.[18] The Karachi daily, *Dawn*, owned by the wealthy Haroon family, tried to compete with the government-controlled *Pakistan Times* by printing Ayub's photograph sixty-nine times in one issue of the newspaper! What all this demonstrated was that, for the second time in two decades, the bureaucracy had succeeded in isolating itself completely from the people. Within a month of the celebrations marking the 'Decade of Development', the country was engulfed in a spontaneous mass upheaval which shook the state apparatus to its very core.

The Decline of the Left

Before we discuss the 1968 uprisings, which transformed the political life of the country, and the social forces that were unleashed by them, a brief survey of the Pakistani left is essential. This is necessary in order to comprehend the virtual eclipse of the traditional left, in the crucially important years that followed 1968, and the rise of a nationalist populism in both parts of the country.

The Sino-Soviet split had divided the left in Pakistan as elsewhere. For old communists schooled in the Stalinist tradition, politics, on both a strategic and tactical level, meant applying the line handed out by Moscow and faithfully following its twists and turns. The schism between Peking and Moscow, however, had created two centres, posing subcontinental Stalinism with a massive dilemma. In Pakistan, as we described earlier, the communists were active in the National Awami Party. With Mian Iftikharud-Din's death in 1962, the NAP had declined in the Punjab. Its main bases were Baluchistan, the NWFP and East Pakistan. Its leaders, all of them non-communists (a few were fellow-travellers), were Wali Khan (NWFP), Ghaus Bux Bizenjo, Attaullah Mengal and Kair Baksh Marri (Baluchistan), Mozaffer Ahmed and Maulana Abdul Hamid Bhashani (East Pakistan). The Eastern province also maintained a separate, underground Communist Party, whose leaders were Moni Singh and Sukhendu Dastidar.

The East Pakistan Communist Party (EPCP) was bitterly divided on

Sino-Soviet lines in 1964 and split two years later. The handful of communists in West Pakistan followed suit, with C. R. Aslam, Mirza Ibrahim and Sardar Shaukat moving to pro-Peking positions, while others remained with Moscow. Following the division in the ranks of the CP, there ensued a bizarre development. The NAP, a petty-bourgeois democratic party, split as well. With the exception of Maulana Bhashani and Masihur Rehman, all the other leaders remained with the pro-Moscow communists. The division reflected the East–West divide. Communists in the West were a minute force, parasitic on the more powerful positions and bases of the non-communist NAP leaders. In East Pakistan, the situation was reversed: the communists were an important segment of NAP's base. There, the (initially) pro-Moscow East Bengal Communist Party (EBCP) had won a sizable section of the former EPCP leaders, whereas the pro-Peking EPCP (Marxist–Leninist) had gained only a minority. Maulana Bhashani, however, sided with the pro-Peking wing, and the NAP was split on the Peking formula of 'unity – struggle or even split – a new unity on a new basis'.

Bhashani had been arrested by the Ayub régime after returning from Egypt, where he had been a guest of President Nasser in 1961. Released in 1963, he agreed to lead a government-sponsored delegation to China. The Pakistani ambassador to Peking, General Raza, was present during Bhashani's conversations with Chou En-lai and Mao Tse-tung; he reported that the latter had bluntly told the Maulana that the Chinese would welcome NAP support for the Ayub régime. During a visit to East Pakistan in July 1969, Bhashani confirmed this to me in the course of a lengthy tape-recorded interview:

> *T.A.*: When you went to China, what did Mao discuss with you when you met him?
> *Bhashani*: Mao said to me that, at the present time, China's relationship with Pakistan was extremely fragile, and that the United States, Russia and India would do their utmost to break this relationship. He said, 'You are our friend, and if at the present moment you continue your struggle against the Ayub government, it will only strengthen the hand of Russia, America and India. It is against our principles to interfere with your work, but we would advise you to proceed slowly and carefully. Give us a chance to deepen our friendship with your government.[19]

After Bhashani's return, in the year and a half preceding a formal split, the pro-Peking communists first considerably toned down their opposition to the Ayub dictatorship and subsequently defended it as an 'anti-imperialist government'. The pro-Moscow NAP continued to oppose the régime, but essentially in a purely constitutional fashion. The split had seriously weakened the ability of NAP and its separate components to offer a coherent political alternative. The Maoist line had created further confusion. The net result was that the cadres of the left were ill-prepared for the 1968–9 explosions.

The Sino-Soviet rift had marked the first serious breach in the international communist movement for South Asian communists. If it had compelled even a small layer of them to develop a critical relationship to both sides and establish some objective criterion for evaluating the rift, the left would have benefited enormously. Neither side, however, encouraged independent thought, and communists in India and Pakistan were to adopt differential attitudes to their respective state machines, depending on the foreign policies of China and the USSR. Thus, in India, the Maoists were bitterly opposed to the Congress administration and embarked on a suicidal policy of 'armed struggles', while the pro-Moscow veterans acted as the left arm of the ruling party. In Pakistan, the situation was reversed. The Maoists defended a repressive military régime, while the pro-Moscow supporters argued in favour of democratic rights. It was in this overall context that a new party appeared in West Pakistan and an old one was able to revitalize itself in East Bengal. Both these formations were decisively to outflank the traditional left groups and win the allegiance of the masses (with the important exception of Baluchistan, and partially the NWFP).

It was the failures and divisions of NAP that ultimately led a former Ayub minister, Z. A. Bhutto, to organize his own party. He had discussed the political situation in the country with both wings of NAP and with the opposition Council Muslim League, but he found their analyses wanting. In December 1967, Bhutto launched the Pakistan People's Party (PPP), with a tiny handful of supporters.[20] These included a former ambassador to France, J. A. Rahim, a former student leader from Karachi, Mairaj Mohammed Khan, and a slightly unbalanced sycophant named Ahmed Raza Qasuri, together with a few drifters from the Convention Muslim League, such as Mustafa Khar and Mumtaz Bhutto (a first cousin). This motley band had very little in common except a loyalty to Bhutto and a belief in his ability to reach the highest office in the land. If the new party's support had been restricted to this small group, it could not have prospered. It found a new constituency, however, among West Pakistan's large student population, and it also attracted a layer of activists from the NAP, disgusted by the passivity of one wing and the pro-régime stance of the other. Bhutto became the major voice of the anti-Ayub agitation which started in November 1968. His rhetoric embraced a combination of anti-imperialist phrases and much talk of socialism. Bhutto's growing popularity was greatly enhanced by the Ayub administration's absurd campaign of vilification and personal slander. When the régime ordered his arrest, Bhutto became even more audacious and self-confident. The PPP was not so much a political party as a movement against the dictatorship, and as such it gathered support. The traditional left was totally bypassed.

In the colony of East Pakistan, politics were more intense. The ten years of dictatorship had heightened every possible contradiction. The national question was now at the centre of the stage, though a bulk of the Bengali left was remarkably blank on the question. Within the student community, the mass of school and university students were utterly opposed to the Ayub régime. Gangsters who supported the régime on the campuses had organized a reign of terror, but the left was to organize a counter-attack in November 1968. In the province as a whole, it was the Awami League that had supplanted the left. The League was now led by Sheikh Mujibur Rehman, who had been imprisoned by the régime for formulating a six-point programme for regional autonomy. The Six Points were: (1) a federal system of government, parliamentary in nature and based on adult franchise; (2) the federal government to deal only with defence and foreign affairs, all other subjects to be dealt with by the federating state; (3) *either* two separate but freely convertible currencies for the two parts of the country *or* one currency for the whole country, in which case effective constitutional measures should be taken to prevent the flight of capital from East to West Pakistan; (4) the power of taxation and revenue collection to be vested in the federating units and not at the centre; (5) separate accounts for foreign-exchange earnings of the two parts of the country, under control of the respective governments; (6) the setting-up of a militia or para-military force for East Pakistan.

This programme represented the most serious attempt yet by an East Pakistani political organization to reverse a situation that had existed since Partition.[21] When the predominantly Hindu traders and landlords had migrated to India in 1947, the vacuum they left behind had been filled by non-Bengalis, many based in West Pakistan. The economic exploitation of East Bengal, which started immediately after 1947, led as we saw in the last chapter to an annual extraction of 3,000 million rupees from the East by West Pakistani capital. The country's most important earner of foreign exchange was East Pakistan's jute crop, which accounted for over 50 per cent of exports. This money was spent on capital investment in West Pakistan. The discrimination against East Bengal was symbolized clearly by the way in which money was allocated by the Centre for development projects. Between 1948 and 1951, a total sum of 1,130 million rupees was sanctioned for development. Of this, only 22.1 per cent went to East Pakistan. Over the period 1948–69, the value of resources transferred from the East amounted to 2.6 thousand million dollars. The East had become both a field of investment and a captive market for manufactures produced in the West. The Six Points posed a fundamental challenge to this state of affairs. The party which had formulated them became, in the eyes of the people, the only force able to fight for Bengali equality. 'Parity not charity' was the message of Mujibur Rehman. The failure of the NAP to perceive the key importance of Bengali nationalism was not unconnected with its tacit support for the Ayub dictatorship; the old Maulana Bhashani was the first to realize this weakness and attempted to change course, but too late to displace the influence of the League.

In December 1967, Ayub paid his last visit to East Pakistan. He denounced the Awami League as a party of traitors and the rest of the opposition as 'enemies of Pakistan'. A fake case was manufactured against some Bengali soldiers, who were accused of 'conspiring with India'. The aim of the case was to discredit the national movement in East Pakistan: to indicate that Bengalis could not be trusted to remain loyal inside the army, and to divide the East Pakistani masses from their counterparts in the West. The fake trial and tortures of the imprisoned Bengali soldiers shocked the province, and almost all Bengali politicians united to denounce the process as a complete farce and one more manifestation of West Pakistani brutality. As the Ayub régime neared its end, the political situation could be summarized as follows. In the West, Zulfiqar Ali Bhutto had emerged as the only politician who commanded mass support in the Punjab and Sind. In the East, it was the national question that was paramount and Sheikh Mujibur Rehman who topped the popularity charts. In both parts of the country, the old left had failed to make even the correct promises. Thus two populist politicians, both with authoritarian tendencies, stood at the head of the movement which was to engulf the entire country.

The Fall of Ayub

The wave of popular explosions which finally toppled Ayub began on 7 November 1968. They lasted five whole months and saw an incredibly powerful display of mass spontaneity and courage. A combination of student demonstrations, worker strikes and mobilizations by teachers and lawyers brought the country to the brink of a pre-revolutionary situation. The character of the mass movement was unprecedented in the brief history of Pakistan. It was the only upheaval that united the masses in West and East for, at least, one common objective: the overthrow of the hated Ayub régime. The mood of the students and workers in both parts of the country was one of extreme self-confidence. They believed they could change everything. I have recorded my impressions and discussions with leading activists in that struggle elsewhere.[22] They thought that their actions would dictate the future history of Pakistan. Moreover, they were, in a broad sense, proved correct, though not in the way many of them had hoped. It is worth stressing that the 1968–9 mass eruption was the first generalized popular manifestation in the history of the country, going far deeper than the Muslim League agitation of the forties. It was essentially an urban affair: with the partial exception of some rural areas in East Pakistan, the struggle was confined to the cities (though its echoes were beginning to be felt in the countryside when Ayub fell). Over a hundred cities were involved in the agitation.

For the month of November, the students of West Pakistan struggled on their own, confronting bullets and sustained repression. In December, they were joined by workers in the West and by workers and students in East Pakistan. In January, the hybrid state created by Jinnah realized the only unity it was ever to know: on the streets of Rawalpindi, Karachi, Lahore and Lyallpur, as of Dacca, Chittagong, Rajshahi, Khulna and Commilla, the people fought as one against those who wielded state power. A study of the casualties indicates the depth of popular mobilization. November 1968: 4 deaths and over 1,000 arrests; December 1968: 11 deaths, 1,530 arrests; January 1969: 57 deaths, 4,710 arrests and 1,424 injured in street clashes; February 1969: 47 deaths, 100 arrests and 412 injured; March 1969: 90 deaths, 356 arrests, 40 injured. The increase in the number of deaths and the drop in the number of arrests signified a change in the tactics of those heading the mass struggle: in the later stages of the struggle, police stations began to be attacked, dozens of police officers were killed and rifles began to be stolen. The use of troops only made the situation worse, and it became clear to Ayub that isolated cases of officers refusing to issue orders to open fire in West Pakistan could easily become generalized. He accordingly announced his resignation on 26 March 1969. Power was handed over to General Yahya Khan, the army C.-in-C., who proclaimed martial law but promised general elections in the near future. Earlier, Yahya had declined a request to impose martial law in order to save Ayub's régime.

Throughout the upsurge, Ayub had been negotiating behind the scenes with the political leaders of the parties he had once consigned to the wilderness. These parties had formed a Democratic Action Committee (DAC) to participate in discussions with Ayub, who a few weeks before his resignation agreed to a restoration of parliamentary democracy and adult franchise. Bhutto, however, had refused to join the DAC–Ayub parleys (known as the Round Table Conferences), stating that *his* meetings were with the people. Mujibur Rehman had attended the meetings with Ayub, but had dissociated himself from DAC after the talks were over; when West Pakistani leaders had asked him to moderate his demands and not push the full nationalist programme, he is reported to have replied: 'I'll accept every Round Table Conference decision, but this is a prelude to an election and if I'm seen to be giving up any part of my programme, Bhashani will win. I'll yield to you, but after the elections. If you want to help me against Bhashani, you'll help me now.'[23]

Ayub's fall was a tremendous victory for those who had sustained the struggle. However, no theory underlay their practice, and at the end of the day the politicians of the old parties came back. The tragedy was that Pakistan had never possessed a mass socialist party. During the five months of struggle, a number of key cities could have fallen to the masses and created a breach within the army, if there had been a political force capable of transforming the desires of the people into concerted political action. Once Ayub fell, however, the struggle petered out in West Pakistan – though in the East it was to acquire radical new dimensions.

During its last phase, the only support the Ayub régime had received was from abroad. The Western press had remained remarkably loyal, as had the leaders of the Chinese People's Republic.[24] The period of uncertainty opened up by Ayub's humiliating downfall was not welcomed by either China or the West. Especially disappointed were the American academics who had attempted to present Ayub's Pakistan as a tolerably benign model for other countries (not to speak of relics of the Raj like Rushbrook-Williams, who provided profiles of the Sandhurst-trained general and the country he ruled for the *Encyclopaedia Britannica* and similar publications). Typical was Karl Von Vorys, a professor of political science at the University of Pennsylvania, who in 1964 concluded a 341-page book on Pakistan with the words: 'Just six years ago Mohammed Ayub Khan took the helm of the State of Pakistan. Since then he has many accomplishments to his credit. The disintegration of the country, an acute threat in 1958, seems rather remote now.'[25] Four years after these unfortunate sentences were penned, Ayub Khan had been overthrown by an unprecedented popular uprising. The country was far closer to disintegration than it had been in 1958.

4 The Break-Up of Pakistan 1969–71

The Yahya Interlude

The military régime of General Yahya Khan was a surreal development in the brief history of Pakistan. It was extremely weak, its birth having been brought about by a five-month mass rebellion. Its political future was limited, since it was impossible to conceive a powerful and undefeated populace tolerating once again the shameless domination of the peaked cap and the machine-gun. The Yahya régime lost little time in making its intentions known. A general election would take place throughout the country, and the country's future would be circumscribed by the result. Yahya's advisers believed that it was essential to concede on the electoral front in order to contain the upheaval. They were confident that the bureaucracy, from long experience in such matters, would be able to manipulate the results satisfactorily. The elections were postponed once, but finally took place in December 1970.

There was a long run-up to the 1970 elections. This enabled the political parties to explain their ideas and programmes to the people in some detail. It was thought that the long time-lapse between the announcement of the elections and the date on which they were ultimately held would also enable the military to ensure that right-wing parties, aided and abetted by the bureaucracy and the state-controlled media, would gain enough votes to act at least as a bargaining counter. What the régime and its advisers failed to comprehend was that the political consciousness and understanding of the masses had grown by leaps and bounds in the period preceding the fall of Ayub. Growing sections of the urban working class and petty bourgeoisie wanted to go the whole way and overthrow the system, but were severely hampered by the lack of a suitable political instrument. Their independent political capacity being thus reduced, they turned their attention to the ballot-box to achieve what they had first sought to accomplish on the streets. The fact that this was to be Pakistan's first parliamentary election on the basis of adult franchise meant that many people still harboured illusions about the possibility of purely electoral solutions. What no observer can deny, however, is that the largely illiterate rural and urban masses were hungry for politics.

The 1969–71 period in Pakistan was a unique example of the spontaneous democratic urge on the part of a people whose cultural level was extremely low and who had no previous experience of making their voice heard. The parties in both East and West that demanded a mandate for fundamental social change were given the best hearing and their leaders drew the largest crowds. In West Pakistan, it was the Pakistan People's Party (PPP) and its leader, Zulfiqar Ali Bhutto, who reached millions of ordinary people with the message of 'socialism'. In East Pakistan, it was the Awami League and Sheikh Mujibur Rehman who took the Six Points to every street-corner and village. The issues were widely aired. Both leaders were under attack from right-wing obscurantists, but fought back and succeeded in isolating the mullahs and their parties.

Bhutto promised a régime which would guarantee 'Food, Clothing and Shelter' to every Pakistani. His more demagogic lieutenants promised a veritable paradise to the poor peasants and workers who attended their meetings. The PPP promised radical land reforms, extensive nationalizations, an end to the economic power of the twenty-two families and many other improbable things. Because of the virtual eclipse of the left, the PPP appeared as socialists who would clean the dirty stables of Pakistani capital once and for all. The role of Bhutto was crucial in mobilizing the masses. His opposition (albeit belated) to Ayub, his months in prison, his forthright speeches helped to endear him to Punjabi and Sindhi audiences. The party leaders, however, consisted of an unholy amalgam of landlords, racketeers, lawyers and bandwagon petty bourgeois. The PPP reached a pact with Sindhi landlords and confiscated the genuine popular aspirations for social change in the towns and villages of the Punjab. The contradictory aspects of the PPP created extreme class tensions within its structures, reflected in its all-purpose motto: 'Socialism is our economy, democracy is our policy, Islam is our religion.'

Mujibur Rehman's campaign in the East concentrated on the national question. The traditional left was successfully outflanked, since its position on the oppression of the Bengalis by the West was confused, ambiguous and, in some cases, reactionary. The Awami League leaders explained in great detail how their part of the country had been exploited economically and politically (see pp. 45–7 above and Tables 1–3). They pointed out that Bengalis constituted a majority of the country's population, but were treated like second-class citizens. Rehman effectively demonstrated to the population of East Bengal that the taxes they paid were spent on building a large defence apparatus in which Bengalis were virtually unrepresented. The Awami League's election campaign captured the mood and aspirations of the masses. They wanted a confederal Pakistan. If they had in the past been unsure, there were no such doubts after 1969. The callousness with which

TABLE 1

Foreign Trade Statistics   (*Rs. in thousands*)

	Pakistan		East Pakistan		West Pakistan	
	Exports	Imports	Exports	Imports	Exports	Imports
1947–52	8,367,402	6,897,551	4,581,596	2,128,628	3,785,806	4,768,923
1952–7	7,410,137	7,264,645	3,969,766	2,159,552	3,440,371	5,105,093
1957–62	8,232,504	12,386,094	5,508,335	3,831,924	2,724,169	8,554,170
1962–7	12,677,062	23,023,717	6,922,694	7,063,692	5,754,368	15,960,025
Grand total 1947–67	36,687,105	49,572,007	20,982,391	15,183,796	15,704,714	34,388,211

SOURCE: *Monthly Foreign Trade Statistics of Pakistan*, June 1967, Karachi, Central Statistical Office.

they had been treated in the recent upsurge convinced them that they could not travel the same road as their Western counterparts. The night of 18 February 1969 had seen a sharp clash between workers and the army, resulting in many deaths: the killings had inflamed an already bitter public. The election campaign was, in a sense, a logical corollary to everything that had taken place in the preceding months, years and decades. A devastating cyclone struck East Pakistan in November 1970; many lives were lost and hundreds of thousands of families rendered homeless. The callous response of officialdom in the West further heightened nationalist fervour. The pro-Moscow and pro-Peking wings of the NAP now demanded a further postponement of the elections, and when Yahya refused both parties decided to boycott the polls. However, this appeared a somewhat flimsy pretext, since there was little doubt that the Awami League would trounce the NAP in any electoral competition.

The December 1970 election thus took on the character of a referendum on the Six Points, so far as East Pakistan was concerned. The result was a tidal victory for the Awami League. Of the total of 169 seats allocated to East Pakistan in the National Assembly, the League won 167; it gained 291 out of the 343 seats in the Provincial Assembly. Its 167 seats in the national legislature (a constituent assembly) gave the Bengali nationalists an overall majority throughout the country and entitled them to form the central government. The West Pakistani oligarchy was traumatized at such a prospect. The election results in West Pakistan had also seen the emergence of the PPP as the largest party from the Western province in the constituent

TABLE 2

Some Economic Indicators

	East Pakistan	West Pakistan
Area (in square miles)	54,501	310,236
Population (1970 estimate)	70 million	60 million
Five-year plan allocations		
1st	32%	68%
2nd	32%	68%
3rd	36%	64%
4th (unlikely to be implemented)	52.5%	47.5%
Foreign aid allocation	20–30%	70–80%
Export earning	50–70%	30–50%
Import expenditure	25–30%	70–75%
Industrial assets owned by Bengalis	11%	
Civil service jobs	16–20%	80–84%
Military jobs	10%	90%
Resources transferred from East to West between 1948–9 and 1968–9	Rs. 31,120 million*	
Per capita income, official		
1964–5	Rs. 285.5	Rs. 419.0
1968–9	Rs. 291.5	Rs. 473.4
Regional difference in p.c.i., official		
1959–60	32%	
1964–5	47%	
1968–9	62%	
Real difference in p.c.i., 1968–9	95%	
Real difference in average standard of living, 1968–9	126%	
Proportion of income spent on food by industrial workers (1955–6 survey)	69–75%	60–63%

* At the official rate, US $1 = 4.76 rupees (Rs.) (current market exchange rate, $1 = Rs. 11).

SOURCES: *Pakistan Statistical Yearbook* and *Pakistan Economic Survey* for the various years.

TABLE 3

Educational Disparities

	East Pakistan		West Pakistan	
	1947	1967	1947	1967
Primary level				
Number of institutions	29,633	28,225	8,413	33,271
Number of students	2,020,000	4,310,000	550,000	2,740,000
Secondary level				
Institutions	3,481	4,390	2,598	4,563
Students	53,000	107,000	51,000	153,000
General College				
Institutions	50	173	40	239
Enrolment	19,000	138,000	13,000	142,000
General University				
Institutions	1	2	2	4
Enrolment	1,600	8,000	700	10,000

SOURCES: Ministry of Education, Government of Pakistan, *Education Statistics of Pakistan* (*1947–57*); and A. O. Huque, 'Educational Disparities in Pakistan', *Forum*, 20 December 1969.

assembly, but its position was by no means as strong as that of the Awami League in the East. The NAP had emerged with a significant regional base in Baluchistan and the North-West Frontier. The best Bhutto could hope for was to be a junior partner in any coalition government at the Centre. The elections had been fair: no political party raised charges of rigging or other malpractices.

The results were a nightmare for the military–bureaucratic bloc in Islamabad. Immediately after the general elections were over, it became clear that the army would not tolerate an autonomous Bengal within a federal state structure. On 1 January 1971, in a comment on the results I wrote:

> Will the Pakistan Army and the capitalist barons of West Pakistan allow these demands (the Six Points) to go through? The answer is quite clearly no. What will probably happen is that in the short term Mujibur Rehman will be allowed to increase East Pakistan's percentage of import and export licences and will be allocated a larger share of foreign capital investment. These are the 'concessions' which the Army will be prepared to make in the coming few months. If Rehman accepts them, he will be allowed to stay in power. If not, it will be back to business as usual in the shape of the Army. Of course, there is no doubt that in the event of another military coup there will be no holding back the immense

grievances of Bengal and the desire for an independent Bengal will increase a hundredfold.[1]

The problem for the Pakistani ruling class lay precisely in the fact that, even if Mujibur Rehman had been prepared to make concessions, the masses who had voted for him were totally intransigent. Mujib was not a particularly shrewd or intelligent leader. In other words, he was dispensable – and aware of the fact. The dominant bloc in West Pakistan was opposed to *any* fundamental concessions. The Pakistan army was organically hostile to the prospect of a Bengali civilian government, because of the danger that it might reduce the lavish military apparatus which has been an inbuilt feature of every Islamabad régime since Ayub seized power in October 1958. The Pakistani officer corps had an enormous stake in the structures of the unitary state. The military budget had absorbed 60 per cent of total state expenditures throughout the preceding decade. In election year, over 625 million dollars had been allocated for the armed forces. Awami League leaders had understandably denounced these colossal outlays on a military machine which was almost bereft of Bengalis and, as shown in 1965, was incapable of defending Pakistan. The army chiefs were also saturated with a racist chauvinism against Bengalis, and the business community had strong material reasons for resisting the Six Points. The interzonal exploitation which marked the country's complex economy was described in the last chapter.[2] Suffice it to say that West Pakistani capitalism depended on the East for 50 per cent of its exports. The captive market of Bengal had to be retained, or West Pakistan's high-cost manufactured goods would be without buyers.

If the army alone had been opposed to Bengali demands, the conflict that followed might have taken on a different character. The PPP and its leader Bhutto, however, had been equally stunned by the overwhelming electoral success of the Awami League. Bhutto soon emerged as the most vociferous defender of the traditional hegemony of West Pakistan, and embarked on a hysterical campaign of denouncing the Six Points. After consulting senior military officers, he whipped up an atmosphere of frenzied chauvinism in the Punjab. The Constituent Assembly was due to meet on 3 March 1971, Bhutto refused to attend unless Mujib compromised on the Six Points. He simultaneously threatened to unleash 'civil disobedience' in West Pakistan if the assembly met without him. Mujib met Bhutto on a number of occasions following the elections, but they failed to reach any agreement.[3] The fact that Bhutto was colluding with the generals was clear to everyone. If the army had decided to accept the results of the election, the assembly would have met and Bhutto's bluff been exposed to public view. For their part, the minority parties in West Pakistan had stated that they were prepared to participate in the assembly. General Yahya, however, uni-laterally decided to postpone the convening of the assembly indefinitely. Bengal reacted with anger, and in street clashes that followed more Bengalis lost their lives. Unarmed masses had been called out by the Awami League, whose leaders then watched troops firing on them, entirely unable to offer any effective initiative. A continuous general strike soon brought the pro-vince to a standstill.

The Pakistani ruling classes had feared a general election ever since the country was formed. They had manoeuvred and manipulated for ten whole years to deny the Bengali nation a voice in the affairs of the state. When this had failed, they had ruled directly through the army for another ten years. As we have seen, this period had ended in a spectacular explosion of public anger on the streets of West and East Pakistan. Fearful of a developing pre-revolutionary crisis, the ruling bloc had finally attempted to defuse the struggle by promising elections. But an undefeated mass movement had utilized the ballot box to inflict a further defeat on the military–bureau-cratic alliance. By 1971, the Pakistani state had moved full circle. Its ideologues and leaders paused for a while, then headed straight for the precipice.

The Awami League was a reformist formation *par excellence*. Its leaders were not prepared for a frontal assault on the bastions of the Pakistani state. They preferred negotiation and compromise. Their tragedy was that none was possible. The tragedy of the Bengali people was that they were led by a party which had no strategy for winning power, but was forced only through a series of defensive manoeuvres to elaborate tactics to confront the new situation. The decades of suffering had made Bengal desperate. People were prepared to fight and dragged their leaders willy-nilly behind them. The Awami League had little choice but to accept the situation. What resulted was a curious state of affairs which can only be described as a bourgeois caricature of dual power. The League set up committees to take over the administration of key areas in both cities and countryside. Only the army cantonments remained outside its control, and even here the tension was felt very deeply: at one stage, all Bengali cooks, servants and laundrymen left the cantonments; in local food markets, street-vendors refused to sell food to soldiers. But the committees were dominated by the Awami League and lacked an autonomous popular basis. They substituted a new authority for that of the Pakistani-controlled state in East Bengal, but did not significantly alter its functions. No serious effort was made to mobilize or arm the people, in order to prepare them for the confrontation that was plainly imminent.

The other side, in sharp contrast, was preparing for the kill. The governor of East Pakistan, Admiral Ahsan, opposed to a military solution, expressed in strong language his opposition to the bloodbath being prepared. Islamabad ordered his removal. He was replaced by General Tikka Khan (who could not be sworn in, as the Bengali Chief Justice of the High Court refused to administer the oath). Tikka supervised the preparations for the military assault on East Bengal. As troops poured in, Awami League leaders were getting detailed reports of the build-up. Mujibur Rehman, however, was adamant in refusing to declare independence, at a time when the balance of forces was more favourable to the nationalists. He repeatedly declared his aim of a negotiated settlement and pledged to preserve the existing social order. At a mass meeting of half-a-million people in Dacca on 7 March, Mujib fulminated against intrigue, but despite the sentiments of the people refused to declare independence. Having won such a large majority, he could not believe that the army would crush it by force. In a revealingly frank interview with an Agence France Presse correspondent, Mujib complained: 'Is the West Pakistan government not aware that I am the only one able to save East Pakistan from communism? If they take the decision to fight I shall be pushed out of power and the Naxalites (Maoists) will intervene in my name. If I make too many concessions, I shall lose my authority. I am in a very difficult situation.'[4]

In Islamabad, the army had completed its work and staff plans were ready to wipe out the Bengali national movement in a series of sharp and well-directed military blows. The army needed more time, in order to dispatch extra troops to ensure a successful surgical operation. Yahya flew to Dacca on 15 March 1971 and resumed talks with the Awami League. Bhutto was also summoned and participated in these discussions. The Awami League leaders were lulled into believing that a deal was now certain. Yahya dragged out the negotiations for ten whole days, until the requisite number of troops had arrived in the Bengali capital. On 25 March, the Awami League leaders were awaiting the announcement of a settlement. Yahya and other West Pakistani leaders left in the morning. That night the army struck. Mujibur Rehman stayed at home and allowed himself to be captured. Tikka Khan's soldiers destroyed buildings indiscriminately. The Bengali working class and intelligentsia were the first major target.[5] The army shelled Dacca University and wiped out all the students and lecturers it could find; soldiers invaded the women's hostel, raping and killing the inmates. Artillery units flattened working-class areas, and trade-union and newspaper offices were burnt to the ground. Tens of thousands were killed in the first few days. The Bengali people paid a terrible price for the inadequacy of their leaders.

An unarmed and abandoned populace attempted to fight back, but without much success. What the masses possessed in courage, they lacked in material weapons. Multitudes fled to the countryside. Scattered units of the

East Pakistan Rifles and police units, under Awami League leadership, continued the struggle. Their policy of attempting to fortify the towns was a disaster, since they only provided an easy target for a professional and mechanized army. They were rapidly defeated and dispersed. By the middle of April, Tikka Khan was in command of all the main cities. In the countryside, a *Mukti Fauj* (liberation army) had been formed, and its units were beginning to learn the art of guerrilla warfare. Yahya's uniformed hoodlums spread death and destruction in East Bengal. The soldiery had been told that the Bengalis were an inferior race, short, dark, weak (unlike the 'martial races' of the Punjab) and still infected with Hinduism. Junior and senior officers alike had spoken of seeking, in the course of their campaign, to improve the genes of the Bengali people. Fascist talk of this character gave the green light for the mass rapes suffered by Bengali women regardless of class or creed. The generals and their favourite politicians, however, had in reality made a terrible mistake. They had destroyed the only political force that could have contained the mass movement – the Awami League. Bhutto's first reported comment on the butchery unleashed in Bengal was: 'Thank God! Pakistan has been saved.' Rarely has a politician been guilty of such a profound misjudgement. The army had scored easy successes, but it had also signed and sealed the death warrant of Pakistan as a state.

Civil War and the Birth of Bangladesh

> It was an evening in November ...
> And suddenly shouts lit up the silence;
> We had attacked, we the slaves; we, the
> dung-underfoot, we the animals with patient hooves ...
>
> Aimé Césaire

Pakistan was engulfed in a civil war without precedent in recent history. An army representing an ethnic minority was seeking to crush a majority of the country's population and to obliterate its political leaders. It was clear at the outset that the struggle would be bloody and protracted. The Eastern province did not, in the main, favour guerrilla warfare. Over 90 per cent of the population lived in the countryside, but the terrain was almost bare of mountains and forests. The Chittagong Hill Tracts were far too remote to serve as a base of operations. The countryside consisted essentially of plains dissected by numerous streams and rivers. In the first few months, the Pakistan army managed to re-establish control through the use of brute force and an overwhelming military superiority. Gradually, however, an armed opposition began to develop, and as the monsoon season gripped the Eastern province, the army found that the *Mukti* guerrillas were becoming more audacious. A number of bridges were blown up, army units were ambushed and Bengali ingenuity began to adapt the traditional forms of guerrilla warfare to indigenous conditions. The war had begun, and the question immediately arose: how long would it last?

The answer lay in the political evolution taking place in the Awami League and the left-wing parties. The League's leadership had fled to neighbouring India, where it soon formed a government in exile with the full backing of the Indian government. The middle-level League cadres, on the other hand, were involved in organizing the *Mukti Fauj*, and a political differentiation began to take place. Many younger members questioned the entire strategy of the League, and sharply criticized the old leaders. A radical nationalist current developed within the liberation army, which hinted openly that the future state should be socialist. It was, however, not helped theoretically by either the veteran pro-Moscow communists or the Maoists. The latter were in some ways the most dynamic current, but they were split into competing sects. Most were in favour of resisting the army of occupation and those who collaborated with it, but the most orthodox, under the leadership of Abdul Haq and Mohammed Toaha, refused to participate in the struggle. Haq finally moved still further to the right and defended the official positions of Peking. The most effective of the Maoist groups in the first months of the struggle was the East Bengal Communist Party (EBCP), led by Matin and Allaudin. Its guerrilla units in Pabna were led by Tipu Biswas, who soon acquired legendary status as an effective military leader. Biswas continually harassed the army garrison at Pabna, drew it out of its cantonment and, after a week-long battle, destroyed it. The guerrillas then occupied the city and distributed weapons to the populace, after which they left – in sharp contrast with the tactics of positional warfare employed by the Awami League in early April 1971.

It became clear that neither side was going to secure a quick victory. The Pakistan army was confronted by a population whose hostility was almost universal. The main collaborators it secured were members and supporters of the fanatical, semi-fascist Jamaat-i-Islami, who supplied the bulk of the recruits for a volunteer corps that fought alongside the army and specialized in burning books and killing nationalist or left-wing professors, lawyers, teachers, journalists and writers. Other right-wing parties also provided support, in the shape of intelligence (*sic*) operations. But the election results had already revealed the total isolation of these groupings. Rejected by their own people, they now sought sustenance in the armed might of the West Pakistani ruling classes. The more the army and its supporters engaged in indiscriminate violence, the more the strength of the guerrillas grew. By September–October 1971, the guerrilla armies numbered tens of thousands of men and women.

Meanwhile the Awami League leaders in Calcutta were becoming restless. In October 1971, a section of the Awami League put out feelers to the Pakistan army, suggesting a possible agreement based on the release of Mujib (then a prisoner in West Pakistan), autonomy for Bengal *within* Pakistan, and mediation by the United States. This proposal reflected a fear on the part of the Awami League that a continuing liberation struggle in East Bengal might render them redundant, pushing the country irreversibly to the left. But to waste time, energy and resources in hoping that the USA would disarm the Pakistan army – a vital component of its system for blocking social revolution in South Asia – was to harbour and create empty illusions. Washington was certainly aware that an important section of the Awami League leadership was subjectively pro-American, but it regarded the League as a woefully inadequate instrument for guaranteeing imperialist domination in the region. The West Pakistani army, by contrast, was a tangible and reliable entity capable of safeguarding US interests and mediating them through those of the local landlord and capitalist classes. The Awami League's pro-American wing was consequently forced to beat a rapid retreat, and a unified military front was established. The Pakistan army soon found itself confronting a guerrilla force of 150,000 combatants, who were gaining experience with every passing day. They succeeded in effectively disrupting the communications system of Tikka's units, making it difficult for them to be supplied with food or reinforcements. At the same time, the guerrillas began to eliminate collaborators, 20,000 of whom had been killed by the end of October. Despite the growing unity of the fighting units in the field, the political disputes continued unabated. This was hardly surprising, since the entire future of East Bengal was at stake. The left was beginning to gain ground, and there could be little doubt that if the war continued for another year, one of the first casualties would be the traditional political style and ideology of the Awami League. The latter's utter inability to grasp or deal with the dynamic turn of events was not the fault of individual leaders. It was a result of its inherent addiction to constitutionalism. An astute commentator in the Indian press candidly noted this fact, and drew a comparison with India's own constitutionalist political formation:

> The Awami League leadership in many ways corresponds to the leadership of our own Congress – a leadership which, with the backing of peaceful agitation, sought to arrive and ultimately succeeded in arriving at compromises with our colonialist masters. Our independence was the result of an understanding with the British masters. Sheikh Mujibur Rehman hoped to pull off a comparable deal with Islamabad. Like the Congress in India, the Awami League does not have the stomach for the type of war circumstances have forced Bangladesh to wage.[6]

These remarks were accurate enough, but they failed to grasp that Mujib was a victim of his own illusions. There was a crucial difference between British imperialism and the wretched sub-colonialism of Islamabad. Britain was able to grant a political decolonization because this nowhere meant abandonment of its real *economic* empire, whose central segments were Malayan rubber and tin, Middle Eastern oil, South African gold, Indian plantations. But the loss of East Bengal affected the vital interests of the Pakistani bourgeoisie. The weaker a colonial power, the more dependent it is on formal political possession of its subject territories. As the war in East Bengal unfolded, it became more and more obvious that the Awami League 'government' in Calcutta was on the verge of being outflanked by the armed bodies of men and women fighting the Pakistan army. So the League leaders moved simultaneously on two fronts: they formed a 'Mujib Army', consisting of several thousand student supporters of their party, and they opened serious negotiations with the Indian government.

The Awami League had never been a structured mass organization, with a genuine leadership system or party discipline. It was a shapeless collection of political notables and their followers, which had yet to prove that it could really handle the forces to its left and prevent them from capturing its rank-and-file. The Indian bourgeoisie was beginning to get alarmed at developments in its neighbouring country. There had been a growing stream of refugees entering West Bengal, who had begun to pose a number of material and political problems in India. Mrs Gandhi, the Indian prime minister, was shrewd enough to realize that political refugees can be a destabilizing factor – especially ones able to communicate to fellow-Bengalis in the same language. The Indian leader was also aware that it is impossible to fight a protracted armed struggle without mass support, and that the only way of preserving this support is to begin a process of social revolution in the liberated zones. Such a process has an innate tendency to snowball, and the threat of the Awami League being bypassed by events was becoming more real every day. At the same time, the prospect of an Indian military intervention in East Pakistan was always more congenial to the leaders of the Awami League than the prospect of themselves organizing armed struggle for national liberation.

The guerrillas inside East Bengal, by November 1971, had succeeded in paralysing the important port towns of Chittagong and Chalna. Interzonal trade had virtually ceased, and Pakistan's infantry divisions were encountering a more mature and serious resistance. On 3 December 1971, however, the civil war in Pakistan took a dramatic turn when the Indian army crossed the East Pakistan border and moved towards the capital, Dacca. Mrs Gandhi had realized that there was now no chance of the Pakistan army succeeding in holding down the province, and that any delay could be fatal to bourgeois interests throughout South Asia. The intervention was not, therefore, a result of the 'humanitarian ideals' of the Congress Party. It had become vital for India that the Awami League, and it alone, should exercise political power in the new Bangladesh. Otherwise the risk of de-stabilization in Indian West Bengal would be too great: any idea of a United Bengali Republic was viewed with the greatest alarm – in Washington as in New Delhi.[7] Indian intervention thus not only solved the question of who would hold state power in Bangladesh, it also created a basis for defeating the left in West Bengal.

The military successes of the Indians exceeded even their own expecta-tions. In a two-week war, Pakistan lost half its navy, a quarter of its air force and a third of its army. Crucial factors in this success, and in the speed of the Indian advance to Dacca, were the collaboration of the guerrillas and the goodwill of the masses. In addition, once it was surrounded the Pakistani army chose to surrender rather than fight. The military commander, General Niazi, handed himself and 93,000 troops over to the Indians as prisoners-of-war. The result was that an important section of the military apparatus of the Pakistani state was transported wholesale to India, where it was preserved intact and – following a political settlement – handed back to Pakistan. The actual surrender was a bizarre occasion. Senior officers of both armies had been trained in the same military academies. They embraced each other and nostalgically exchanged anecdotes and vulgar jokes while consuming their whisky and soda in the army mess, much to the amusement of British and American diplomats. In the heart of a city where people were dying of starvation and where several hundred intellec-tuals had been cold-bloodedly massacred a few days before, the victors consoled the defeated. The generals of both armies demonstrated that class solidarity remained a more powerful force than confessional divisions.

Once the victory was confirmed, the Awami League leaders were flown home from Calcutta in an Indian air force plane, welcomed at Dacca Airport by a guard of honour consisting of Indian troops, packed into an army truck and displayed to the people. Within the next few weeks Sheikh Mujibur Rehman was released from his West Pakistani prison and flown home to Dacca via London. The scenario was complete and the League was in power. Despite the decisive Indian role in its birth, Bangladesh was now an independent state, with 70 million people and an area of 55,126 square miles. The absence in Bengal of any solid pre-existent state apparatus, and the fact that Bangladesh's army had been formed in a process of bloody struggles, meant that the new leaders would face enormous problems. The lack of an effective social and economic programme to transform the lives of the masses meant that Sheikh Mujib and his supporters would attempt to reconstruct their state on the old pattern. Mujib himself was soon to be assassinated by young army officers, and the country has known only a chronic instability, its left wing dispersed and atomized, its masses prey to greed, corruption and repression. But the story is by no means over.

Retrenchment in the West

The attempt of the West Pakistani ruling class to maintain all its privileges had thus led to the break-up of Pakistan, only two and a half decades after its formation. The 'two-nations' theory, formulated in the middle-class living rooms of Uttar Pradesh, was buried in the Bengali countryside. During the repression in Bengal and following the war, supreme power in Islamabad was exercised by a small circle of military officers, flanked by a few civilian advisers and accomplices. Yahya Khan himself was a dim and slothful alcoholic. There were five generals who ruled behind him: Hamid, Deputy C.-in-C.; Umar Khan, chairman of the National Security Council; Akbar Khan, head of the Inter-Services Intelligence Committee; Pirzada, Deputy Chief Martial Law Administrator; and Tikka Khan, the 'Butcher of Dacca'. The régime's top civilian bureaucrat, M. M. Ahmed, was also a trusted adviser.

Like all political expressions of class rule, the Pakistani army and civil bureaucracy had always enjoyed a relative autonomy from the landlords and capitalists of West Pakistan. But the converse had not been the case. The cohesion of the army was needed as a *political* rallying-point, over and above its purely repressive functions. The Six Points struck at the very heart of oligarchic rule in West Pakistan. This is what explains the refusal to compromise with the Awami League, the ferocity of the measures taken against the East, and the virtual unanimity in West Pakistani ruling circles in support of the 25 March action. The Yahya régime could have been isolated and defeated only if the West Pakistani masses had also risen and expressed their solidarity with the victims of military repression in the East. Here the failure was one of leadership. Bhutto's support for the army effectively defused any possibility of mass action in the West. The pro-Moscow groups were sympathetic to Bengali aspirations, but lacked a popular base to oppose the régime. The Maoists were hostile to the 'secessionists', in line with the Chinese government's support for Yahya Khan.

On the external front, the United States, faced with a choice between Mujib and Yahya, had naturally and unhesitatingly gambled on the latter, and decided that the Islamabad régime must be sustained. Henry Kissinger was widely quoted as saying at a top security gathering: 'I am getting hell every half hour from the President that we are not being tough enough on India. He has just called me again. He does not believe we are carrying out his wishes. He wants to tilt in favour of Pakistan.' The Soviet Union, for reasons of its own, gave tacit backing to the Bengalis, and Soviet President Podgorny sent a message to Yahya Khan 'insistently appealing for the adoption of urgent measures to stop the bloodshed and repressions against the population of East Pakistan and for methods for a peaceful political settlement'. The Chinese leaders, for their part, gave unconditional and blanket approval to the Yahya régime in its attempt to crush the Bengali resistance. Their support extended far beyond state diplomacy; it faithfully echoed the ideological justifications offered by the Islamabad military clique for its genocide in Bengal. In a warm personal letter to Yahya Khan, Chou En-lai openly accepted and defended the right of the Pakistan army to trample on the aspirations of an oppressed people.[8]

The Chinese justification that they were upholding the 'unity and sove-reignty' of Pakistan was outrageous. The Pakistani state, as we have sought to explain in preceding chapters, was a uniquely reactionary and anti-national construct. It was one of the only two confessional states in the world – the other being Israel. The Chinese appeared to be saying that the sacred ties of religion were indissoluble. In fact, of course, the basic right of national self-determination, a fundamental principle of Marxism and Leninism, belonged unequivocally to the oppressed masses of East Pakistan. Not only were they ethnically, historically, linguistically and culturally a distinct community, they also constituted a majority of the population of 'Pakistan'. The class character of the state machine that attempted to enforce the 'unity of Pakistan' was equally plain: it was the repressive weapon of a landlord–capitalist–bureaucratic ruling bloc against millions of workers and peasants. It was a shock force of imperialist-trained and Pentagon-backed coercion, an integral component of CENTO and SEATO which, for instance, had provided mercenaries to defend feudal despotism in the Arab Gulf against the popular revolt in Dhofar.

China did not limit itself to verbal support for the military dictatorship in Pakistan. It provided crucial military and economic assistance. It was Chinese-made tanks that were used to raze workers' districts in Dacca and it was Chinese-constructed fighter bombers which bombed Bengali villages. At the height of the war, Peking provided the generals with a 100-million-dollar interest-free loan. The modern highway linking Sinkiang with North-West Pakistan across the Karakorum range, from Sufu to Gilgit, was a constant conduit for military and civilian supplies from China throughout the crisis. When a general strike in East Bengal had halted shipments of newsprint, Chinese trucks brought newsprint south to keep the official presses running in Pakistan. During the war a hundred lorries a day were leaving China for Gilgit, with military supplies for the ordnance depots in Peshawar and Rawalpindi. Chinese aid was thus of direct benefit to the counter-revolution. China's cynical attitude to the Bengali masses marked the deepening of a turn away from policies even remotely connected with any form of internationalism. The Sino-US partnership, which was to flourish in later years, was sealed with the blood of Bengali peasants, students and workers.

Yahya and his clique of generals and civilian advisers were only able to prosecute the war because of internal backing from the PPP and external support from China and the United States. Yet the depoliticizing effect of the war in West Pakistan should not be underestimated. The Punjabi province was the focal point of mass chauvinism. The bulk of the soldiers fighting in the East were from this region, and Bhutto had received strong backing in the recent elections from these areas. The failure of the PPP to challenge the army during the fateful year of 1971 was to have deep repercussions. The defeat of the Pakistan army traumatized West Pakistan and considerably dented the prestige of the armed services. This was a golden opportunity permanently to weaken the position of the army in national politics and ensure that it could never rule again. Within the army itself, there was a strong mood of revolt against the high command. A crack armoured division was on the verge of open mutiny after the war. A large number of junior officers met and decided to march their troops to Islamabad and overthrow Yahya by force, despite the risk of civil war. This situation was averted by the commanding officer, General Karim. He persuaded the officers to postpone their projected action, went himself to Islamabad and made it clear that unless Yahya and his fellow generals were ousted, the country would be engulfed in civil strife. At a stormy meeting of senior officers, General Hamid was abused and almost physically assaulted. A new military leader was considered inappropriate. The dissident officers decided to send for Zulfiqar Ali Bhutto. The old Pakistan was dead. Could the new one survive?

5 The Populist Experiment: Bhutto in Power 1971–7

On 20 December 1971, the military high command handed over power to Zulfiqar Ali Bhutto, chairman of the Pakistan People's Party. It was a somewhat bizarre occasion, Pakistan scoring another historical first when the civilian Bhutto was appointed Chief Martial Law Administrator. This fact reflected the changed realities that confronted the military–bureaucratic bloc in Islamabad. The defeat suffered in Dacca and the break-up of the country traumatized the population from top to bottom. History has recorded that military defeats feed the processes of social revolution. The army is the spinal cord of a state apparatus. In Pakistan the army had been in direct political command as well. The defeat suffered by this army created conditions of extreme uncertainty. The mood of the country was such that a radical overhaul of the social and economic structures of the truncated state would have won massive support. A socialist régime could even have pushed through measures that demolished the crumbling edifice of the military–bureaucratic complex. It was awareness of their isolation that had compelled the generals to send for Bhutto, who at that moment was to be found addressing the Security Council in characteristically emotional style. When he received the message from Islamabad, he had in fact already been cleared by the State Department; a formal meeting with Nixon ratified the decision of the Pakistani high command. Bhutto's assumption of power was welcomed by the *Washington Post* and the *New York Times*, on the grounds that he was the only politician in the country who could preserve the existing social order.

Bhutto's take-over was thus arranged by the army. Although he dismissed the generals who had formed the mainstay of the Yahya administration, and some months later pushed through a further purge when army chief General Gul Hasan, Air Marshal Rahim and other senior officers were removed and dispatched abroad as ambassadors, and although he fulminated against 'Bonapartist influences' in the armed forces, Bhutto did nothing qualitatively to alter the army's character or function. He replaced Gul Hasan with Tikka Khan, a veteran of 'anti-insurgent operations' in the province of Baluchistan prior to his more recent role as the 'Butcher of Dacca'. Tikka's appointment served a dual function. On the one hand, himself a Sindhi, Bhutto felt that it would be advantageous for the army boss to be a Punjabi. On the other, Tikka's ruthlessness as a military commander was an added advantage, as it delivered a veiled warning to the nationalists in the Frontier and Baluchistan provinces, where the PPP was in a minority and the National Awami Party constituted the major political force.

In acting to modify somewhat the command structure of the army – Bhutto abolished the post of C.-in-C. and replaced it with that of Chief of Staff – and to ensure that generals personally sympathetic to him occupied the top positions, the PPP leader was following a conscious plan. More than any other politician, he had observed the army functioning at first hand. His ministerial posts during the Ayub military régime, and his collaboration with Yahya Khan during the war in Bengal, had given him a unique education in the mentality and operational style of the army top brass. Aware that the army had been gravely weakened as an institution and widely discredited in the country, he saw this as an opportunity to reinforce civilian rule. However, what he failed to perceive was that as long as the army was allowed to continue to exist in its present form, it would soon recover its standing and succeed in crushing any civilian politician without *organized* mass support.

The military officers who had sent for Bhutto had, for their part, by no means learnt any correct lessons from the disintegration of their state. A typical example of the superficial analysis widely accepted amongst ruling circles in Pakistan was contained in a book by General Fazal Muqeem Khan. The general, who sees himself as a friendly historian of the institution which he helped to build, spoke for many officers and bureaucrats when he wrote:

> The macabre events of 1971 showed clearly that the country was not prepared to meet the challenge politically, economically or militarily. The war in East Pakistan was brought on by the political chaos created by the idiocy of Yahya Khan and his advisers. The humiliating surrender at Dacca was the result of ineptness of the high command and the commander appointed by him. It is no less than a miracle that in spite of indecisive and indifferent leadership, the lack of weapons and equipment, and the defection and treachery of Bengalis, the formations and units in the field still fought so tenaciously . . . It is most unfair and unrealistic to ask soldiers, sailors and airmen to fight a war without proper weapons and equipment, a coherent political leadership . . .[1]

This view was reiterated with greater vigour by others who had observed the débâcle. Bhutto was fond of referring to Yahya's love of alcohol and prostitutes, and his fellow-officers were often described as corpulent and isolated incompetents. Soon after Bhutto assumed power, it became a national pastime to mock and abuse the fallen generals. Few, very few, attempted to analyse why the Pakistan of 1947 no longer existed. This did not simply reflect the inability of the country's intelligentsia to subject political developments to a searching inquisition. It was a deliberate attempt to prevent the people from gaining access to ideas that could encourage a challenge to existing state institutions. For General Muqeem to suggest that Bengal could have been subjugated by more effective generals and more advanced weapons of mass murder was immoral, to say the least. For Bhutto to blame everything on the 'fat and flabby generals' was to miss an enormous opportunity to establish democratic institutions and emasculate the army and civil service. This mistake was ultimately to cost him his own life.

The problems that confronted the PPP and its leader cannot be under-estimated. The truncated state they inherited was in the throes of a quad-ruple crisis: a crisis of legitimacy, and the pressing need to salvage the coun-try's damaged political institutions, to restore its economy and to re-fashion its external relations. Bhutto's flamboyant populism was not pleasing to the military–bureaucratic patricians of Pakistan's political order; yet they toler-ated his demagogy, being only too aware that he was the one political leader standing between them and complete chaos. For his part, Bhutto mistook their temporary subservience for permanent weakness. He genu-inely believed that he had tamed the generals and bureaucrats, and that under his benign control the same old structures would suffice. His reforms were essentially cosmetic, designed to mask the PPP's inability to deliver all it had promised to its voters. Bhutto's years in power are best discussed by considering separately his attempts to reconstruct the Pakistani state in the spheres of domestic politics, foreign policy and the economy.

The Economy

Bhutto came to power after the disintegration of the country. During the civil war, the economy – depressed since 1968 – had received a body blow. Foreign-exchange reserves had dwindled to a minimum. Prices and un-employment had mounted steadily. The collapse of jute exports had pre-cipitated a steep decline on the Karachi stock-exchange. The cost of Yahya's expeditionary force in East Bengal had approached two million dollars per day. The burden this imposed on the economy can best be understood if put in the context of West Pakistan's chronic import deficit of 140 million dollars a month. The Pakistani state was compelled unilaterally to suspend pay-ment on foreign debts, and to appeal for more foreign aid.

The choices which faced Bhutto and the PPP were limited. The revolutionary ardour of the urban masses had been diminished by an upsurge of anti-Bengali chauvinism in the main cities of the Punjab and Karachi. None the less, many of the most depressed urban strata expected some fundamental social change from the new government. Bhutto had never intended a socialist transformation, but the dynamics of third-world development dictated priorities far removed from the classical schemas of the bourgeois–democratic revolution. The three goals of the latter had been national independence, capital accumulation and political democracy. In the third world, however, though it had on occasion been possible to achieve one or other of these aims, there had been no instance (since the implosion of capital in Japan) of any country reaching Western European standards. In some cases, the capitalist class of certain third-world territories or countries had abandoned the goals of national independence and democracy, in order to achieve a phenomenally high rate of growth and exceptional privileges in the markets of advanced capitalism: Hong Kong, Puerto Rico, South Korea and Taiwan are the examples that immediately come to mind. This economic growth, however, had been of a distorted type, accompanied by super-exploitation of the majority of the toiling population in town and countryside.[2] There were other cases where national independence went together with economic autarky (that is, stagnation) and political repression: Haiti and Burma, for instance. But though many different permutations existed, one fact had become clear since the sixties: the only long-term solution for the bourgeoisie of the third world was a régime that concentrated brutally on accumulating capital, disregarded the democratic rights of the masses and compromised its national independence. Régimes of this sort are the rule in the third world today – their success or lack of it being determined by geography, size, guerrilla wars, urban unrest and the direct presence of foreign powers. Ruling groups based on popular revolts they had themselves helped to abort through triumphant counter-revolutions were usually in the strongest position to promote capital accumulation, in collaboration with and dependence on the capitalist strongholds in the West. It is true that rises in the market price of certain raw materials (especially oil) have occasionally improved the bargaining capacity of some third-world states; but even where this has occurred it has in no way eliminated their subordination to the world market itself. This subordination is anchored in fundamental production relationships, not in mere terms of exchange.

The Bhutto régime attempted, for a short period, to defy the objective realities of the economic system of which it was a part. It did so in a feeble, half-hearted fashion and, more importantly, by suppressing rather than encouraging mass mobilizations. 'Those who only make the revolution half-way,' the French revolutionary Saint-Just had said in the eighteenth century, 'only dig their own graves.' In Pakistan, the revolution did not even go half-way. The key to transforming the country as a whole lay in a revolutionary transformation of the countryside; but such transformations cannot be carried out by those who are not revolutionaries. Bhutto's excited rhetoric had enabled the peasant to lift his head, but the series of land reforms introduced by the new régime in fact changed very little in terms of production relations in the countryside, and utterly failed to destroy the grip of the landlords (hardly surprising since the PPP leaders, especially in Sind where rural life was virtually medieval, were predominantly scions of landowning families).

The effective land ceiling was indeed reduced from 36,000 produce index units to 18,000. But while this might appear a radical change, the important fact, as one economist pointed out at the time, was that 'the key unit in determining the ceiling of land to be owned by an individual *is not* the acreage but the produce index unit. Produce index is a measurement for determining the gross product of various classes of lands and is calculated at the time of land settlements.' Since such land settlements can only be revised after a period of forty years, the produce index calculations are completely out of date. The last settlement had been made in the thirties at the peak of the great depression, which was when the existing unit had been established. Writing in the Karachi daily *Dawn* on 6 March 1972, this economist, prudently signing himself 'Observer', shrewdly pointed out the lacunae in the land reforms:

How the produce index is likely to defeat the objective of the Reforms can be judged from the fact that the value of an acre in terms of produce index units ranges from 10 units to 110 units. Where an acre is equivalent to 100 units, 18,000 units will form 180 acres, but where it is equivalent to 10 units the ceiling will come to 1,800 acres. And this difference will not reflect the difference in productivity of the two but only their status in the mid-thirties. In actual fact, the former may be less productive today than the latter. Hence the effective ceiling may not be 150 acres of irrigated land and 300 acres of unirrigated land, as is the intention of the President, but anything up to 1,800 acres or even more.

Furthermore, the reforms made the usual allowances for exempting orchards, stud farms, stock-rearing and hunting grounds (!) from the ceiling limitation.

The net result of the 1972 reforms was to push the large landlords towards a more active interest in capitalist farming. Cash crops became immensely profitable and many landlords began to eject tenants and replace them with hired labour. Even conservative observers have criticized Bhutto for strengthening the big landlords at the expense of the 'kulaks'. Burki, for instance, has pointed out accurately that the decision to impose state ownership over the wheat-flour, rice-milling and cotton-milling industries, far from being a leftward move, was in reality designed to aid the rural gentry by removing the links between middlemen and the rural middle classes. The latter's challenge was thus made impotent right from the beginning. Burki is correct to stress that 'the real political and economic significance of this measure was that it resulted in the vertical integration of the agricultural sector in the sense that the landed aristocracy now had a share not only in producing a sizable part of the output traded in the market, but also in the marketing, processing and distribution of this output'.[3]

For many liberal–conservative economists, the problem with Bhutto's reforms was that they did not engender the creation of a dynamic layer of small capitalist farmers, but concentrated on measures that cemented political alliances in the countryside. The real problems, however, lay elsewhere. The fact that the 1972 land reforms were utterly inadequate was to be admitted by the régime itself five years later. In January 1977, a further series of reforms was announced. Since this was election year, the reforms had a dual function: they were more radical, in order to convince those on the lower rungs of the rural ladder that the seemingly immutable pyramid of power was to be altered; simultaneously, the decisive instruments for implementing change were left in the hands of the administration, so that landlords were made fully aware that their future lay with the PPP and a transference of allegiance to the opposition could lead to punitive measures. The new reforms proposed to reduce the size of holdings from 150 to 100 acres for irrigated and from 300 to 200 acres for non-irrigated land. They abolished land revenue, and in its place instituted a new agricultural income tax. This was an undoubted step forward, since it ended an anachronism whereby those who tilled their land in order to survive had to pay the same rate of tax as the large landlords. The abolition of the old system also reduced the oppressive powers of the village bureaucrat, more often than not on the payroll of the local feudal potentate.

There were, however, a number of problems with the new reforms, hinted at by left-wing analysts otherwise well disposed to the measures. Writing in the Lahore weekly *Viewpoint*, I. A. Rehman drew attention to the fact that the 1977 reforms were offering compensation to landlords who willingly surrendered land. More acutely the same writer noted that:

> It could be argued that anything that has the possibility of diverting the landless tenants, the small cultivators, the idle land workers from their revolutionary role, by stimulating the process of Kulakizing the more privileged among them and driving the rest away from the land,

into the slums of the towns, pushes the goal of establishing an order based on social and economic equality that much farther . . .[4]

In other words, even pro-Bhutto writers expressed certain doubts. What none of them spelt out in detail was the measures that were needed if the countryside was to be transformed. These would have included expropriating large estates; total abolition of share-cropping, giving the land to the tillers; immediate annulment of all peasant debts; a maximum landholding of twenty-five acres of cultivated land; utilization of expropriated land to resettle landless peasants within a cooperative framework; a minimum wage for agricultural workers, coupled with a forty-hour week, trade unions and a compulsory day of rest; a rationalization of the water supply, by nationalizing the tubewells and placing them under the direct control of elected peasant committees; state-instituted cheap rural credit and the outlawing of money-lending by private individuals; restricting the distribution of fertilizers and seeds to cooperative societies at controlled prices; the allotment of one school and one medical centre (with a doctor) to every village and a hospital and agricultural university or technical college to every sixty villages. It is true that all this would have amounted to a social revolution in the countryside; but it is the minimum needed to transform existing social patterns in the rural areas of Pakistan. Bhutto merely tinkered with the system in the countryside. In the process, he consolidated the position of the landlords at the expense of the urban industrialists. His aim was to 'frighten' the landlords, rather than liberate the peasantry.

The failure of the PPP government to destroy the grip of landlordism, either in the countryside or in national politics, constituted a rank betrayal of those whose votes had elected it to office. The land question was the key to transforming the country as a whole. When the PPP came to power in 1972, infant mortality was among the highest in Asia (120 per 1,000 live births). In 1977, the figure had not undergone even the slightest alteration. The number of doctors and hospital beds had risen only marginally: there were twenty-five doctors and fifty beds per 100,000 people. These figures refuted the propaganda of the régime far more effectively than the rhetoric of the opposition parties. The bulk of the country's population was rural. There had been no qualitative change in their lives since 1947, despite frequent changes in government, military dictatorships and now the 'people's government'.

Once the PPP had decided to leave property relations in the countryside intact, most of their other economic reforms proved to be merely cosmetic. No amount of ideological henna or demagogic mascara could prettify the beast that was the Pakistani social formation. In the absence of change in the countryside, the nationalizations of the banks and insurance companies, and the take-over of thirty-one large businesses (including iron and steel, heavy engineering, motor-vehicle assembly, chemicals, petro-chemicals, cement and public utilities) were simply a powerful dose of state-capitalism. This frightened the industrialists and led to a massive decline in investment and a flight of capital; but it brought no real improvement in living standards for the vast majority of urban dwellers. Nationalization was, in reality, used as a political weapon against the country's leading industrialists and the civil servants on their payrolls. In this regard the measures were not without success. But they did not succeed in boosting production, nor did they ameliorate the plight of the workers in any significant way. Supporters of the PPP were merely given an opportunity to extend their patronage in employing managers and providing official backing for some trade unions. Chicanery and corruption continued unabated and the scale of bribery became a national scandal. Many of the country's top industrialists took their money to the Gulf states, East Africa and into the heartlands of capitalism itself, with New York and London becoming their new centres for investment.

This flight of capital created a tremendous burden for the country's fledgling public sector, which was compelled to concentrate on investments unlikely to pay off in the short term. There was, accordingly, a sharp decline in industrial output during the Bhutto years. While Bhutto was correct to point out that international recession had exacerbated the problems of third-world states, he failed to perceive the structural impossibility of piecemeal reformism in countries where large rural hinterlands account for a majority of the total work-force. There were certainly secondary factors as well: the growth of the sixties had been financed essentially with the aid of foreign capital, leaving a debt which in 1980 still totalled 9,164.8 million dollars, the equivalent of half the country's GNP. The major 'success' of the seventies was the creation of agencies to export a commodity always in demand somewhere in the world: cheap labour. It was export of labour and workers' remittances that helped offset the losses incurred in the balance of payments after the detachment of Bangladesh. Foreign remittances in the shape of money and consumer goods helped both to reduce the deficit and to redistribute income within the Pakistani economy.

The tragic fact, however, is that the economic growth achieved during the sixties and the nationalizations of the seventies alike failed fundamentally to alter the living conditions of the majority of the country's population. The problem was aptly stated by Dr Rashid Amjad, a leading Pakistani economist:

After over 30 years of high economic growth, only 29 per cent of the population has access to safe drinking water. The adult literacy rate is 21 per cent, which is even lower than the average of the low-income countries

(36 per cent). Only 50 per cent of the population in the age-group 5–9 years is enrolled in primary education, compared to an average of 73 per cent for low-income countries and 92 per cent for middle-income countries. Only 17 per cent of the children of schoolgoing age attend secondary school, a figure which is lower than the average of 24 per cent for the low-income countries ... Less than 30 per cent of the population has access to adequate health services or adequate shelter. About 33 per cent of the population live below the poverty line, i.e. have a level of per capita expenditure that fails to satisfy even the minimum needs of the average individual.[5]

Such an assessment provides, in reality, a far more fitting epitaph to the economic policies of the PPP government than the propaganda of its apologists. The régime attempted to tinker with the system, but did not challenge the effective power of property-owners, the army or the civil service. It was this, as much as Bhutto's political strategy, that led ultimately to the tragic débâcle of July 1977.

Domestic Politics: Democracy and the National Question

In his campaign against the military régime of Field-Marshal Ayub Khan, Bhutto had stressed the importance of human rights. In one of the first pamphlets produced by the PPP, its leader had argued: 'Civil liberties hold the key to our future happiness ... All fundamental rights are important and stand or fall together. Genuine freedom of speech cannot function genuinely without freedom of the press or without a proper opportunity for free association.' In a ferocious literary onslaught, Bhutto had compared Pakistan in 1968 to the Kuomintang régime in pre-revolutionary China, and insisted that 'the present conditions must give way to a democratic dispensation in which the entire population participates ... All power must pass to the people. This can only be done by democracy.' It was a combination of democratic demands and socialist promises that helped Bhutto to win the 1970 elections in West Pakistan.

All the surveys conducted in their aftermath told the same story, especially in the crucial province of Punjab. There the PPP bandwagon had swept aside the old feudal families in their own rural strongholds, for the first time since the birth of electoral politics in 1921. Ten districts had a particularly high PPP vote – Lahore, Rawalpindi, Lyallpur, Multan, Jhelum, Gujranwala, Sahiwal, Sialkot, Sheikhupura and Gujrat – whereas in more backward areas such as Jhang and Mianwali (lower level of industrialization and literacy, combined with large estates and tenant farming), the party did not fare so well. Overall the PPP obtained 41.66 per cent of the votes polled in the Punjab. In Sind, the voting followed more traditional lines, with competing alliances of landlords and their favoured politicians. But here, too, landlords backing the PPP were able to utilize the party's popularity to win seats. Of major cities in the Punjab and Sind, Karachi, the largest industrial conurbation in the country, was alone in defying the PPP: the fact that large numbers of immigrant refugees from India had settled in the town had given it a conservative flavour. In the border provinces of Baluchistan and the NWFP, regional autonomists of the National Awami Party succeeded in maintaining their hegemony.

What was beyond question was that, overall, people had utilized the ballot-box to make clear their desire for fundamental social change. It was, in some ways, the most striking argument against those (on left and right) who argued that elections in backward countries like Pakistan were useless, since the masses were too backward to understand the complexities of the ballot-box or could be easily manipulated by rural bosses. As on numerous other occasions in history, the common people confounded their detractors. Despite the traumatic impact of the civil war which had led to the establishment of Bangladesh, the ordinary citizens of the country had enormous expectations when Bhutto took office. They hoped that, if nothing else, the new régime would restore fundamental rights and promote a democratic interregnum which would make dictatorships a nightmare of the past.

A useful start could have been made by transforming the PPP into a genuine political party. Populist dictators like Peron and Sukarno, whom Bhutto resembled in politics and temperament, had either created a stable apparatus or depended on some real political force in the country.[6] Bhutto was soon to discover that he, too, needed organized political support. The PPP could have been organized from the grass-roots upwards. There was every possibility of developing a party cadre composed of trade-unionists, peasant leaders and students, who could have pushed through a campaign of political education to arm their supporters. However, in this field as in many others, Bhutto preferred to utilize the PPP as a family heirloom. He frowned upon dissent, treated his colleagues as inferiors and established a party régime which was blatantly dictatorial. In keeping with this image, Bhutto stated that he would like the new constitution to be based on a presidential system. He clearly believed that the country's entire political system could be a replica of the PPP.

The very fact that the PPP had led the movement against dictatorship meant that many of those who had participated in the struggle were within its ranks. Bhutto's reluctance to implement the PPP's official positions on democracy led to the emergence of an opposition within the party. This was ruthlessly suppressed, and the founder-Secretary-General – a somewhat eccentric former diplomat, J. A. Rahim – was dismissed from both party and government posts and severely beaten by police. Bhutto justified the episode with the remark: 'I am the People's Party and they are all my creatures.' It soon became obvious that Bhutto regarded his political party essentially as a bargaining instrument vis-à-vis the opposition. For his real support, he built specialized sections of the state apparatus such as the Federal Security Force (FSF), which acted as a political police for the PPP régime. The force was headed by veteran policemen notorious for their corruption and sadism; the foot-soldiers were recruited from *lumpen* layers in the cities, armed with repressive powers and weapons. Simultaneously, Bhutto sought to 'politicize' the civil service.[7]

As we explained in Chapter 3, the scale of the mobilizations which toppled Ayub was massive. The country's new working class was an active participant and, during the process, acquired the political consciousness that helped the PPP to win the elections in the West. These workers were now hoping that *their* government, as they saw it, would act on their behalf. Six months after assuming office, Bhutto revealed himself a classic Bonapartist leader, swaying above all social classes in order to build his power. In June 1972, the police opened fire on the workers of Feroz Sultan Textile Mills, Karachi, killing an unspecified number. This was greeted by an eleven-day strike throughout the province of Sind, which forced the government to convene a Tripartite Conference (workers, employers and government) to discuss the workers' demands. The outcome was an uneasy truce. In the industrial estates of Karachi, the country's largest proletarian stronghold, a seething anger gripped the workers in the months that followed. Since such trade unions as existed were in the main either government or company unions, the workers resorted in most cases to direct action. Factory occupations laid the basis for a new unionism, symbolized by the United Workers' Federation. New leaders such as Bawar Khan (a mill-hand) and Usman Baluch attested to the militant mood in the factories.

The Landhi/Korangi industrial belt in the suburbs of Karachi contained 300 industrial units, employing 80,000 workers. It was here that the first major clash between the Bhutto régime and the working class took place. On 15 September 1972, Bhutto had been chief guest at a chamber of commerce banquet, where he had given the bemused businessmen a potted and schematic account of world history. He had pointed to the war in Indo-China as representative of a revolutionary breeze which might blow aside everything in its way. He had appealed to capitalists to accept workers as a legitimate interest group. If they rejected his advice then 'if trouble comes, and I hope it does not, because the interests of the management and labour are not incompatible at this juncture, I can tell you frankly that we will be with labour'. Phrases like this were music to the ears of the working class, which preferred to ignore evidence of the régime's real intentions.

In October, machine-tool workers came out on strike. Their factory was government-owned. The government declared the strike illegal and arrested the leaders. Workers in other factories, who had come out on a two-day token strike in support of their comrades, were faced with a hardened management which decided to deduct two days' wages. Two mills were occupied by the work-force, and in one of them strike leaders warned the police that if there was an attempt to enter forcibly the boilers would be blown up. On 18 October, police and specialist paramilitary units, acting under the orders of the labour minister, launched a surprise assault on the occupied factories and 'captured' the plants. Hundreds of workers were injured and four killed during this episode. Government forces had used tear-gas and opened fire many times. The entire industrial estate reacted with anger and a strike stopped all factories. The workers demanded the unconditional release of all imprisoned strikers, and compensation for the families of those killed or disabled. On 22 October, the police led another attack on a workers' meeting in the nearby hills. Two more workers were killed and dozens arrested and injured. The hill where the workers were killed was named 'Red Hill' and became a shrine for trade-unionists. The strike lasted for several weeks, but was ultimately defeated because it was isolated: it did not receive the support of other workers, and the students remained passive. Furthermore, the weakness of the trade unions meant that those who negotiated with the government did not represent the views of shop-floor militants. The strike ended in despair.

It soon became obvious that, despite his threat to the chamber of commerce, Bhutto did not back labour. Throughout the years of the PPP government, attempts were made to pre-empt strikes by cajoling workers and buying off their leaders. Such an approach worked, but it led to increasing cynicism. Those workers who refused to accept bribes and persisted in defending their living standards soon found themselves incarcerated under Defence of Pakistan Regulations (DPR). The régime also turned a blind eye to murders carried out by goons in the pay of management. The case of Usman Baluch, president of the left-wing United Workers' Federation, is symbolic of the approach of the PPP régime. Baluch was a self-educated working-class leader with a long history of trade-unionism. As a leader of the Karachi Gas Employees' Union, he had struggled for workers' rights under the Ayub dictatorship. He was first arrested in 1969 and imprisoned for a year. In 1971 he led a strike and factory occupation at the Valika textile mills, and was imprisoned for thirteen months in March of that year. After Bhutto's rise to power, Baluch led an eleven-day protest strike against the government's proposed labour laws. In October 1972, he was arrested under DPR for organizing protests against the killings of workers in the Landhi/Korangi clashes. He was released after six months, when the High Court declared his detention illegal. In August 1973, he was forced to go underground to avoid arrest, but was picked up in January 1974 and kept in prison for five months. In July of the same year, he was re-arrested and charged with thirteen cases of breaching the DPR, but was released on bail in December 1974. The aim of this series of measures was to break Baluch's resistance and force him to accept the policies of the PPP. The government failed in this instance, but there were many cases where they succeeded, leaving behind a trail of bitterness and disgust.

It was not only the working class which felt deceived and disappointed. In the realm of democratic rights and civil liberties too, the PPP admini-stration was to disappoint those who had voted it into office. The press laws were not repealed, and the lofty promises made about this at mass meetings during the upsurge of 1968–9 were never to be fulfilled. With the exception of two weeklies, *Outlook* in Karachi and the *Frontier Guardian* in Peshawar, the press tended to be conformist in outlook. The Karachi daily *Dawn* had at first attempted to service the opposition, but the arrest of its chief editor had brought it back into line (though for eighteen months it continued to publish reports which were 'constructively' critical and sought to defend the PPP administration against the inevitable time-servers who had climbed onto its bandwagon). The bulk of the media at all events was kept firmly under government control, serving the Bhutto régime as loyally as it had done its predecessors, and as it serves Bhutto's executioners today. The Pakistani journalist had already been transformed, during the Ayub period, into an unimportant cog helping to run the ideological machinery of the government in power. Bhutto did nothing to alter this state of affairs but, as in other fields, appointed his own nominees to run the National Press Trust. In 1972, he punished three Lahore periodicals for stepping out of line: *Punjab Punch* (a scurrilous scandal sheet), *Zindagi* and *Urdu Digest* were banned and their editors and publishers arrested. A special military ord-nance was even promulgated, to prevent the latter from publishing any other journal. These events took place a mere four months after Bhutto had told a mass meeting in Karachi that Pakistan's press would be free of all fetters. The reality was exactly the opposite, and the Karachi daily *Dawn* com-mented in an editorial on 7 April 1972 that 'the harsh action against the three Lahore periodicals probably represents the severest penalties ever imposed on journals and journalists in the history of the Press in Pakistan'.

For many PPP partisans, the repressive measures employed by their government appeared as a thunderbolt from a clear blue sky. Their expecta-tions were never to be fulfilled. The first measures of the post-1971 régime in Pakistan were ominous pointers to the direction which Pakistani politics was to take in the years that followed. The PPP's 'supreme leader' permitted the tame media to dub him Quaid-i-Awam (Leader of the People) and devoted his energies to framing a new Constitution, the country's third in seventeen years. The disintegration of the Pakistani state should have been sufficient stimulus to prevent a repetition of mistakes which had culminated in the débâcle of 1971. The first elected assembly in the history of the country was now given the task of elaborating constitutional principles to guide the new state. The PPP's overall majority did, of course, mean that Bhutto's views would predominate; but opposition parties were consulted and voted for the new Constitution. This established a federal parliamentary system, but with a strong centre. It also guaranteed fundamental rights, but allowed for their suspension during 'states of emergency'. The DPR remained on the statute book, and in the years that followed a series of constitutional amendments further reduced the ability of the citizen to safeguard his or her civil rights through recourse to the judiciary. It is somewhat pointless to get too immersed in a discussion of the rights and wrongs of the Bhutto Constitution. All constitutions represent an institutionalization of a particular status quo, and the chronic political instability which characterized the Pakistani state meant that this one was virtually ignored.

The Pakistan that survived the formation of Bangladesh was no more a cohesive nation-state than its predecessor. If anything, its idiosyncrasies became more pronounced, and the 'national question' acquired a new relevance. The former province of East Pakistan had provided the smaller western provinces with a certain guarantee that they would not be totally crushed by the Punjab. The defection of the Bengalis now exacerbated national tensions in West Pakistan itself: the Pathans, Baluch and Sindhis felt more exposed and vulnerable. Bhutto's inability to arrive at a rapprochement with the Baluch and Pathans was to play an important role in his downfall. The PPP leader considered himself a master of the art of *Realpolitik*, but he severely underestimated the festering contradictions that lay beneath the surface of Pakistan's political structures. The PPP leaders had failed to implement a drastic land reform. They had antagonized a large section of the industrial working class. Bewitched by the music of their own trumpets, they now proceeded to trample the rights of the Baluch and Pathan provinces under foot.

The 1970 elections had given Bhutto an overall majority in West Pakistan, but on a provincial level he could form governments only in the Punjab and Sind. The National Awami Party was the largest political force in the NWFP and Baluchistan. After assuming power, Bhutto wisely appointed NAP governors in the two provinces, and accepted the right of the NAP to form provincial administrations in coalition with their parliamentary allies in the two regions. The situation was an uneasy one, since the NAP formed the opposition in the National Assembly. Bhutto was thus confronted with a situation in which the leading lights of the parliamentary opposition controlled two provinces. For a politician who regarded himself and his party (in that order) as the saviours of the nation, this was a galling state of affairs. Instead of making a concerted effort to allay the fears of the minority provinces and reach an agreement with their elected representatives, Bhutto chose to form an alliance at the national level with corrupt and discredited reactionary politicians who had been rejected by the electorate in the NWFP and Baluchistan. The veteran Muslim Leaguer from Peshawar, Khan Abdul Qayyum Khan, was appointed to the sensitive post of minister for home affairs in the Central cabinet: Qayyum was thus nominally in charge of the entire apparatus of 'internal security', though in practice he did nothing without consulting Bhutto. An offensive plan was devised at cabinet level to destabilize the NAP provincial governments through a set of well-orchestrated provocations.

In the NWFP, Bhutto sought to utilize a radical demagogy and encouraged his own cabinet ministers to attack the NAP leaders as landlords. Simultaneously, the Centre turned a blind eye to a series of peasant upheavals led by the Maoist Mazdoor-Kissan Party (MKP). Wali Khan, the Pathan leader, was later to allege that the MKP was financed by the home ministry, and that one of its leaders, Afzal Bangash, had been given asylum in Qayyum Khan's official residence in Islamabad. In Baluchistan, the Centre attempted to create a 'law and order' crisis by withdrawing non-Baluch policemen and preventing the more radical NAP government from abolishing the antiquated Sardari system of tribal leadership (a measure which would have threatened the system of tribal hierarchy and severely damaged reaction in the province). A presidential visit to Baluchistan by Bhutto in 1972 was utilized to create disorder. Bhutto was accompanied by Qayyum Khan, who took with him a gang of forty armed retainers. The NAP government insisted that they be disarmed, but when its instructions were carried out, Bhutto intervened personally and had their weapons restored. The armed hooligans then provoked an argument on the street with Baluch nationalists and used their guns to seal the debate. At least one person died and several were injured.

What appeared a small, albeit unpleasant, incident was in fact far more symbolic in character. The armed clash took place on the same day as Princess Ashraf, sister of the then Shah of Iran, had arrived in Pakistan as a special guest of the president. The entire provocation had undoubtedly been organized for the benefit of the distinguished Iranian visitor. It was a well-known fact that the Shah of Iran was extremely unhappy with the election results in Baluchistan. He feared that if the NAP succeeded in pushing through a set of radical reforms in the province or gaining a meaningful autonomy, the impact on Iranian Baluchistan would destabilize Iran as a whole. In an interview with the *New York Times*, the Shah had stated that in the eventuality of a further disintegration of Pakistan, the Iranian army might be forced to intervene in order to prevent instability from enveloping the whole region.[8] In the light of subsequent events in Iran, such views may appear somewhat bizarre, but the impact of Iran's ruler on Pakistani politics at that time should not be underestimated. The years 1972 and 1973 were crucial for Pakistan and the Bhutto régime. In May 1973 Bhutto paid a state visit to Iran, where he was told in no uncertain terms that the Shah viewed demands for provincial autonomy as dangerous. Some years later, Bhutto admitted to America's most intelligent South Asia expert, Selig S. Harrison, that the Shah 'had been very insistent, even threatening, and he promised us all sorts of economic and military help, much more than we actually got. He felt strongly that letting the Baluch have provincial self-government was not only dangerous in itself, for Pakistan, but would give his Baluch dangerous ideas.'[9]

Some months prior to his Iranian visit, Bhutto had dismissed the elected Baluch government, on the charge that Ghaus Bux Bizenjo, the governor, and Ataullah Mengal, the chief minister, were involved in a plot with Iraq and the USSR, designed to break up Pakistan and Iran. A cache of arms had been discovered at the Iraqi Embassy, which Bhutto claimed were destined for Baluch supporters of NAP. A plot certainly did exist, but it was one hatched by Pakistani and Iranian intelligence services, in order to provide a pretext for dismissing the Bizenjo government. Bizenjo, Mengal and the president of the Baluchistan NAP, Khair Bux Marri, were arrested and taken to a government rest house in Sihala, not far from the military–political capital of Islamabad/Rawalpindi. Bhutto now attempted to form a new government in Baluchistan by offering bribes to NAP members of the provincial assembly, but all his efforts resulted in miserable failure. Within six weeks of the overthrow of the elected government, hundreds of students and others had fled to the Baluch hills and the province was engulfed in a civil war.

In an interview with me in 1969, Bhutto – as I recounted earlier – had criticized my refusal to join or support the PPP in the following way: 'There are only two ways to get rid of these bastards [the army]. Mine or that of Che Guevara. It's either me or the Baluchs in the mountains with their guns.' I had politely rejected his choice. Now, less than four years later, he was repeating a slightly different message to the Baluch nationalists: either join the PPP or be crushed. Most Baluch chose to fight back. The war did not reach the proportions of that in East Bengal, for reasons that we shall discuss below, but it did succeed in poisoning Pakistani politics and sounding the death-knell of civilian rule. The NAP governor and administration in the NWFP were also removed at this time, so that the PPP now dominated the whole country. In an interview with the Karachi weekly

Outlook (which was banned as a result), the NAP leader Wali Khan expressed the feeling of the disenfranchised regions:

> If you want to settle it bullet by bullet, you will find people who will meet your bullet with their bullet. You can't stop it. If you have legitimate means of political agitation here, people will go to legitimate means. But if you stop all conventional and traditional methods of constitutional and legal agitation, people will pick up unconstitutional, illegal methods for furthering their political cause. It is so very simple.[10]

Wali Khan was permitted to remain leader of the opposition for another two years, then he too was arrested and charged with masterminding a plan for the 'dismemberment of Pakistan'. The NAP was banned and many of its cadres imprisoned.

The War in Baluchistan

Baluchistan has 'plagued' every government in Pakistan since 1947. The reason for this lies in the fact that the Baluch were not allowed to decide for themselves whether or not they wished to accede to the new state in 1947. The most influential Baluch ruler, the Khan of Kalat, was initially opposed to accession and claimed the right to form an independent state on the model of Nepal. The Khan pointed out to the Cabinet Mission in 1946 that Nepal and Kalat were the only two states in India which negotiated with Whitehall rather than Delhi. The Baluch nationalists of the Kalat National Party were equally adamant. Accordingly, the Khan of Kalat declared his state independent twenty-four hours after the formation of Pakistan. It was not until a year later that the Pakistan army occupied Kalat and forced the Khan to sign accession documents. Despite his capitulation, moreover, his younger brother Prince Karim led several hundred retainers in an attempt at resistance (though this was easily crushed).

The first political justification of Baluch independence was contained in a speech by Bizenjo in the Kalat Assembly. Though favouring close relations with the new Pakistani state, the young Baluch nationalist attacked the whole underlying thesis of the 'two nations' (Muslim and Hindu):

> We have a distinct culture like Afghanistan and Iran, and if the mere fact that we are Muslims requires us to amalgamate with Pakistan, then Afghanistan and Iran should also be amalgamated with Pakistan. They say we Baluch cannot defend ourselves in the atomic age. Well, are Afghanistan, Iran, and even Pakistan capable of defending themselves against the superpowers? If we cannot defend ourselves, a lot of others cannot do so either. They say we must join Pakistan for economic reasons.

Yet we have minerals, we have petroleum and we have ports. The question is, what would Pakistan be without us? I do not propose to create hurdles for the newly created state in matters of defence, external affairs and communications. But we want an honourable relationship and not a humiliating one. We don't want to amalgamate with Pakistan ... If Pakistan wants to treat us as a sovereign people, we are ready to extend our friendship. But if Pakistan does not do so and forces us to accept this fate, flying in the face of democratic principles, every Baluch will fight for his freedom.[11]

Baluchistan was to become the largest province of West Pakistan, but the least populated, with some 40 per cent of its area but a mere 4 per cent of its population. Its social structure was dominated by nomadic tribalism, and the tribal chiefs dominated the tribesmen. The British had entered the regions inhabited by Baluch simply to control the frontier with Afghanistan. The Baluch capital, Quetta, had acquired its prominence when the British constructed a military cantonment there, and developed road and rail links with the provinces of Sind and the Punjab. The Baluch intelligentsia, of course, was minute, consisting essentially of those children and relatives of the chiefs fortunate enough to have obtained an education. This layer, together with a sprinkling of poets and balladeers, had helped to awaken a Baluch national consciousness during the thirties and forties, and the high point of this entire movement was Bizenjo's speech in the Kalat Assembly. But the military intervention by the Pakistan army in 1948 was to inaugurate a process of forced integration within the Pakistani state.

At every key moment in Pakistan's history, the Baluch were opposed to the machinations and intrigues of the military–bureaucratic complex that ruled the country. When the four provinces of West Pakistan were amalgamated into One Unit in 1954, the Baluch protested but their cries were ignored. Three years later, discontent in Baluchistan was utilized to justify the coup d'état of General Ayub. In 1959, there was a campaign of repression against the Baluch: several hundred armed men, led by the eighty-year-old Nauroz Khan, took to the arid hills of the province and fought back. A concentration camp was set up near Quetta, and Baluch political prisoners were tortured. Bizenjo and Mengal both served time in prison. The Ayub régime offered to negotiate, promising a free pardon to the guerrillas if they laid down their arms. When they agreed to the terms, however, and surrendered their weapons to a force commanded by Colonel Tikka Khan, Nauroz's son and six others were arrested and hanged. Pakistan had tricked them.

The Baluch patriots went to the gallows chanting: 'Long Live Baluchistan!' Nauroz was sentenced to life imprisonment, and died in prison after a protracted illness. The resulting anger created a chronic state of tension, which was released in the 1970 elections, when Baluch voted overwhelmingly for the NAP. In 1972, Bizenjo and Mengal, veterans of numerous prison camps, became governor and chief minister respectively. This was the first popular representation that Baluch had enjoyed since the creation of Pakistan. However, when I met Bizenjo that same summer in Pakistan, he was not optimistic. 'The Baluch students have been welcoming me with cries of *"Baluchistan surkh hai"* [Baluchistan is red]', he told me, 'but I would be happy if the Centre simply lets us modernize Baluchistan. There is plenty of time to make it red.'

During a lengthy discussion with the author in London in 1981, the exiled Baluch leader Ataullah Mengal confirmed the distance that existed between Baluchistan and the Pakistani state. He explained matters in the following way:

Till the assassination of Liaquat Ali Khan in 1951, the army and bureaucracy had not decided how to run the country. After that they became the effective rulers. The question they posed to themselves was: How can we retain colonies without provoking a challenge to our rule? For us in Baluchistan, it was an uncomfortable situation from the very beginning. As you know we were forced to accede to Pakistan. We decided to adjust to the new situation, but all the bureaucrats treated Baluch as traitors to be dealt with as such. The mistrust of the ruling class was phenomenal. They started to flood Baluchistan with refugees who had fled from India during the Partition. They thought they could politically overpower us by a numerical trick!

When I was in Mach gaol in Baluchistan, the situation was brought home to me very vividly. A prison warder is the lowest-paid government employee. There were 120 warders in the gaol, but only eleven of them were Baluch. If anyone had stated this, he would have been denounced as a traitor. When we took office in 1972, there was a total of 12,000 government employees in twenty-two grades. Only 3,000 were Baluch (including Baluch Pathans, Hazarewals, local Punjabi settlers). There are only a few hundred Baluch in the entire Pakistan army. The famous Baluch Regiment has no Baluch in it! The Kalat Scouts was a paramilitary force raised during the Ayub dictatorship. There were only two people from Kalat recruited to its ranks. The same is the case with the Sibi Scouts, created to police the Marri areas. Not a single Baluch in its ranks. The officers were from the Punjab and the soldiers from the Frontier. If you land at Quetta airport today and visit the city, you will soon realize that 95 per cent of the police constables have been brought from outside. When we tried to correct the balance, Bhutto and his Punjabi aide Khar organized a police strike against our government. Bhutto's aim was to destabilize the situation and pave the way for a Central government intervention. This merely added fuel to the fire of nationalism. The students, in particular, wanted to go the whole way. Bizenjo and I told them: 'These are temporary phases. We don't have another alternative.' Governments, military régimes have come and gone, but they have shared one attitude in common. They have mistreated and oppressed the Baluch.[12]

Bhutto's ploy was to force the Baluch leaders to negotiate from a position of weakness. He tried to divide Bizenjo from Mengal, and Marri from the others, but his stratagems were frustrated at every stage by the political intransigence of the Baluch and their refusal to compromise on basic principles. Bhutto's motives for the crackdown were a combination of domestic and international pressures. The PPP leader was undoubtedly surprised by the vehemence of the reaction in Baluchistan. According to Mengal, 'when Bhutto came to meet us in prison, he treated us like children. He did not understand the character of our grievances.' Bhutto appointed a Baluch tribal chief, Akbar Bugti, as the new governor; but the latter was regarded as a quisling, and even his own brother Ahmed Nawaz supported the imprisoned triumvirate. Bugti attempted to act as a broker on behalf of Bhutto, but the Baluch leaders refused to compromise unless the dissolved assembly was re-convened and allowed to re-establish its authority. Bizenjo, regarded by Bhutto as the softest of the three, was offered conditional release and a trip to Baluchistan, where he could assess the situation for himself. The trap was obvious: Bizenjo would have been regarded as a traitor if he had been seen as an unofficial envoy of the régime. The veteran Baluch refused unless all Baluch political prisoners were released. Mengal was then approached, but replied in the same vein – though using stronger language.

During the first phase, the three leaders were kept in relative comfort in Sihala Rest House. When Bhutto realized, however, that they were adamant in their refusal to negotiate or be utilized, they were dispatched to separate prisons: Marri was interned in Lyallpur, Bizenjo in Mianwali and Mengal in Sahiwal. When Bhutto's messenger came to inform them that they were being separated and sent to three Punjabi prisons, Mengal smiled and replied: 'Tell Bhutto we're glad you've decided that it is useless negotiating with us. We'll now teach you what resistance means.' The PPP leader did not know it, but in ordering the army into Baluchistan he had put a noose around his own neck and doomed democracy in the country. The Pakistan army, discredited after the débâcle of Bangladesh, was now given a new opportunity to re-occupy the country's political stage. It is worth stressing that the longest military campaigns conducted by Pakistani generals since 1947 have been directed against Bengalis and Baluch inside Pakistan. One led to the disintegration of the state; the second paved the way for the post-1977 military dictatorship.

For five years, Baluchistan was torn apart by a cruel civil war. Four Pakistani divisions (100,000 men) were given the task of subjugating the recalcitrant Baluch. Almost every section of the Baluch population was affected by the fighting, which was to change the character of Baluch nationalism for ever. As the guerrillas grew in number, army casualties grew heavier. By the middle of 1974, the guerrillas had effectively destroyed the road and rail links between Baluchistan and the rest of the country. Coal from the Baluch mines was inordinately delayed, and Punjabi industry began to be adversely affected. The guerrillas also carried out a daring series of raids on the oil-drilling operations of Western companies. General Jahanzeb, the army chief in charge of the Baluch war, told Selig S. Harrison that 'the hostiles were becoming quite bold as the year [1974] progressed. They thought they had reached the stage of confrontation with the armed forces in which they would actually be able to drive us out of Baluchistan. They were determined to stop oil exploration. We knew that we had to respond very forcefully or we would simply be unable to bring the situation under control.'[13]

The Pakistan army's offensive was culled from the classics of counter-insurgency manuals. It concentrated on destroying the base of popular support on which the guerrillas depended. In August–September 1974, Punjabi soldiers under Jahanzeb's command encircled the Marri tribal areas. A massive artillery bombardment was coupled with strafing from the air by French-supplied Mirages before soldiers moved in, many of them descending from US Cobra helicopters flown by Iranian pilots. These Cobra gun-ships had a devastating firepower of 750 rounds per minute, emanating from 20-mm automatic cannon. Despite the scale of this offensive, many guerrillas escaped the siege, thanks to their unrivalled knowledge of the terrain. The Pakistan army, however, had scored an undoubted victory against the unarmed people of Baluchistan. They had captured 50,000 head of cattle, an impressive haul by any standards but crippling for a nomadic society. Thousands of Baluch were forced to leave their homelands and placed in 'strategic hamlets' at Kolu, Loralai and Quetta. Some were to flee and seek refuge in neighbouring Afghanistan. Thirty guerrillas were killed (though the army's casualties approached the 300 mark). The whole operation was a devastating blow against the Baluch resistance, but out of it emerged a new organization: the Baluchistan People's Liberation Front (BPLF).

The BPLF developed a network of armed militants that cut across tribal bonds and rivalries. It established a series of mobile camps, based on military units which were self-sufficient. A campaign was launched to eradicate illiteracy, and the Front distributed antibiotics to combat malaria and pneumonia. These activities went side by side with attempts to create a general political awareness. On the thorny question of women's rights, the BPLF proceeded with caution.[14] Fully aware of the dangers of military élitism, the BPLF leaders encouraged debate and democracy within their ranks. Every plan of action, however large or small, was discussed openly before it was acted upon. The guerrillas operated their ambushes on the principle: 'three ways of retreat, one way of battle'. In other words, the Baluch resistance avoided set-piece confrontations and did not make the mistake of gathering all its forces in one camp.

Crushing the guerrillas had become a matter of pride for the military high command in Islamabad, since the Shah of Iran was threatening direct military intervention. The régime in Teheran was not prepared to tolerate any national liberation struggles on its borders. It had provided weapons, aid and men to defeat the Dhofari insurgents in Oman, and it would have done the same in Baluchistan.[15] Bhutto stated after the 1974 offensive that the movement in Baluchistan had been crushed, and some collaborators were produced on Pakistani television, to deceive viewers. Press censorship with respect to Baluchistan was of a different calibre from that imposed during the genocidal operations against the Bengalis. In the latter instance, the régime had practised a simple Goebbelsian policy: untruths were repeated daily and *ad nauseam* in the press and on radio and television. However, no one could have been in any doubt as to the seriousness of the situation in East Bengal. In Baluchistan, the tactics were the exact opposite: very little of import was actually published in the press, the aim being to avoid any real movement of support from developing in the other provinces.

In the summer of 1975, the BPLF launched a new offensive and Pakistani troops were ambushed throughout the province: in one ambush alone, several officers were killed. But BPLF policy (inspired by Che Guevara's writings) was to release all rank-and-file soldiers captured during the fighting, *after* explaining the rights and wrongs of the conflict. However, *Jabal*, the English-language bulletin produced by the BPLF, was to claim that Baluch prisoners were treated somewhat differently by the Pakistan army. Given the independently attested accounts of the savagery inflicted on Bengalis, there is little reason to disbelieve the following description published in *Jabal* in 1977:

> In contrast [to BPLF treatment of prisoners] the enemy carries out savage tortures and summarily executes our captured compatriots. The

army has captured over 5,000 men, women and children from BPLF zones. 95 per cent of these have been brutally tortured. Apart from the standard practice of severe beatings, limbs are broken or cut off; eyes gouged out; electric shocks are applied, especially to the genitals; beards and hair are torn out; finger nails ripped; water and food are withheld, which in the summer months often turns out to be fatal. Ten fighters have become permanently deranged due to electric shock and torture. Women, in addition to being subject to these tortures, are also raped. After this they invariably commit suicide because they are too ashamed to return to their families. The prisoners who are released as being of no further use to the enemy all immediately return to the BPLF and insist on fighting again, although many of them are so badly cut up that they cannot hold a rifle or walk properly.

The repression against the Baluch was decided on at the highest levels, and there can be little doubt that the Islamabad government was kept well informed. Bhutto certainly could not have doubted the existence of a large torture and interrogation camp established near Malir, on the outskirts of Karachi. A special commando unit headed by Colonel Bashir had the authority to capture and kill Baluch anywhere in Pakistan. It was Bashir who ordered a trap to be set in Karachi for Ataullah Mengal's son Asadullah. Mengal has described this painful episode:

I was in hospital in Karachi, being treated for a heart complaint. Asadullah came to see me one day before he was killed. He told me that the surveillance on him was getting very close. I warned him that, from my experience, this meant they were on the verge of picking him up. He had a phone-call from Quetta, from a man who pretended to be an underground fighter, but about whom I had always had my suspicions. This man arranged to meet Asadullah in Karachi on Bashir's instructions. When they met, the commandos surrounded their car. Asadullah was shot in the process. The commandos had come in a special plane from Quetta to Karachi to kill him. Bhutto was reportedly very angry and he clearly was unaware of this, but he did nothing. Zia-ul-Haq told me that the culprits would be traced and punished, but nothing happened. I've lost so many 'sons' in Baluchistan, and I felt: So another of them is dead . . .[16]

The agony of the Baluchistan province left the rest of the country largely unmoved. In the NWFP and Sind there was sympathy, but it was never to find any political expression. In the Punjab there was silence, except for a handful of Punjabi radicals who left the comfort of their middle-class families and joined the guerrillas, gradually winning their respect. One of them, Asad Rehman, son of a former Justice of the Supreme Court, under the *nom-de-plume* of Chakar Khan (a legendary Baluch chief), was to play an important role in organizing some of the most effective guerrilla attacks of the war.[17] It was probably the presence of a tiny layer of Marxists which helped the BPLF to develop a fairly accurate analysis of the Pakistani social formation. The BPLF defined the Pakistani state as a reactionary construct governed by a military–bureaucratic dictatorship, which defended the interests of the propertied classes in town and countryside and was, in its turn, backed by the United States and its leading relays in the region: Saudi Arabia and Iran. The Bhutto régime was designated as the 'most advanced political representative' of 'feudal, bourgeois, bureaucratic and military interests'. The national question and agrarian problem were characterized as the central contradictions of the Pakistani state. The Baluch struggle was visualized as the starting-point for a more generalized assault on the Islamabad régime. The hope was expressed that the peasant masses of the Punjab would soon emulate the Baluch and rise up to combat their traditional oppressors. The BPLF and other Baluch leaders were perfectly aware of the fact that they alone could not defeat the armed bodies of men who occupied their province in the name of the Pakistani state.

Military struggles alone have never been sufficient to win decisive victories. Even where martial skills and well-honed tactics have played a crucial role, it has required an overall *political* strategy to ensure success. Baluchistan could not have been more different from Bangladesh. Its mountainous terrain, sparse population and antiquated social structure meant that, at best, the guerrillas could harass and disrupt the operations of the Pakistani troops. In order to defeat them, they needed new bases of support elsewhere in the country, or dramatic openings on the external front. The rest of Pakistan, however, remained aloof; and the Baluch resistance was contained *before* the 1978 left-wing coup in Kabul and the 1979 overthrow of the Shah in Iran brought about startling changes on Pakistan's frontiers. The heroism of the Baluch struggle has been depicted with passion and feeling by balladeers.[18] But its lessons were only too obvious: the Baluch could not win on their own. Since the guerrillas refused to contemplate surrender, the core of the units under BPLF command sought and obtained refuge in neighbouring Afghanistan, where they were provided with camps outside the city of Kandahar. Islamabad was to find that the Baluch political leaders too were unwilling to compromise. Mengal summed up the outraged feelings of Baluch nationalism in the following words:

> Khair Bux Marri and myself had reached the conclusion that nothing was possible any longer within the old framework. Short of a major confrontation nothing will satisfy us. We want cast-iron guarantees. We

want to emasculate the Centre. When we asked for provincial autonomy they treated us like secessionists. So we have lost all faith and trust. Even if a 'wise person' comes to power in Islamabad there can be no trust. We will not compromise again. Tell them that, so that there is no doubt in their minds. We will not compromise.[19]

We shall return to the thorny problem of Baluchistan in the final chapter, where we shall discuss its relevance to the overall dilemma posed by the submerged nationalities for contemporary Pakistan. But for the present, we can summarize the impact of the Baluch crisis on Pakistani politics under Bhutto. In our opinion, Bhutto's downfall and the end of civilian rule can be traced directly to the PPP's refusal to tolerate a meaningful regional autonomy or accept the principle of power-sharing within a federal framework. Bhutto's Baluch adventure was thus a disaster on every count. It poisoned the political atmosphere of Pakistan, and the country is still suffering from the pollution. It thus laid the basis for the military coup of July 1977. When Bhutto and his defence minister General Tikka Khan ordered four army divisions to crush the Baluch, they sealed the fate of their own régime. The offensive against Baluchistan permitted a discredited, enfeebled high command to recoup what it had lost with the débâcle in East Bengal, and re-enter the political stage.

Bhutto assumed that his ability to communicate directly with the masses would serve as a sufficient deterrent against the army. He also believed that, since he had removed all senior military officers with evident Bonapartist ambitions, he was fairly safe. His chief military commander, General Zia-ul-Haq, had been promoted because Bhutto was convinced – by his servility and lack of intelligence – that he represented no danger. However, the PPP boss fatally underestimated the autonomous power of the army as a *political* institution in Pakistani politics. There is strong evidence to suggest that Bhutto had himself been unhappy and apprehensive regarding some details of the army's operations in the Baluch province. What he failed to grasp, however, was that the army was utilizing Baluchistan as a political laboratory, and that sooner or later its experiments, culled from counter-insurgency manuals in Fort Bragg, would be tried out on the population of Pakistan as a whole.

Foreign Policy: Something Old, Something New, Something Borrowed, Something Blue

'Foreign policy,' wrote Trotsky, 'is everywhere and always a continuation of domestic policy, for it is conducted by the same ruling class and pursues the same historic goals.' This crisp and definitive formula appears somewhat dogmatic, but in reality expresses a profound truth often lost in the mist of obfuscatory rhetoric which emanates from so many third-world capitals. Pakistan's foreign policy has always been closely related to its internal economic and political priorities. It is necessary to state this unambiguously in rebuttal of a tendency prevalent among Pakistani historians to isolate foreign policy (supposedly based on certain undefined moral or religious precepts) from domestic realities. The most classic exponent of this trend was, of course, Zulfiqar Ali Bhutto himself. As Pakistan's foreign minister during the Ayub dictatorship, he developed an interest in world politics and later contributed a number of useful essays on the subject.

The determining factor in Pakistan's foreign policy has been India. Protectionist measures devised to keep out Indian capital were not unrelated to India's refusal amicably to settle outstanding problems following Partition. Pakistan's rulers embarked on an anti-Indian policy, and embraced an option which helped them in this regard. So whereas Nehru's India, taking full advantage of the semi-autonomous strengths of indigenous capitalism, sought to cultivate a policy of non-alignment – tilting towards the Soviet Union and (initially) China, while at the same time mythologizing the Commonwealth – the Pakistani foreign office settled for becoming a loyal and unquestioning ally of the United States.

We discussed Pakistan's foreign relations under Ayub in Chapter 3. Here, therefore, we shall simply assess the subsequent development of foreign policy under Bhutto. The post-1971 Pakistan confronted a totally new situation vis-à-vis India and the rest of the world. Secession of the Bengali province had inevitably reduced the country's international standing. One thing, above all else, was patently obvious: any new armed conflict or confrontation with India would be suicidal for the truncated Pakistani state. Bhutto's first major priority was to reassure the Indians and secure the release of 90,000 prisoners-of-war captured in Bangladesh. The second was to recognize Bangladesh as an independent and sovereign state. In June 1972, Bhutto, the arch-chauvinist who had vowed to fight the Indians for 'a thousand years', left for the Indian hill-town of Simla to meet Indira Gandhi, prime minister of India. The summit was a success for both sides. Bhutto returned with an agreement that led to the release of the Pakistani soldiers. Gandhi was assured there would be no more attempts to gain Kashmir by force. In reality, Simla symbolized the new respective positions of Pakistan and India in South Asia: Islamabad accepted there that New Delhi was the dominant political capital of the region.

Prior to the disintegration of the old state, Pakistan had been heavily dependent on American aid. By 1970, Pakistan had received assistance to the tune of 7 billion dollars, largely from the United States and the World Bank. The crisis of 1970–71 resulted in Pakistan declaring a unilateral moratorium on repayment of its foreign debts: these were later rescheduled, after the International Monetary Fund had agreed to a loan – on its usual stiff terms. The fact that Pakistan had lost its captive market in East Bengal compelled the new régime to look elsewhere: the oil-rich Gulf kingdoms provided the obvious choice for the shell-shocked confessional state. Accordingly, from 1970 to 1975 Pakistan's economy underwent a major shift of emphasis. In a useful analytical survey of this change, Feroz Ahmed pointed out:

> The share of nine major Muslim trade partners, namely Iran, Iraq, Abu Dhabi, Dubai, Kuwait, Oman, Saudi Arabia, Libya and Indonesia, in Pakistan's total exports increased from 6.6 per cent in 1969–70 to 24.8 per cent in 1973–4. During the first nine months of the fiscal year 1974–5, exports to Middle-East countries accounted for 30.8 per cent of Pakistan's total exports, as compared with 17.2 per cent for the same period of the preceding year.[20]

One of the commodities exported was labour (both unskilled and skilled), and the remittances sent back by migrant workers provided nearly 20 per cent of the country's foreign-exchange earnings. It was also reported that 10,000 Pakistani prostitutes had been dispatched to the Gulf states by the United Bank, to strengthen its reserves of foreign currency. Soldiers and officers were also leased out as mercenaries to a number of states in that region. In some ways it was a telling indictment of the Pakistani state that it could only survive by selling itself to the oil-rich Sheikhs. The loss of skilled professionals and craft-workers – nurses, doctors, engineers, electricians, plumbers, masons, carpenters and others – left Pakistan depleted. Its economy became parasitic in the extreme, dependent on Arab finance-capital. It was these circumstances that necessitated new foreign-policy initiatives by Bhutto.

The Islamic Summit – a conference attended by heads of state from every Islamic state – which took place in Lahore on 22 February 1974 was nothing more than a gigantic exercise in public relations. Symbolizing the changing economic horizons of the new Pakistan, it was partially designed to show the rest of South Asia that even a less significant Pakistan could retain its importance through links with the world of Islam. The one concrete use of the occasion was that Bhutto effectively manipulated mass euphoria to win acceptance for the recognition of Bangladesh. The domestic implications of the turn towards Islam had not been foreseen clearly by Bhutto. He had hoped that by appropriating the confessional mantle, he would be able to outmanoeuvre and outflank the right-wing religious opposition in Pakistan. The exact opposite, however, took place: the Islamic fundamentalists, delighted that Bhutto had decided to fight the ideological battle on their terrain, put forward more and more outrageous demands. Three months after the Summit, moreover, New Delhi fired an unexpected shot across Islamabad's bows: it exploded a nuclear device.

While the Islamic Summit reflected the shift in Pakistan's external priorities, it would be wrong to assume that it meant a fundamental break with the past. The United States remained a major factor in Pakistani politics. The fact that it now acted through its continental relays, Saudi Arabia and Iran, indicated that only the form of Pakistani's foreign policy had altered. As far as China was concerned, there was no change in policy by either Peking or Islamabad: indeed, the Sino-US *rapprochement* meant that apparent contradictions in Pakistan's foreign policy were now resolved. China had been loyal to every régime in Pakistan since the late sixties. It backed Ayub against the popular upsurge of 1968–9.[21] It supplied moral and material aid to Ayub's successor Yahya Khan, and opposed the struggle of the Bengali people for national self-determination. After Yahya was compelled to resign, Peking transferred its support to his successor.

Bhutto did not scruple to utilize private conversations with Chou En-lai and other Chinese leaders, to curb recalcitrant leftists inside his own party: he told an internal party meeting on one occasion that Chou En-lai had told him to 'go easy, as you will need a few hundred years before you'll get socialism in Pakistan'. China's influence on the Pakistani left has been even more disastrous than that of the USSR. Many of the most dangerous Stalinist formulae were given a new lease of life through their endorsement by Chinese leaders: the notion of a new democratic revolution separate from the socialist revolution; the slurring over of any distinction between the roles of the urban and rural proletariat; reliance at one moment on the adventurist moods of sections of the petty bourgeoisie, and at the next on sordid alliances with reactionary political forces.[22] The ultra-opportunist twists and turns of Chinese foreign policy served to compound the demoralization and disorientation of the Pakistani left. China's deals with the United States at the expense of the Vietnamese, its support for reaction in Pakistan, its cordiality towards the Chilean military junta and the South-African-backed forces in Angola – all contributed to a cynical degradation of the enthusiasm inspired by the Chinese revolution.

The increased dependence of Islamabad on the oil-rich kingdoms of Iran and Saudi Arabia led to a blatant political intervention by Riyadh and Teheran in Pakistani politics. We have already seen how the Shah of Iran was decisive in pushing Bhutto to dismiss the elected government in Baluchistan. He also acted as a go-between in order to decrease tensions between Kabul and Islamabad. The Pakistan–Afghan conflict had its origins in the international frontiers imposed on the region by British colonialism. Kabul refused to recognize the Durand Line – the border between

Afghanistan and Pakistan – as final. It should be stated that Afghanistan's case was not without logic. Outcome of a geo-military decision, the Durand Line was not based on respect for nationality. Kabul consequently developed an implacable hostility to the border. It constantly encouraged the nationalist aspirations of the Pathan people, and referred to the North-West Frontier Province of Pakistan as Pakhtunistan (literally 'land of the Pathans'). The tension between the two countries was yet another manifestation of the irrationality that underlay the confessional division of 1947. Islam, of course, was quite unable to transcend the diplomatic, military, national and class differences between the two states. An exchange of visits by Bhutto and the Afghan president Daud was the only tangible result of the Shah's mediation.

The Saudi Arabian princes were not interested in Pakistan merely because its principal cities catered for 'delights' prohibited in their own kingdom. They also, for example, utilized Pakistan to educate and train Saudi students in medicine and engineering. But their main intervention was at the ideological level. The Saudi royal family belonged to a purist sect of Islam, and they backed similar groupings elsewhere. In Pakistan, it was the semifascist, obscurantist Jamaat-i-Islami ('Party of Islam') which was the major recipient of Saudi patronage. The Jamaat's leader, Maulana Maududi, a veteran theologian, was a much respected visitor to Riyadh. His views were heard with patience and reverence by the Saudi King. As the Pakistani state's trade with Saudi Arabia grew, the influence of the Jamaat *within* the state apparatuses (and especially the army) grew in parallel. Bhutto's attempts to pacify the Saudis with a set of half-baked Islamic measures hastened the processes which were inexorably leading to his downfall. There can be little doubt that Saudi money was instrumental in financing the campaign of the Pakistan National Alliance, the heteroclite opposition which challenged Bhutto in the 1977 elections.

Bhutto attempted to balance Saudi pressure, on occasion, by developing closer links with Libya and its leader, Ghaddafi. Libyan aid was a vital component of the plan to establish a nuclear re-processing plant in Pakistan. The aim was obvious: Pakistan was attempting to develop an independent nuclear deterrent. When the United States, enraged by a French government agreement to help Pakistan, put sufficient pressure on Paris to force unilateral abrogation of the agreement, the indignant Bhutto protested vigorously that this was a crude attempt to prevent a Muslim country from developing an 'Islamic bomb'. During a visit to Lahore in August 1976, American secretary of state, Henry Kissinger, offered Bhutto material and political support if Pakistan would abandon its plans to acquire nuclear weaponry. Bhutto was later to describe this approach as follows: 'This was the carrot – the stick was held out brazenly when, in reply to the Prime

Minister's refusal to accept dictation on policies considered vital for Pakistan, Kissinger said "we can destabilize your government and make a horrible example out of you".'[23] The American's characteristically blunt language demonstrated the continuing master–client relationship between Washington and Islamabad: in the fifties it had been more pronounced and open, but two decades later it was still intact.

The irony of the situation lay in the fact that Bhutto's flights of rhetoric regarding the 'Islamic Bomb' were designed largely for public consumption at home and abroad. The true reason for agreeing to the nuclear project was pressure from Pakistan's military establishment. The generals wanted a bomb at all costs, in order to maintain some 'self-respect' vis-à-vis India. Bhutto agreed, thinking that this would help to keep the army top brass under his control. He failed to perceive the obscenity entailed in a poverty-stricken state like Pakistan devoting precious resources and skills to pro-ducing a nuclear bomb. Bhutto had shrieked that 'we will eat grass, if necessary' in order to get the bomb. It was always obvious, however, that Pakistan's ruling gentry would never eat grass. It would be the common people who would pay for military extravaganzas. The most common de-mands of working people were for food, clothing, shelter, education, medical care and employment. The surreal nuclear fantasies of the army were a far cry from these social goals.

Bhutto's tragedy lay in his inability to perceive that he had been tolerated by the army only because he was the one politician in the country with mass popular support. Once this support began to drain away, he became ex-tremely vulnerable. Bhutto imagined that the close relations he had culti-vated with the Shah of Iran, the Saudi royal family and the rulers of the oil-rich Gulf kingdoms would immunize him against US intrigue, and disarm fundamentalist plots inside the army. In fact, Bhutto became so self-satisfied and complacent about his 'skilful' handling of foreign relations that he ignored the objective political processes which were fuelling the rise of a right-wing opposition inside the country.

Last Phase: The Fall of Bhutto

In January 1977, Bhutto advised the president to dissolve the National Assembly: the country's first general election since 1970 was scheduled for March. Preparations for such an event had been inaugurated in January 1976, when hardly a day had gone by without the tame media announcing thousands of new members for the PPP. Bhutto, realizing that he needed an organization of sorts, had resorted to the time-honoured traditions of Pakistani politics which the PPP had wisely eschewed in 1970. The PPP leader began to utilize the extensive powers of patronage at his disposal, in order to secure the support of leading representatives of the Punjabi rural élite. The old families had made their peace with the régime, and were only too pleased to collaborate with the PPP.

The opposition parties united under the banner of the Pakistan National Alliance (PNA): a motley alliance of right-wing religious groups, Asghar Khan's Tehrik-i-Istiqlal and the secular-democratic National Democratic Party (the name assumed by NAP after it was banned). The PNA bore a marked resemblance to the Janata Party which was attempting to topple Indira Gandhi in India. Both were heteroclite cartels united by one overriding aim: to remove their respective prime ministers. It was thus obvious that the March 1977 general elections would not be fought on the basis of political programmes, but would effectively be viewed as a referendum on the personality, political style and defects or otherwise of Zulfiqar Ali Bhutto. The PNA proved incapable of producing a coherent programme. It was, however, adept at coining anti-Bhutto slogans and mobilizing an important section of the urban masses against the régime. Political repression, inflation and the spiralling costs of corruption (the going-rate for essential bribes) had generated widespread discontent.

A hope was expressed by critical supporters of the régime:

> We hope, therefore, that the coming elections will, unlike most previous polls, be entirely free and fair, and that the contest will be conducted on a purely political plane. For the first essential, the ruling party bears the main responsibility. It must break away from the tradition and resist the temptation to use bureaucratic or other pressures to suborn the voters, and, as has already been done in Sind, remove all restrictions on public meetings and allow Opposition parties to conduct their campaigns without any interference.[24]

The break from tradition, however, proved difficult. Party and state functionaries, aided by the powerful apparatus of repression, ensured that there would be no 'mistakes'. The media kept up a barrage of pro-PPP propaganda, and Bhutto himself embarked on a tour which took him to every major city in the country. In some areas the reception was warm but, in general, the difference between the campaigns of 1970 and 1977 was clearly visible. In 1970, Bhutto had promised massive social changes and had been believed. Seven years later, he promised similar changes; but this time he was accompanied by the landed aristocrats of the Punjab and Sind. The PNA leaders may have been politically bankrupt, but they were not short of funds. They waged an effective campaign pointing to broken promises, widespread arrests, conflict in Baluchistan, corruption, arbitrary use of the Federal Security Force and intelligence services. Their message was simple: Bhutto had promised both bread and freedom; he had delivered neither.

It was not the PNA alone which felt the lash of the PPP whip. Attempts by independent left-wing candidates too were mercilessly disrupted. Feroz Ahmed has described (see Appendix Three below) the case of a talented peasant leader, Ismail Soho, who was prevented from winning in a rural constituency in Sind: he had supported Bhutto in 1970, but been disappointed by the subsequent performance of the PPP government.[25] At all events, after polling was completed on 7 March 1977, it was announced that the PPP had won 154 National Assembly seats out of a total of 200. It soon became clear that large-scale rigging had taken place. The PNA leaders denounced the result as a farce, and stated that they would boycott elections to the provincial assemblies, due to be held on 10 March. Bhutto contemptuously dismissed opposition claims. The boycott of the provincial elections, however, was largely successful and was accompanied by massive street demonstrations and partial strikes in a number of cities. The Election Commission – a body designed to supervise the electoral process – announced a month after the elections that they were preparing to charge a senior PPP cabinet minister, Hafeezullah Cheema, with electoral malpractice.

The PNA campaign was given an unexpected impetus by the stunning electoral defeat suffered by Indira Gandhi and the Congress Party in neighbouring India: Mrs Gandhi's graceful withdrawal after accepting the verdict of the electorate was in marked contrast to Bhutto's refusal to acknowledge what had taken place in Pakistan. There were very few politicians or seasoned observers who had thought that Bhutto would be overwhelmingly defeated in a fair and impartial poll. Even Bhutto's staunchest opponents believed that the result would be close. But planned subversion of the electoral process brought about a result that was unacceptable to decisive layers of the population. As street demonstrations mounted, Bhutto began to make concessions, but he offered too little, too late. If he had declared the initial results null and void and sanctioned new polls, he might have averted the tragedy that was to befall Pakistan. Instead, on 21 April, he authorized the proclamation of martial law in the three important cities of Lahore, Karachi and Hyderabad.

Once three major urban centres had been handed over to the army, it was hardly surprising that the generals would plan a total take-over. Bhutto was aware that he was cornered. In an emotional address to the National Assembly on 28 April 1977, he stated that there was an international conspiracy to unseat him and implied that it was the CIA which was masterminding the plan. 'The bloodhounds are after my blood,' Bhutto told a silent chamber. But it was not till June 1977 that an agreement with the opposition parties was worked out. Before the deal could be announced and a date set for new elections, the army implemented 'Operation Fairplay' and seized the country, on 5 July 1977. General Zia-ul-Haq appointed himself Chief Martial Law Administrator and promised elections within three months. Bhutto, at first confined to a government residence in Murree, twenty-five miles from Islamabad, was soon released. However, when he started touring the country again, the size of his meetings indicated to the army that he was not as much a spent force as they had thought. He was accordingly soon re-arrested and accused of murdering a political opponent. The populist tide in Pakistani politics had come to an end.

It is tempting to speculate on the tactical options open to Bhutto in 1977, but this is to avoid confronting the central problems. We have argued that the PPP régime elected in 1970 had enormous possibilities, which were squandered. It would be foolish to ascribe the vices of the PPP to Bhutto alone (though we have already indicated that he was far from blameless). Bhutto attempted to construct a populist state and to conciliate conflicting social classes through his own person. A key element of all populist régimes is the 'man on horseback' who for a period reflects the hopes of both oppressor and oppressed classes, but who ultimately destroys the illusions of the latter and is then struck down by the former. If anyone is 'to blame' it is the historical process. Populism, of course, is simply a further concretization of Marx's concept of Bonapartism, which entails a temporary equilibrium of all social and class forces. The exact character and form of Bonapartism differs from state to state. During his Mexican exile, Trotsky had the opportunity to study the Cardenas régime at first hand. Cardenas was a forerunner (and as such far more radical than those who followed him, elsewhere in the colonial world, in subsequent decades). Trotsky argued that:

> In the industrially backward countries foreign capital plays a decisive role. Hence the relative weakness of the *national* bourgeoisie in relation to the *national* proletariat. This creates special conditions of state power. The government veers between foreign and domestic capital, between the weak national bourgeoisie and the relatively powerful proletariat. This gives the government a Bonapartist character *sui generis* (of a special type). It raises itself, so to speak, above classes.[26]

The most common form of Bonapartism in the third world today is military dictatorship. Bhutto attempted to avoid this variant, but he failed to construct a strong base in any social class. Instead, he gave a special twist to the Pakistani variety of populism: he sought to compensate for his lack of *institutionalized* political support by constructing extremely powerful extra-state apparatuses designed to coerce. At the head of these, he placed men whom he regarded as personally loyal. Most of them were subsequently to provide evidence against him to the military rulers. Bhutto's trusted agents inside the police and army are now serving his successor with the same zeal. It is not accidental that the Pakistani ruling class should have utilized a populist leader *after* the break-up of 1971, when every state institution was in danger of collapse. Once Bhutto had put the state back on its feet, however, he was dispensable, and the army eliminated him at the first possible opportunity. The tragedy of Pakistan is that Bhutto's successors in the PPP have so far made no real attempt to analyse the causes of his downfall. This is not a point of pedantry. If the lessons are not learnt, even more drastic mistakes will be made in the future. For the point, as the old philosopher Spinoza once wrote, is 'neither to laugh nor to cry, but to understand'.

6 The Crisis of Legitimacy:
Martial Law with an Islamic Face 1977–?

Pakistan is like Israel, an ideological state. Take out Judaism from Israel and it will collapse like a house of cards. Take Islam out of Pakistan and make it a secular state; it would collapse. For the past four years we have been trying to bring Islamic values to the country.

General Zia-ul-Haq, Chief Martial Law
Administrator [1]

With the declaration of martial law by General Zia-ul-Haq on 5 July 1977, the state had returned to its most primitive form. Once again the status quo could be preserved only by 'armed bodies of men'. It was as if Pakistan's entire history had turned full circle. General Ayub had seized power in 1958 to prevent elections: a mass movement led to his fall in 1969. His successor General Yahya agreed to allow the people the right to choose their own government: when they did so, he embarked on a bloody civil war to negate their choice, which led to the disintegration of the old state. Pakistan's military high command had suffered a devastating blow in Bengal; it waited five years before embarking on a new adventure. It was the large-scale rigging of the 1977 elections which provided the pretext.

It is true that the failure of Bhutto's populism laid the basis for Zia's coup, but there were additional factors at work. Of these, the most important was dissension within the officer corps. The generals acted partly to preempt a coup attempt by junior officers, many of whom were strongly infected by reactionary ideologies.[2] There was never any real intention of permitting fresh elections on the old model. Zia's address to the nation on the evening of 5 July 1977 was a *mélange* of duplicity and straightforward untruth:

> It must be quite clear to you now that when the political leaders failed to steer the country out of a crisis, it is an inexcusable sin for the Armed Forces to sit as silent spectators. It is, primarily, for this reason that the

Army perforce had to intervene to save the country ... I would like to point out here that I saw no prospects of a compromise between the People's Party and the PNA ... It was feared that the failure of the PNA and PPP to reach a compromise would throw the country into chaos ... This risk could not be taken in view of the larger interests of the country ... I want to make it absolutely clear that neither have I any political ambitions nor does the Army want to be distracted from its profession of soldiering ... My sole aim is to organize free and fair elections which would be held in October this year ... I give a solemn assurance that I will not deviate from this schedule.[3]

There are no details available of the discussions inside the army that preceded the July coup, but it was a known fact that the generals had a number of contingency plans at their disposal. Most of these were the direct result of US involvement with the Pakistan armed forces. One of these plans, Operation Wheeljam, designed to destabilize a civilian government, was similar to US-sponsored projects in Chile during the Allende period. Bhutto was later to claim that the army and General Zia had 'played a prominent part in encouraging, aiding and manipulating events to exacerbate civil strife in order to overthrow the legal government'.[4] Some of the evidence provided by Bhutto and confirmed by PNA leaders indicated that the army had decided to take over the country soon after the March 1977 elections.

A key demand of the PNA during its negotiations with the PPP following the March elections was that the crudely manufactured cases against Pathan and Baluch leaders be unconditionally withdrawn, the detainees released and the army recalled to barracks in Baluchistan. Bhutto finally agreed to these demands, but was told by Zia and the senior corps commanders that the army would simply refuse to accept such a settlement. A few days prior to the coup, Zia attended a meeting of PPP and PNA leaders with a lengthy document arguing that 'secessionists' and 'traitors' should not be released. At the same time, the generals insisted that unless an immediate agreement was reached between the government and the opposition parties, they would not be able to control the situation. Bhutto was effectively trapped by this pincer movement.

In the weeks before the coup, a series of desperate meetings was organized with the Saudi Arabian ambassador, through whom the Pakistan army and the United States regularly exchanged information. There were also unconfirmed reports that Bhutto, accompanied by his military aide General Imtiaz, had secretly crossed the border into Afghanistan for a meeting with Soviet officials. The army's plans, however, had been carefully worked out. It got rid of Bhutto and placed him under 'protective custody', at the very moment when he had reached an agreement with the PNA. Zia's speech announcing martial law stated the exact opposite. The high command, moreover, was perfectly well aware that immediate elections were not on the agenda. Zia's reference to elections within ninety days was a deliberate misstatement, designed to reassure a few dissenters within the armed forces: in both the navy and the air force, there was a feeling that new elections were both desirable and necessary.[5] It was also aimed at stifling any public outcry and dividing the political parties. On every count, the tactic was successful. It is possible that if the army had been totally confident that a low-key election would result in an electoral victory for the extreme right-wing parties, Zia, Chishti and Iqbal – the leading advocates of a coup – could have been restrained. It soon became obvious, however, that any new election would not produce the results desired by the army.

On 28 July 1977, Bhutto was released from house-arrest. The PPP leader did not waste a single moment, but immediately began a tour of all four provinces. What disconcerted the martial law authorities was the large crowds that came to his meetings in the Punjab. It was clear that Bhutto and the PPP would win the two most populous provinces: Punjab and Sind. The army high command had discussed, but rejected, the possibility of killing Bhutto at the time of the coup itself. They were later to regret this omission. At all events, on 3 September 1977 Bhutto was arrested and charged with 'conspiracy to murder'. The alleged victim was a former member of the PPP, Ahmed Raza Kasuri, whose political instability was a byword in Pakistani political circles.

A judicial farce now commenced, during the course of which it became clear that the generals and a majority of the judges were determined to rid themselves of the 'turbulent' PPP leader. The Pakistani judiciary was not known for its impartiality. It had accepted Ayub's martial law in 1958. It had accepted Bhutto's dictates, authorizing the proscription of the National Awami Party and tamely accepting the establishment of a Special Tribunal at Hyderabad to try detained NAP leaders, denounced in the PPP-controlled media as 'secessionists' and 'traitors'. It enjoyed very little respect amongst the population as a whole. Very few judges were regarded as upholders of the law. When their lordships of the Supreme Court invoked the dubious 'doctrine of necessity' to provide the army coup with a judicial seal of approval, few observers expressed surprise. The Supreme Court had a long history of legalizing régimes which violated every tenet of the Constitution which the judges were sworn to defend.[6]

Bhutto's trial provided the first major test for the military régime. The mechanics of how Zia both secured the judgement he wanted *and* managed to avoid generalized discontent have yet to be analysed fully. A number of useful articles and books on the trial and subsequent execution of Bhutto have already been published, but it is not intended to recount here the sordid details of the judicial farce that was enacted in Pakistan over the nineteen months from September 1977 to April 1979, since these can be studied elsewhere.[7] What is far more instructive is to examine the political processes which enabled the army to tighten its grip on the country. Undoubtedly, the major obstacle standing between the military dictatorship and political stability, however temporary, was the person of Zulfiqar Ali Bhutto. It was not simply that Bhutto might win any democratic electoral contest. What frightened the corps commanders was that Bhutto alive represented a permanent potential alternative to military rule. At the first sign of unrest, the rural and urban masses would have turned to the country's foremost populist politician. Few had doubts as to who would emerge victorious in any frontal clash between the army and the masses, with a Bhutto-led PPP at the helm.

General Zia-ul-Haq had been dismissed by both friends and enemies as a simpleton, mere front-man for a junta, who could be easily swept aside.[8] What such views ignored was the fact that the state had precisely required a 'low-profile' leader. Appearances in this case were deceptive. Zia emerged as a shrewd political operator, who knew when to assert his authority. His handling of the country's political parties revealed a Machiavellian streak, which surprised the politicians who allowed themselves to be manipulated. Throughout the period of Bhutto's trials, the Chief Martial Law Administrator maintained the pretence that he was ultimately going to permit elections to take place. This was necessary to keep the support of the political parties grouped under the PNA umbrella. While a few parties did withdraw from the PNA, the majority accepted martial law and their leaders accepted posts in Zia's re-organized federal cabinet in 1978. Thus, when Bhutto was hanged on 4 April 1979, the act was defended by civilian politicians serving in a military government.

From 1977 to 1979, the generals continuously reneged on Zia's initial promise to organize fresh elections. In 1978, Zia informed a bewildered nation that he had been overpowered by a dream in which a voice (presumably that of the Almighty) had suggested that elections were un-Islamic. This, of course, was nothing but a cynical attempt to manipulate mass consciousness in rural areas where superstition is rife. Zia had not dreamed anything. He had been informed in no uncertain terms by the six corps commanders – Generals Chishti, Iqbal, Jehanzeb, Sarwar Khan, Ghulam Hassan and Ghulam Mohammed – that elections could not be held. It was these six generals, in addition to Zia and Arif, who constituted the highest decision-making body in the country during the two critical years that followed the declaration of martial law. Iqbal and Jehanzeb are said to have warned Zia that if he allowed political parties to dominate Pakistan's political stage once again, he would confront a mutiny by junior officers from within the army.

A similar argument was utilized to ensure unanimity among the seven generals on the decision to execute Bhutto. Zia was to be given full backing to take all necessary steps to control any discontent that might result from killing the country's last elected prime minister. In the event, the much-feared spontaneous upsurge did not materialize. Bhutto's death undoubtedly traumatized the vast majority of the population,[9] but the masses saw little reason at this stage to risk their own lives. The limited response by no means implied support for the army; it merely demonstrated the lack of political organization at the grass-roots level. But the military high command was certainly emboldened by its success. It soon evicted the civilian politicians from the cabinet, and sought to rule once again in league with its old friend, the civil bureaucracy (though on this occasion with the bureaucrats in an extremely subordinate position).

In order to quell discontent with continued military rule in the armed services – the navy and air force were reportedly restive – and to demonstrate that even in death Bhutto had not lost his hold over the masses, the martial law régime permitted non-party elections to local bodies in September 1979. All the major political parties contested the local elections, under appropriate disguises. PPP candidates postured as 'friends of the people' on printed posters; 'for an honest leadership' was the signature-tune of the fundamentalist Jamaat-i-Islami (which interestingly enough did not utilize Islam in its appeal); the discredited Muslim League (now an unrepresentative feudal rump) appeared as 'old servants', much to the amusement of those whom they claimed to have served in the past. Despite a low poll (below 50 per cent), the PPP won a decisive majority, though inner-party squabbles denied them a more substantial victory. The local election results were thus a clear confirmation of the military junta's assessment of the political crisis. All dissenters were silenced inside the armed forces: there were very few senior officers, in any of the three services, prepared to tolerate the return of a PPP government. Zia had promised that general elections would follow in November 1979, but on 16 October the army felt sufficiently confident to announce their indefinite postponement. For good measure it banned all political parties, forbade political activity of any kind, shut down most opposition newspapers and tightened censorship.

The banning of 'political activity' as such was necessitated by the spread of rural discontent in a number of areas. Exactly a week before Zia's announcement, a hurriedly prepared and little publicized peasant conference in the interior of Sind had been attended by several thousand peasant delegates. Sindhi peasant and national leaders – Rasul Baksh Palejo and Fazil Rahu being the best known among them – were arrested at the conclusion of the conference. Brought before a summary military court, they were sentenced to be publicly flogged and imprisoned. This was among the first instances of political activists being whipped in public. At a press conference in Islamabad, Zia explained the army's case:

> Martial law is a temporary phenomenon, but it could go on for two years, four years, or ten years. Ultimately a government has to come into existence that should enjoy the confidence of the people. I want to introduce Islam in Pakistan, in the true sense. Our present political edifice is based on the secular democratic system of the West which has no place in Islam . . . In Pakistan neither anarchy nor Westernism will work. This country was created in the name of Islam, and in Islam there is no provision for Western-type elections.[10]

For over two years Zia consolidated his rule through a combination of repression, the shameless utilization of Islam and an elaborate series of carefully orchestrated political initiatives designed to lull the masses. On the two crucial issues – Bhutto and elections – he followed a similar pattern of procrastination. Bhutto's trial was permitted to last for nineteen months. This both created a feeling of hope that the deposed prime minister might win through in the end, and simultaneously encouraged a mood of fatalism and despair, so that the final verdict appeared almost as an anti-climax. The execution, of course, was *not* delayed, since that could have allowed a dangerous head of steam to build up. Throughout the period of the trial, Zia reassured politicians hostile to the PPP that once the Bhutto affair was over he would allow elections. Baluch and Pathan leaders were released from Hyderabad gaol, and the tribunal which had condemned them disbanded. This was the supreme irony, and demonstrated Zia's audacity as a politician. Freeing the NAP leaders from detention had the effect of reassuring many people that an election could not be indefinitely delayed. This, in its turn, encouraged a certain passivity.

Zia's measures of 16 October 1979, while not exactly a bolt from the blue for some commentators, were none the less the equivalent of a second coup for most of Pakistan's politicians. Islam was the cloak with which the generals sought to cover their nakedness. A repressive code, partially modelled on medieval Islamic punishments, was introduced to punish social and political dissenters: public flogging, amputation of the hands of burglars and criminals; stoning to death of adulterers; execution of political activists; torture of women political prisoners.[11] These were some of the measures put on the statute book by the military régime. This is what Zia was referring to when he later stated that 'for the past four years we have been trying to bring Islamic values to the country'. At the moment of writing, no one has actually been amputated or stoned to death, though many have been sentenced to receive these punishments. The whole plan is 'aimed at brutalizing our political culture, at preparing people to accept repression and repressive measures'.[12] The institutionalized brutality is designed to ensure a semi-permanent passivity. Only partial success, however, has been achieved on this front, and the silent anger that undoubtedly exists in many parts of the country could soon erupt into a violent explosion on the streets.

The severity of Zia's rule reflected the extreme character of the crisis afflicting the Pakistani state. Ayub's 1958 coup, by contrast, had symbolized a very different state and army. The semi-patrician, Sandhurst-trained style of the high command in the fifties and early sixties had gone together with a less aggressive, almost avuncular approach to Pakistani politics. Ayub had not allowed his own staunch anti-communism to mingle with that of the more plebeian sections of urban society. Nor had he been besotted with religion: this had not been necessary at the time. But now times had changed. In the truncated, strife-ridden state of the seventies, the army was larger, the social and class composition of its officer corps had altered, and the military campaigns in Bangladesh and Baluchistan had brought to the fore a new type of officer: a man trained and prepared to root out and kill all 'subversives'. Moreover, Zia now felt it necessary to utilize Islam to combat the PPP and groups further to the left.

This was done with the sometimes open, sometimes covert, support of the Jamaat-i-Islami (the Party of Islam). The Jamaat, an extreme right-wing organization closely linked to Saudi Arabia and the United States, was the closest thing in Pakistan to a fascist party. Concentrated in the cities, it drew its support from the poor petty bourgeoisie. Unlike every other political formation in the country, including those on the left, the Jamaat was an extremely efficient grouping which took party organization seriously. It had a structure built from the top down, consisting of a rigid hierarchy of command based on a cell-system. Recruitment was on a strict basis, and a great deal was demanded even of sympathizers. The leader – veteran theologian Abul-Ala Maududi, who had presided over the organization since before Partition – had virtually unfettered control.[13] For the Jamaat, the country which served as a model was the backward-looking, oil-rich kingdom of Saudi Arabia, where the brand of Islam preached was an austere variety of Sunniism: the Saudis and their votaries in the Jamaat rejected every other variant of Islam as impure.

The Jamaat had acquired a strong base among the immigrant-refugees from central India and East Punjab who had settled in Karachi, or replaced departing Sikhs and Hindus in the Western Punjab. This was hardly surprising, since those prepared to leave their ancestral homes and trek to a new country based on religion must have had stronger religious beliefs than those who chose to stay behind. One of those millions of Muslims who left

India to become a citizen of the new state had been the twenty-three-year-old army lieutenant named Zia-ul-Haq. During a visit to Teheran in September 1977 to explain his actions to the Shah – then still in power and the major US relay in the region – Zia gave an unusually frank interview to the editor of the Teheran daily *Kayhan*. In response to a question about Islam, he replied:

> The basis of Pakistan is Islam and nothing else. I could have stayed on in India. But I did not, because I was a Muslim. We left everything we had in East Punjab and arrived in Pakistan destitute, but rich with hope and faith . . . seven generations of my family were born and brought up there. When the break-up came we were not rich; ours was an ordinary family. Nevertheless we sacrificed all we had and moved to Pakistan. With such a background how would you expect me to forget, after a mere thirty years, what the basis of the Islamic Republic was. The basis is Islam and shall be so.[14]

When Zia became Chief Martial Law Administrator in July 1977, his personal beliefs neatly coincided with the ideological needs of the debilitated state machine in Pakistan. Whether or not Zia was ever a card-carrying member of the Jamaat-i-Islami is not a matter of great interest. What is beyond doubt is his affinity to the political programme of that organization. This fact has been commented upon by a number of American political scientists specializing in Pakistan.[15] The one aspect of the Jamaat's influence which has rarely been discussed, however, is its leverage inside the Pakistan army. One reason for this absence in most scholarly accounts is lack of concrete information: the Jamaat's inner-party structure being based on a system of interlocking cells, the top leaders enjoy a monopoly of information regarding all functions of the organization. None the less, on the basis of conversations with former and present junior army officers, it can be stated that the Jamaat's influence inside the army grew rapidly during the Bhutto years. Its literature and propaganda were widely circulated, and the more regrettable excesses of the Bhutto régime (perpetrated by such lieutenants as Mustafa Khar) were effectively utilized by the Jamaat to widen its network inside the armed forces.[16]

There was, however, as we have already indicated, a more fundamental shift assisting the Jamaat to extend its influence in the army. In Chapter 3 we briefly discussed the class background of army officers in the post-Independence period. Contrasting it to that of the officers in the Egyptian army, we suggested that it was the latter's urban base which explained the explosion of petty-bourgeois radicalism that overthrew the monarchy and saw the emergence of Nasserism throughout the Middle East. Changes in the Pakistan army over the last two decades, however, have altered it in a number of significant ways. It would be wrong to see this as a qualitative break, but the changes in the social composition of junior officers do merit some discussion. In the past, the overwhelming majority of officer-cadets were recruited from the rural gentry. More often than not they were second or third sons (the eldest male child being kept for better things). The majority of non-commissioned officers came from the upper and middle strata of the peasantry, while poor peasants comprised the rank-and-file. Thus the rigid class and caste divisions of the South Asian countryside were reproduced inside the British Indian army, and helped to preserve 'stability' at home and abroad. This tradition still continues to dominate the armies of India and Pakistan. We have already explained how the concept of 'martial races', based on a cynical estimate of where the most down-trodden and politically backward peasants lived, was utilized in post-Independence Pakistan by successive ruling groups, and how it led to the disintegration of the state created in 1947.

What has changed in this old equation? The most striking alteration since Partition is that there has been a sharp decline in recruitment of officers from the upper reaches of the rural gentry. The old families, whose rise to fame and fortune had been guaranteed by their loyalty to the British Raj, had felt that they had to repay imperialist generosity by providing a son to serve in the army. But Independence opened up other and more profitable channels: industry and commerce, politics and government service were to prove more attractive. The shift, of course, was gradual, and its effects were not really felt in the army till the seventies. Officers trained by the British, who had served the empire loyally during and after the Second World War, were to provide the first generation of commanders after Independence. But promotions were rapid for Muslim officers in the new army. The period of industrialization in the late fifties and sixties saw a growth in the population of every city in West Pakistan: with no statistics available, it is difficult to provide even an approximate estimate of how many more cadets were now enrolled from the cities, but there can be no doubt that urban representation underwent a sharp proportional increase.

Most cadets accepted as potential officers at the Pakistan Military Academy at Kakul now came, in any event, from petty-bourgeois layers in town and countryside. The era of the gentleman-cadet carefully nurtured and developed by the British had come to an end. The Jamaat-i-Islami, most influential amongst the city petty bourgeois, having encouraged its supporters to enlist in the army during the sixties and seventies, probably now has some dozens of officers at colonel or brigadier level, backed up by a bevy of more junior recruits. The Jamaat's penetration could have been counter-balanced if there had been a hard core determined to preserve the secular traditions of the army. But here Bhutto had made yet another mistake. Under pressure from the fundamentalists he had decreed that the Ahmediyyas (a heretical sect of Islam, to which many officers belong) were no longer Muslims. At a single stroke he had eliminated the influence inside the army of one layer of middle and senior officers strongly opposed to the Jamaat's fanaticism. Actions such as this could only increase the weight of fundamentalist forces inside the armed services.

Martial law was imposed in 1977 by generals fully aware of the political sympathies and orientation of their junior officers. Bhutto was still widely popular among the *jawans* (soldiers), but his standing in the officer corps was at its lowest ebb. Islam appeared to the intelligence agencies as the obvious solution. The fact that Zia appeared to believe in Islamic measures and presented himself as a devout Muslim was an additional bonus for those who cynically sought to exploit religion in order to establish their hold over the rural masses. The first two generations of senior officers had been heavily imbued with the old ideology. Even when they had intervened to take direct control of the state, they had done so with an old-fashioned conservatism, which had won them the plaudits of the Western press. The new breed, however, had no time for niceties. They acquiesced in Bhutto's take-over, since a direct military intervention could have led to civil war in West Pakistan itself. The campaign in Baluchistan then enabled the army to use the province as a laboratory for counter-insurgency operations. Bhutto had committed his fatal error: by bringing the army into politics, he had tightened the noose around his own neck. The roots of the martial law established in July 1977 stretched back to the Central government's coup against an elected provincial government.

One writes this not simply with hindsight: I made the same points much more emphatically in discussions with numerous PPP partisans at the time. Nor was this view confined to people like myself. Bhutto's political secretariat warned him repeatedly of the dangers inherent in the military intervention in Baluchistan. Rao Rashid, a senior adviser, drafted a paper in which he spelt out how the junior officers were reacting:

> Power has its own taste, and in the course of time the army officers, especially in the middle ranks, start relishing power in the form of arrests, searches and interrogation which gives them the feel of authority. They also develop contempt for the ways of the politicians and the civil servants, and a general impression in the army circle starts gaining ground that everybody in the field of civil administration and politics is incompetent and corrupt ... The army should be divested of powers of arrest, house-searches and keeping civilians in military custody even for a short period. The withdrawal of the army, which may be gradual, might lead to more incidents but that risk should be taken ... The impression amongst the

junior army officers that the army is a panacea for all ills, which had received a severe blow after the débâcle in East Pakistan, is again gaining ground. It can be very infectious and cannot remain confined to one province. This infection may not be allowed to spread.[17]

The Rashid Memorandum would appear to confirm the harsh verdict of the Baluch leaders. They have always been sceptical of the reputed rift between Bhutto and the army during the civil war in Baluchistan. Mengal, for example, while accepting that the army jealously preserved its autonomy of action, insists:

> Bhutto cannot be absolved. He was an autocrat and kept himself informed of everything that was going on. It was Bhutto who gave the army a blank cheque. They then carried on as they chose. It is true that Bhutto was not consulted on everything, but *he* gave them the authority.[18]

The changes in the social and political composition of the officer corps, coupled with the experiences in Baluchistan, produced sinister results. Pakistan's third period of military rule was designed to brutalize the population into passivity. Bhutto's execution, public floggings, routine torture of political prisoners (including women), harassment and intimidation of opposition politicians – all were designed to frighten the people and atomize any potential dissent. There can be few doubts as to the initial success of the régime. Zia-ul-Haq has succeeded in holding office for over five years, with the support of the army and a handful of chosen civil servants.

The power of the civil service has diminished considerably under Zia's dictatorship. During the Ayub period (1958–68), civil servants had co-ruled the country with the army: the last six years of Ayub's régime, indeed, had seen the civil service in effective command of the country. The civil service of Pakistan, like its military counterpart, had represented a Muslim breakaway from the Indian civil service. This institution had been the pride of the Raj and had governed the country unfettered by democracy or politicians. It had, in reality, been the ruling party of British imperialism in India. The civil servants of the early twentieth century were even referred to as 'politicals' in the lexicon of the empire. Lord Curzon, in particular, had sung their praises in semi-lyrical prose:

> There is no more varied or responsible service in the world. At one moment the political [civil servant] may be grinding in the Foreign Office, at another he may be required to stiffen the administration of a backward native state, at a third he may be presiding over a *jirga* of unruly tribesmen on the Frontier, at a fourth he may be demarcating a boundary amid the

wilds of Tibet or the sands of Seistan. I hope that the time may never come when the political department will cease to draw to itself the best abilities and the finest characters that the services in India can produce.[19]

With only a few changes Curzon's description retains its validity in the states of contemporary South Asia, especially India and Sri Lanka. In both Pakistan and Bangladesh, however, the civil service has shared power with the army, which in Pakistan today is the dominant political force: it is an army-party, running the country on behalf of a state that has run out of steam. The authority of the civil service has declined, even top bureaucrats now being dependent on military patrons. Military rule or Bonapartism has become the religion of the Pakistani ruling classes. But the latter now confront a fearsome dilemma: if they keep the army in command indefinitely, the state will begin to break up sooner rather than later; if they send the army back to barracks, they have to find a credible alternative, which at the moment does not exist. It is this insoluble predicament, above all, which has helped General Zia-ul-Haq to stay in power.

A second factor, however, has been the changed situation on Pakistan's borders. Just when Zia's position was becoming shaky and unrest was spreading in the upper reaches of the army, the Soviet entry into Afghanistan provided the Pakistani dictator with a new lease of life. This could be seen most clearly in the sudden change of attitude displayed by the Western press. The sordid hangman of an elected prime minister was soon transformed into the plucky defender of the frontiers of the Free World. Prior to the Russian invasion, most Western observers had been in favour of a return to civilian rule, but this theme virtually disappeared in the years that followed. For example, on 28 September 1979, three months before Soviet tanks rumbled into Kabul, the *Financial Times* commented editorially:

> General Zia has been no more successful than the three [*sic*] military régimes before him in finding a satisfactory balance between the demands of the provinces for more autonomy and the claims of the central government for sufficient power to hold the country together . . . His régime has brought the army – which has traditionally believed that it has a special role as defender of the nation's integrity – into disrepute by the oppressiveness of its rule.[20]

A few years later the same newspaper (and the same leader-writer?) was stating that: 'President Zia's rule has been firm, somewhat harsh. But he is not a dictator. What he lacks in depth he makes up for in guile.'[21] A report by Amnesty International on Pakistan in 1982 was to provide a sober and chilling corrective to the Foreign Office propaganda regularly reproduced by Fleet Street leader writers.[22]

Army rule has brought all the contradictions of the Pakistani state to a head. Lack of political democracy, economic inequality and the oppression of minority nationalities have become deeply embedded in the consciousness of a mass which increasingly begins to question the very basis of the state. It does not, after all, require a university degree to realize that something has gone seriously wrong with the state of Pakistan. Apportioning blame among individual politicians or military leaders is clearly insufficient. Stressing the fact that Jinnah died prematurely, or that he left behind only a bunch of mediocrities, is to be crassly superficial. All that is true, but evades the real issue, the more fundamental problem which needs to be grasped, analysed, understood and acted upon. To state it bluntly has always been unpopular in Pakistan, but to remain silent today is a crime: the truth is that there was no real basis for carving out an independent 'Muslim' state from the Indian subcontinent. For the overwhelming majority of Muslim toilers, it could have no economic or political justification. A confused demagogy and sinister emotionalism became substitutes for a sober, realistic appraisal of the condition and objective interests of Muslims in India.

True, imperialism was a messy and unpleasant business. The break-up of the old colonial empires witnessed a hasty evacuation of South Asia and much of Africa by the European powers. They left behind a wide variety of bastard bourgeois states: modernized mutants of pre-capitalist social formations. Victims of the law of combined and uneven development, these states were trapped in a circle of poverty and dependence. The only way out of this prison was through social revolution – as attested by China, Indo-China, Cuba and Nicaragua.[23] Otherwise, the picture is grim. Of the dependent post-colonial states, the only ones which have succeeded in separating the political from the economic sphere are India and Mexico.

In Pakistan, the state has overpowered civil society and with a vengeance. Pakistan was an irrationality, a product of imperialist penetration of the subcontinent. Its makeshift political and social composition indicated that its interior was diseased from birth. The disintegration of 1971–2 was not the result of a foreign conspiracy or an Indian plot. It was the dispassionate verdict of history on an experiment doomed to failure. The process is by no means over, as the imposition of martial law in July 1977 vividly demonstrated. What sort of a state is it that can exist only by an indiscriminate use of the mullah, the gun and the latest torture equipment imported from the West? Whatever its other demerits, we can say that such a state is built on foundations of sand. It cannot last indefinitely. When military rule becomes the first rather than the last response of a frightened ruling class; when elections can no longer be tolerated, because the masses might utilize them to impose their will; when the army and civil bureaucracy lose all credibility or trust and are regarded as usurpers – then we may indeed say that the end cannot be far away.

The future trajectory of the Pakistani state, however, does not depend exclusively on the correlation of social, class and national forces in the country itself. Pakistan's future is inextricably linked to the turn of events in Kabul, the tense confrontations in Teheran and the strategic options chosen by the Indian ruling class in New Delhi. We will discuss these geopolitical factors in some detail in the concluding chapter. For the moment, we will concentrate on the internal contradictions confronting the state and evaluate the strength and weaknesses of indigenous political institutions.

Centralism, Democracy and the Question of Nationalities

The peculiar history of Pakistan's establishment lent the state certain quite specific features, of which the most pronounced was the attempt to construct a strong Centre and ignore the democratic rights of the vast majority of the population. Inevitably, this came into conflict with the multi-national character of the Pakistani state. Denial of the democratic rights and linguistic and cultural freedoms of the bulk of the population gave birth to a powerful national movement in East Bengal, which culminated in a civil war and the establishment of Bangladesh. The military–bureaucratic élite responsible for this débâcle learnt the wrong lessons from the break-up of the old state, and sought to make religion the organizing principle of the new one. This enterprise, which reached its peak with the military coup of July 1977, has failed to solve the intractable structural problem confronting Pakistan. The only viable solution (even within the existing socio-economic framework) would have entailed a loose federation of the four provinces, with a Centre responsible only for defence, foreign affairs, currency and communications. Such a solution, however, would undoubtedly have weakened the hold of the army and bureaucracy, and opened up the possibility that some of the provinces might experiment with radical socio-economic programmes for change. A voluntary federation, or ultimate disintegration? This was the real question confronting the state. Rejecting the first option, it sought to avoid the second by institutionalizing a form of political rule based exclusively on coercion. In denying themselves any popular legitimacy, however, the military rulers were weakening the legitimacy of the Pakistani state itself.

The 'nationalities question' has become a central point of dispute in Pakistan. The debate on nationalism, nationalities and the right of nations to self-determination has a distinguished pedigree in Marxism and liberal-democratic political theory alike. As we indicated in the opening chapter, for Marx and Engels the old nation-states of Europe were a product of the development of capitalism. A bourgeois nation was a synonym for the modern state, with its separation of political and civil society. This separation arose out of the very nature of the capitalist mode of production. Capitalism, dissolving nationalities, and languages and cultures, tends towards universalization. The world market creates a 'universal interdependence of nations'. Michael Löwy has pointed out that, despite some brilliant generalizations, Marx did not develop a 'systematic theory of the national question', nor even a precise definition of the concept of a 'nation'.[24] It was left to Lenin to develop and struggle for the principle of self-determination as a *political* and democratic right of all nationalities who were oppressed. There is nothing in Lenin's writings which indicates a rigid dogmatism, or enunciates some set of abstract criteria to define a 'nation'. Neither religion nor language, it should be stressed, were important criteria for Marx or Lenin in their writings on this question. Both stressed that bourgeois society tended, objectively, to decompose ethnic, linguistic or religious affinities.

The uneven global spread of capitalism; the capricious asymmetry imposed on three continents by decades of imperialist domination; the unfinished character of the socialist revolutions that transformed Russia, China and Indo-China; the revealing failure of advanced capitalism in the West to satisfy all the democratic aspirations of its subjects – all these factors have prevented a dissolution of the national question. In other words it is politics, much more than economics, which lies at the root of the problem. We stress this point to challenge the view that there is somehow a pre-ordained evolutionary sequence from a tribal/feudal nationality to a bourgeois nation – an argument advanced, for example, by the distinguished Soviet orientalist Y. V. Gankovsky, whose writings are influential in South Asia.[25] Gankovsky's rigid theses are refuted by the entire development of European history over the last seven centuries. There was a crucial distinction between the ways in which bourgeois nations emerged in the West and East of Europe respectively.[26] The Western states were not based on the existence of one strong nationality oppressing lesser nations. A polyglot state apparatus helped to lay the basis of unified nation-states. In the East the political landscape was profoundly different: the Romanovs and Hapsburgs ruled their empires at the head of numerically large and militarily strong oppressor nationalities. The development of capitalism thus coincided with the national oppression of a vast array of small nations. Consequently, the birth of modern states in the East involved a necessary detour: a bitterly contested struggle for national independence, against a ruling class based on a hegemonic nationality. It was political factors rather than inexorable economic laws that determined the parameters of modern states.

If we now contrast the colonial state created by the British in India, we perceive a much closer similarity to Western Europe than to Tsarist Russia on the crucial issue of nationalities. Political power was held by a foreign ruling class, which based itself locally on a small number of civil servants and soldiers in alliance with native rulers and élite social layers. But the colonial structures could, at best, create a deformed and misshapen bourgeois state. This was by design, not accident. The colonial authorities only permitted such political, cultural and economic development as was absolutely necessary to preserve the empire. If they had allowed an untrammelled social and economic advance, the entire pattern of post-Independence South Asia might have been different. Even the limited reforms from above had *begun* a process of merging nationalities, while simultaneously encouraging the emergence of an all-Indian *national* movement against colonial oppression. Like the post-1848 bourgeoisie in Europe, the colonial state halted reforms from above to prevent a revolt from below.

In post-Independence Pakistan, the 'national' contradiction became dominant largely because, as we have seen, the ruling-class apparatuses excluded the majority of the population from representation. This was coupled with the national oppression of Bengalis, and attempts to suppress their democratic rights and their language. In contemporary Pakistan, the four major nationalities are the Punjabis, Sindhis, Pathans and Baluch. Of these the Punjabis are the largest, comprising over 60 per cent of Pakistan's population, followed by the Sindhis, Pathans and Baluch respectively. The Punjab, known in the colonial period as both the granary and the 'sword-arm' of India, has succeeded in retaining these characteristics, but within the framework of a much smaller state. It also benefited most during the period of industrialization initiated by the military régime of General Ayub Khan. Today the Punjab is militarily, economically and politically the dominant province in Pakistan. At the other extreme, Balachistan contains only 4 per cent of Pakistan's population, though it forms 42 per cent of its territory. Successive governments have left the province almost entirely undeveloped. Per capita income, the level of adult literacy and life expectancy are lower than anywhere else in the country. The struggle between Baluch nationalists and a Punjabi-dominated military–bureaucratic élite has symbolized the difficulties that confront Islamabad. At the same time, since Bhutto's execution the national movement in Sind has acquired a new dynamism and been subjected to direct military repression in the interior, while the Pathans of the NWFP are also showing signs of disaffection with the régime. The competing hierarchy of intelligence agencies who are the real political advisers to the military chiefs, not surprisingly, are obsessed with the nationalist dimension of Pakistani politics.

Successive régimes have not discouraged the movement of labour, so that Pathans and Baluch are a strong component of the urban proletariat in Karachi, while Punjabi policemen and government officials are a common sight in Quetta. Nevertheless, there has been neither an even process of industrialization nor a modernized political order. As a result, all the minority nationalities jealously safeguard their identity. A new layer of Pushtu, Sindhi and Baluch poets has arisen to proclaim the vitality of their respective languages and cultures, and to complain against oppression: nothing concentrates the mind so wonderfully as a military government. Nor are Punjabi workers or peasants contented with their lot: there is in fact growing discontent among them. In a recent interview, the Baluch leader still resident in Pakistan, Ghaus Bux Bizenjo, made a strong plea for a democratic federal state, arguing that 'the bitterness and tension that has built up over the years is not only adversely affecting the people's relations with the government, but has also become a source and cause of doubts. There are today misgivings about the efficacy, viability (and justification) of the State itself and about whether the people can any longer live together.'[27]

The point we are stressing is a simple one. The main reason for the smouldering national discontent in Pakistan's three minority provinces is political discrimination. The refusal to tolerate representative governments in the provinces has exacerbated the problem tenfold. Islam did not prove strong enough to hold East and West Pakistan together. Why should it then become the cement to unite the remaining four provinces? If 20,000 Baluch guerrillas could tie down four Pakistani divisions (100,000 men) and numerous air-force squadrons, with Iranian helicopters and pilots, inflicting heavy casualties before retreating, how could conflicts on three fronts be contained? It is true that there are hardly any Baluch in the armed forces and very few Sindhis; but there is a substantial minority of Pathans, so that trouble in the NWFP could create serious dissensions within the army. (The lack of Baluch recruits in the army is, of course, blatant political discrimination. Certainly, the macho rhetoric behind the racist theory of 'martial races' so popular with the Pakistani high command could hardly exclude the Baluch. According to the classic exposition given by General Sir O'Moore Creagh, C.-in-C. of the British Indian Army in 1909–14: 'In the hot, flat regions, of which by far the greater part of India consists . . . are found races, timid both by religion and habit, servile to their superiors, but tyrannical to their inferiors, and quite unwarlike. In other parts . . . where the winter is cold, the warlike minority is to be found.'[28] But leaving aside the fact that this gibberish has been repeatedly refuted by history – in Vietnam, China, Bangladesh, etc. – such arguments cannot affect the Baluchis, who fulfil all the 'martial' criteria laid down by the military ideologies of the Raj and their native successors.)

There is an additional factor, which we will discuss in detail in the next chapter. Three of Pakistan's provinces – the Punjab, the NWFP and

Baluchistan – were bisected by Lord Curzon's civil servants and their successors. One half of the Punjab is in India, part of Baluchistan is in Iran and the Durand Line demarcating the Pakistan–Afghanistan border was drawn with total disregard for the integrity of peoples or nationalities. So can the national question be solved within the existing framework of the Pakistani state? Only if there is a fundamental change in the character of the state and its machinery. This is impossible without a social revolution. It is one of history's ironies that 'Muslim' Pakistan could only survive as a stable entity if it were a secular-democratic, socialist republic, with safeguards for all nationalities and religions. It is true that such a future appears utopian at the moment; but there is no other long-term solution.

In that sense, the problems of democracy, federalism and the national question are not the sole responsibility of General Zia-ul-Haq: his departure, however it comes about, will not lead to their automatic solution. The crisis of nationalities is far too advanced to be cured by a mild dose of reforms from above, coupled with a limited industrialization programme. The torture, floggings and executions imposed by the military régime on the people of Sind and Baluchistan has hardened attitudes considerably. An Indian journalist travelling through Pakistan in January 1982 reported that: 'A Sindhi militant asked me in all seriousness why the Indian army withdrew in 1971, why it did not move in deeper into his part of the country at a time when the Pak army was in shambles.'[29] Such a question reflects both demoralization and despair, but it also signifies a growing anger and alienation from Islamabad and everything that it represents. The national question is the time-bomb threatening the very structures of the post-1971 state. The hour of the explosion cannot be too far away.

Political Parties

The break-up of Pakistan in 1971 did not, as might have been expected, result in any serious split within the country's political parties. Politics had become so thoroughly regionalized that the decomposition of the 1947 state did not seriously affect the parties, in any of its component parts. The Muslim League had represented the first major attempt to construct a national political party in Pakistan. Its roots, however, had remained extremely weak and, failing to acquire a mass base, it disintegrated soon after Jinnah's death. There were a number of reasons why the latter failed to create a substantial party organization: Uttar Pradesh, one of the main regions of the Muslim petty bourgeoisie which he represented, did not become part of Pakistan; the post-Partition refugees from India, moreover, did not constitute a numerically significant or politically stable force; hence, without a base in the present provinces of Pakistan, Jinnah tended to confirm provincial landlords as the representatives of the Muslim League. The low level of productive forces (the virtual non-existence of capitalism) in the areas that now constitute Pakistan meant that landlords were the dominant social force inside the ruling class.

The Muslim League, unlike the Indian Congress, was never able to become a reliable political party for the ruling class, capable of either mystifying or controlling the masses. After Jinnah's death, it discredited itself permanently, when it was reduced to a clutch of corrupt and bickering factions. Hence, from the outset Pakistan was dominated by the army and bureaucracy. It was the latter which was crucial in the development of capitalism in Pakistan. The links between the new entrepreneurs and the civil service were always close and mutually beneficial. As long as the civil servants exercised untrammelled power, there was no reason why the new ruling class should develop its own political party. The army and bureaucracy guaranteed its interests more effectively than the Muslim League or any other surrogate could have done. The failure of the Pakistani ruling class to produce a political instrument also prevented the emergence of a national alternative from the centre or left.

Pre-Partition politics continued to dominate Pakistan's provinces well after Independence. In the NWFP and Baluchistan, the Muslim League had enjoyed little organized support. The Pathan and Baluch leaders engaged in the struggle against imperialism were part of a nationalist offensive which the Muslim League was precisely created to sabotage. The two border provinces remained under the strong influence of anti-League nationalists. For a long period they worked in concert, but the growing political crisis separated them. The civil war in Baluchistan transformed the political life of that province: the birth of the BPLF and the subsequent split between Bizenjo and Wali Khan was the consequence. In the Punjab and Sind, landlords dominated politics and feudalist hegemony made political parties almost redundant, though this hold was partially broken by the emergence of populism under the banners of Bhutto's PPP.

It is unnecessary to repeat what we wrote in the last chapter, but the PPP's popularity was based on what it promised rather than what it achieved. In Pakistan, no major political leader had ever argued that the interests of the common people were paramount. However, Bhutto's place in Pakistani history is assured because he encouraged the downtrodden to speak their bitterness.[30] That was novel. But since Bhutto's death, the PPP remains a shell. It has two courageous women at its head (Bhutto's widow and eldest daughter), but it lacks a cadre, experienced and dedicated organizers, a trade-union and peasant base or even a politically stable student organization. Its ideology remains confused.

Few doubt that the PPP would win a majority in any election. The question, however, is whether any of Pakistan's political parties are sufficiently well-organized to initiate a mass movement that could force a general election. The Punjab is here the crucial province. If the Punjabi masses take to the streets, the present military régime will fall. But the political parties in the Punjab are weak. The PPP has support, but no serious network. The Tehrik-i-Istiqlal led by Air Marshal Asghar Khan is a typical Pakistani organization, consisting largely of national or provincial leaders, together with bandwagon careerists who hoped that the army might tolerate the moderate Tehrik as a counter to the PPP. The Tehrik's political programme is based on a limited modernization of the state and a sprinkling of reforms. Committed to the 'mixed economy', it is ambiguous on every major question confronting the country.

There can be little doubt that, in the eventuality of a spontaneous mass uprising, it would be the PPP (in the Punjab and Sind) that would reap the harvest. Its difficulty lies in the fact that it is not strong enough to initiate such a rebellion, but is dependent on the mood of the masses. Political consciousness is difficult to gauge when there are no elections. The failure of mass protests to materialize after the execution of Bhutto was an indication that people were tired. They had struggled for five months to overthrow Ayub in 1968–9. They had protested against the election-rigging of 1977. Many had indeed voted against Bhutto, but not with the intention of bringing about martial law. Blame has been attached to Bhutto's lieutenants, in particular Hafiz Pirzada and Mumtaz Bhutto, for the lack of any mass action preceding or following his execution: to be sure, the PPP leaders can not totally evade responsibility, but they were paying the price of the earlier failure to construct a political party in the real sense of the word. Nor could they simply leap over the masses, to unleash strikes and demonstrations. At all events, the fact that the people remained passive, if anguished, spectators throughout the trial and execution of Bhutto was a sufficient indicator that the army would have an easy run for a few years.

Subsequently, the trauma that followed Bhutto's execution brought about a detachment from politics. This was not a de-politicization, but reflected a feeling of helplessness and demoralization, a combination of sadness and fear. It was quite common to hear a Punjabi say: 'If they could kill a powerful man like Bhutto, who are we? We are nothings.' The brutalization of Pakistani politics helped to atomize popular consciousness. The military régime hoped that in this way it could expunge from the historical memory of the masses all recollection of their collective strength. This, however, it has not succeeded in doing. There are signs that change is not far away. How it will come is uncertain: few can ever accurately predict the creativity of the masses in movement. None, however, believe that Pakistan's political parties, as they exist today, could be the motor force for removing the army permanently from the political scene.

Problems of the Pakistani Left

The history of the communist movement in South Asia is inextricably linked to the Russian revolution and its aftermath. The fall of Tsarism and the establishment of a soviet republic in Petrograd had a profound impact on a layer of revolutionary nationalists in India. Instinctively many ordinary people felt they were witnessing the birth of a state that would be the friend and ally of oppressed peoples everywhere. The unilateral abrogation of all former imperialist treaties, and the publication of secret protocols designed to prolong colonial subjugation in the Near East, won the new revolution approval in many parts of the world. The internationalism displayed by the Bolsheviks was concretized by the formation of the Communist International in 1919.

At its Fourth Congress in 1922, the Comintern established certain guidelines designed to aid the fledgling communist parties in the colonies. These were, of necessity, extremely general, schematic and abstract; but compared to the 'advice' proffered from Moscow in the thirties, forties and fifties, they appear as models of clarity:

> The refusal of the communists in the colonies to participate against imperialist oppression on the pretext of alleged 'defence' of independent class interests is opportunism of the worst kind, calculated only to discredit the proletarian revolution in the East. No less harmful must be recognized the attempt to isolate oneself from the immediate and everyday interests of the working class for the sake of 'national unity' or 'civil peace' with bourgeois democracy. The communist and working-class parties in the colonies and semi-colonial countries are confronted by a two-fold task: on the one hand to fight for the most radical solutions of the problems of bourgeois-democratic revolution, directed to the conquest of political independence, and on the other to organize the workers and peasants to fight for their special class interests and to take advantage of the antagonism existing in the national bourgeois-democratic camp ... The working class must know that only by deepening and extending the struggle against the imperialism of the great powers can its role as revolutionary leader be fulfilled.[31]

The tragedy of Indian communism was that its main period of growth was the forties, when the revolutionary potential of October 1917 had already been squandered and falsified by the emergence of Stalinism. From then on, the policies and perspectives of the Comintern parties were to be determined by the needs of the Soviet bureaucracy.[32] Accordingly, the 1922 Theses became a dead letter. Indian communists, far from avoiding the twin errors outlined above, pursued a policy which alternated between a grotesque sectarianism towards the national movement and outright class-collaboration. The result was a dismal failure with respect to the crucial question of winning power. Why did the Indian communists fail, while the Chinese and Vietnamese parties succeeded? Were the latter not part of the Comintern as well? These questions have been raised by Indian communists themselves over the last three decades. The answer is not a simple one. This is not the place to enter into a detailed comparative survey of Chinese, Vietnamese and Indian communism. However, a few elementary features differentiating the three parties can briefly be mentioned.

The Chinese party does not possess an unblemished record of linear ascent from a handful of militants to the seizure of power. Disastrous advice from the Comintern was accepted by the Chinese communists in the late twenties. The result was catastrophic: in 1927, Chinese communists were butchered in cold blood by troops in Shanghai acting under the orders of General Chiang Kai-shek, characterized by Stalin and his associates as a 'progressive' leader of the 'democratic bourgeoisie'. The subsequent re-building of the party was a lengthy process, aided inadvertently by the Japanese invasion of China. Mao's partisans built a party-army that won mass support by becoming the most effective means of defence against the Japanese colonialists. After the defeat of the Japanese, Mao effectively disregarded Stalin's advice in practice by refusing to disband the Chinese communist armies. A peasant uprising in the North saw a renewed civil war in which the Maoists triumphed over Chiang Kai-shek without too much difficulty. Chiang's soldiery deserted with its weapons in tens of thousands.

The Vietnamese party was aided by the virtual non-existence of an indigenous bourgeoisie or political parties allied to the latter's cause. In 1960, under questioning from an Indian communist leader, Ho Chi Minh was blunt and to the point:

He gave a characteristic reply when I asked him [Ho Chi Minh] how in his view the Vietnamese party, which in the thirties was not much bigger than the Indian party, had succeeded whereas we had failed. He replied: 'There you had Mahatama Gandhi, here I am the Mahatama Gandhi!' He then went on to explain how they had utilized the anti-imperialist struggle to build their hegemony over the masses. They had become the leading force in the anti-imperialist struggle and moved on to socialism. The clear implication was that in India it was Gandhi and the Congress who had kept control and that the CPI was at fault. He also explained as did other Vietnamese leaders the endemic weaknesses of the Vietnamese bourgeoisie, which of course contrasted very vividly with the strength of the Indian bourgeoisie.[33]

Indian communists were confronted with an extremely strong and powerful enemy in the shape of the colonial state, as well as with a nationalist party, the Indian Congress, which had direct links with indigenous capitalists and the landowning classes. Bourgeois nationalism in India was not something which could simply be swept aside, a fact never properly understood by the Comintern (even during its revolutionary phase).[34] A further difference with respect to China was the diversity of the rural structures pertaining in the two largest Asian states. The role of religion and caste in the Indian villages was coupled with the existence for centuries of a layer of intermediary exploiters: both were preserved and extended by the British, creating a potent counter-revolutionary stability. The major differences between the two countries, however, existed at the level of the state machine. In China, throughout the pre-revolutionary periods and revolutionary upsurges of the twenties, thirties and forties, the state machine was either weak or distracted or both. It is true that the Kuomintang state apparatus, albeit more unstable than the colonial state in India, was much more repressive: the systematic elimination of communists and progressives of all hues by the KMT was far more savage than British repression in Amritsar or crushing of the Moplah uprising in Malabar. Executions of political prisoners remained a novelty in twentieth-century British India. However, the strength of the British colonial state lay in its whole relationship to the social formation over which it ruled, rather than in pure coercion: as we have already seen, Britain never needed more than 50,000 troops to maintain control of India's multi-millioned masses.[35]

In China, the explosive impact of an expanding capitalism wreaked havoc on existing social relations and laid the basis for the first Chinese revolution in 1911. Subsequent depredations by the contending forces of the major imperialist powers further undermined the remnants of the traditional social order. In India, meanwhile, the development of the colonial state paved the way for a unique amalgam of pre-capitalist social relations with aspects of a modern state machine, complete with the trappings of a bourgeois democracy albeit tightly controlled by Whitehall: Indian judges and local councils could already be observed in the closing years of the nineteenth century. Marx had forecast that the British would bring a bourgeois revolution to India, and though he was wrong, the colonial state did achieve a very partial and deformed variant of such a revolution. It is this that explains the *relatively* smooth transfer of power: 'smooth' in the sense that it averted a social revolution, not that it saved lives, since nearly a million people died as innocent victims of communal violence and ten million bitter refugees sought new homes across confessional frontiers.

The point of this lengthy digression has been to drive home the fact that the weakness of Indian communism cannot be explained simply by Comintern blundering. Mistakes, after all, were committed on an extravagant scale in China, Vietnam and India alike. It was the misfortune of Indian communists to be confronted with a far more cunning and powerful opponent than their Chinese and Vietnamese comrades in the thirties and forties. Here the Comintern's failures were multiplied by the deadening impact of Stalinism, whose theoretical absolutism and rigid ideological monopoly were especially damaging in India. Critical thought was vital to comprehend and analyse the complex structures of the colonial state and the vagaries of bourgeois nationalism, and to evolve a strategy that could win over the masses. Its absence led to costly political blunders. Bipan Chandra, the well-known Indian Marxist historian and political scientist, attempting in a constructive and non-sectarian fashion to analyse the weakness of Indian Marxism, has concluded:

> Almost all aspects of the weakness of the Indian Marxists in analysing the social reality, in applying Marxism to India, in evolving correct political practice, and in the failure to correct mistakes in time, are linked to the virtual absence of free discussion amongst them . . . the Indian Marxist, political worker or intellectual has learnt to exercise drastic, and disastrous self-censorship . . . The cult of the great man or men has greatly eroded the democratic and scientific notion that the acquisition of knowledge of society is a collective activity . . . The average Indian Marxist therefore genuinely believes that he is not *fit* to think on or debate matters of theory, ideology, and higher or broader political practice.[36]

The two great errors committed by Indian communism were both related to its subordination of workers' and peasants' interests to the wishes of Moscow. The failure to participate in and help the Quit India movement of 1942 handed India over on a platter to bourgeois nationalism and simultaneously weakened the left inside the Congress Party. The second misjudgement was grounded in a theoretical incapacity to comprehend the complexities of the national question. The CPI failed to analyse the forces motivating Hindu and Muslim communalism. It supported the demand for a confessional state of Pakistan, disguising its ignorance by arguing that communalism was a 'problem of growing nationalities'. At the most critical period in the history of the subcontinent, the CPI, congenitally incapable of developing an independent policy, prostrated itself before the Congress and the Muslim League. In March 1946, the British communist R. P. Dutt intervened in an attempt to lift the mist of confusion, maintaining that the demand for Pakistan was based on religion, not nationality. Five months later, the CPI obligingly altered course. They now explained that the demand for an independent Pakistan was a reactionary one, based on the needs of 'Muslim bourgeois and feudal vested interests, who are seeking a compromise with imperialism for a share of the administration in divided India'. What the comrades could not explain was how the League had managed to build an element of mass support. We are not suggesting that a correct evaluation by the CPI would have avoided the bloodbath of 1947. What it would have done, however, was help to lay the foundations for a strong and powerful communist movement throughout South Asia in the period following Independence.

When Partition came, the tiny band of Pakistani communists active in the Punjab, Sind, the NWFP and Baluchistan saw their numbers depleted by the mass migration of Hindus and Sikhs. The refugees arriving from Uttar Pradesh or Indian Punjab were unlikely recruits to the communist cause. The history of communism in this region is not particularly edifying or instructive. The weaknesses of Indian Marxism were reproduced in an exaggerated form in Pakistan, and with tragic consequences. Pakistani communism never succeeded in implanting itself as a national, political current, except in East Pakistan prior to 1971. The movement was utterly disoriented by the Sino-Soviet split: the Stalinist tradition had not prepared the cadres for the existence of *two* centres of the world communist movement. A majority of Pakistani communists, brought up in the stultifying atmosphere of monolithism and stunned by the split, finally decided to back Peking. This, however, was not for 'leftist' reasons as in India. Peking's break with Moscow and conflict with India had led to its adopting a friendly attitude towards the Pakistani military régime under Ayub Khan: many communists who became Maoists accordingly found themselves, for the first time in their political lives, the beneficiaries of state patronage.

The results were extremely negative for the entire Pakistani left. Its opportunist attitude to the régime meant that the 1968 wave of revolt from below which toppled Ayub also bypassed the Maoists, who had initially opposed the mass movement or remained passive. It was the PPP which gained the allegiance of the 'new left' which emerged at that time. The populist years with Bhutto in power generated more disillusionment on the left. At the time of the military coup of July 1977, the Pakistani left was much weaker than it had been in 1947 or 1968. This was an unmitigated disaster for any hope of social transformation in the country. Unlike its Indian counterpart, the Pakistani left from 1947 on confronted a weak and unstable state. As the decades went by, the crisis of legitimacy mounted. Yet it was not the left, but Bengali nationalism which triumphed in the East and a populist-nationalism which grew in the West prior to the collapse of the old state and the civil war.

The situation today is extremely bleak. Splinters from the early Communist Party still survive, but they are shadows of their former selves. Maoism is in total decline: few former enthusiasts of the cult could swallow the drastic turn in Chinese foreign policy. Some have returned to Moscow's fold, thus tragically confirming that the fundamental problems of South Asian Marxism have yet to be resolved. Others have retreated from politics. There are Marxist study-circles in a number of cities, and of late there has been a limited resurgence of interest in the classics of Marxism. It would, however, be foolish to imagine that Marxist forces stand poised to bring down the régime. If the state is threatened, it is not the sudden, subterranean growth of a renovated Marxism that provides the challenge. The experience of communist governments in West Bengal and Kerala, the murky situation in Afghanistan or the role of the Tudeh Party in Iran are not designed to inspire a new generation of militants. The current world outlook of the Chinese leaders and the Vietnamese embroilment in Kampuchea have also helped to create a sense of despondency and gloom. Only when the reasons for past failures are thoroughly assimilated on the plane of theory, and when the masses re-enter the political stage from the left, could this crisis of perspectives be overcome. In that sense, the situation of the left, though bad, is certainly not permanent.

Crisis of Legitimacy: Can Pakistan Survive?

Soon after he took power in December 1971 as the first civilian to be appointed Chief Martial Law Administrator, Zulfiqar Ali Bhutto was confronted with the problem of the army. He understood the dimensions of the difficulty. In one flight of rhetoric, he went so far as to state: 'We must take a leaf or two out of North Vietnam's military textbook. A People's Army rather than a conventional army, that is the philosophy that will guide us in our new defence policy.'[37] It was a pleasing thought, but what Bhutto should also have understood was that the Vietnamese army was not a product of French or American imperialism. It was a 'people's army' precisely because it had been built by the people in a struggle *against* four colonial powers: France, Japan, Britain and the United States of America. Whereas the man who was to be the first C.-in-C. of the Pakistan army, General Sir Douglas Gracey, had as it happened led many future soldiers and officers of that army precisely to reoccupy Saigon and hold it till the French could muster a sufficient force to reassert their authority. The Pakistani army could not be transformed by decree, but only by a social revolution: an understanding of this fact is central, if we wish to ask how the army could be removed from power on a permanent basis. As we have stressed above, the army is in power to preserve the Pakistani state.

When General Zia says that Pakistan would collapse without Islam, he is utilizing an ideological fig-leaf to cover the naked realities of power. What he really means is that, without the army, Pakistan would not exist as before. Islam is a convenience designed to maintain iron control over every different aspect of political and social life. The economy is now in the trusted hands of Dr Mahbubul Haq of the World Bank, who will re-build the private sector in the name of 'Islamic Justice'. How long can this farce continue? What strategy should be pursued to bring an end to this régime? The choices vary, depending on which layer one chooses to question. The politicians want to see a return to the 1973 Constitution, through peaceful means. They maintain that there is only one appropriate demand: general elections. Is this a realistic prospect? In our opinion, a civilian government is unlikely unless there is mass pressure on the streets or a new turn of events on the external front. A voluntary transfer of power by the generals can virtually be excluded.

There is now more than a simple political reason for the army's desire to remain in power – though that remains a fundamental factor. The officer corps is also the recipient of considerable largesse in the shape of bribes, foreign currency, patronage rights, etc. There is, of course, a hierarchy of corruption, with a general making more money than a captain. But the officers as a whole are reputed to be contented with their lot. The perquisites of power are now their privilege. Moreover, a layer of these officers have been trained at CIA and DIA (Defence Intelligence Agency) centres in the United States and are aware of what is expected of them in emergencies. The Pakistani army today is a mercenary force in every sense of the word: soldiers and officers are regularly sold to the Gulf states and Saudi Arabia; the USA maintains its network of agents and informers; and since 1977, martial law has provided ample bounty for the executioners of the elected prime minister. Such an army has no reason to relinquish political power. It is true that the longer it stays in office, the more advanced is the crisis of legitimacy. But that is not how the high command views the situation.

If it is utopian to expect (as all the country's political parties do) the generals voluntarily to quit the stage, what then can be done? Is terrorism (dignified by the phrase 'armed struggle') the answer? We think not. Terrorism is, after all, not a newcomer to the subcontinent. There was an active and vigorous terrorist movement in the Punjab and Bengal in the twenties. The Chittagong Armoury Raid, with the trial and hanging of the legendary Bhagat Singh, forms part of South Asian folklore. What is recalled less often is that it was a miserable failure, as Bhagat Singh in his prison cell understood better than most. The question of terrorism is no abstract one today. Al-Zulfiqar (based in Kabul and under the political direction of Murtaza Bhutto, eldest son of the executed political leader) has claimed credit for the hijacking of a Pakistan International Airlines plane, which secured the release of some dozens of political prisoners. A reactionary politician has been shot dead in Lahore. On 7 February 1982, an Al-Zulfiqar squad fired a SAM-7 missile at a plane carrying General Zia soon after it had taken off from Islamabad, but the missile narrowly missed its target: repression inside the country increased. Other acts of sabotage have been carried out in the Frontier province.

When Lenin described a terrorist as a 'liberal with a bomb', he was not being facetious. Terrorism is the most dramatic form of pressure-politics. The perpetrators of terrorist acts believe that, by heroic actions, they can accomplish change over the heads of the masses. Terrorism is apolitical, precisely because it ignores the level of mass consciousness. It seeks in vain to substitute for the masses; it seeks in vain to arouse them, independently of the objective conditions that prevail in the country. In this respect, terrorism is the exact opposite of a viable strategy of protracted armed struggle. For the latter can only be successful where it is based on the support of the people: the Cuban, Vietnamese, Yugoslav, Chinese or Nicaraguan revolutions, the French and Italian resistance movements during the Second World War – these are all examples of a protracted struggle with popular support. The gigantic insurrection that overthrew the Shah of Iran – and in the process severely dented the Iranian army, the strongest and best-equipped force in the region – revealed the enormous capacities of the masses, for whose mobilization there is no substitute. The activities of Al-Zulfiqar, by contrast, have so far not seriously damaged the régime, but rather provided a pretext for intensifying repression at home.

The only effective basis for overthrowing the military régime would be a mass movement repeating in more difficult circumstances what it accomplished in 1968–9. The task today, therefore, is the political arming of the masses, so that at the right moment they can both acquire and utilize weapons to defend themselves. It is worth bearing in mind Trotsky's powerful and evocative description of a fighter: 'What distinguishes a revolutionary is not his ability to kill, but his readiness to die.' It is only when the masses are ready to die (as they were in 1968–9) that the army régime will fall. The time-scale or pattern of such a movement cannot be predicted with certainty. Nor can one point to the particular spark which might ignite a large-scale revolt. What can be stated is that this régime is, without doubt, the most unpopular administration in even Pakistan's chequered history. The hour of reckoning, in historical terms, cannot be all that distant.

Military rule has suffocated politics and society in general. However, it is worth stressing in particular that the oppression suffered by political prisoners is also now the daily diet of all Pakistan's women, for whom life itself is a prison, the Islamic code having reduced them (after the limited gains of the preceding decade) to ciphers and objects. Puritanism of this variety in fact seeks to conceal the sexual misery of everyday urban life (rural areas are marginally less oppressive in this regard). It is a remarkable feature of Pakistani cities that sexual tensions are always high: their victims are mainly women, but young boys are also a frequent target of repressed minds and bodies. In its own peculiar way the current régime, based as it is on coercion, backed by a competing network of intelligence agencies, has concentrated brutality on more sections of the population than its predecessors.

Despite all this, the state will not disintegrate of its own accord. There is is

no reason why, in the absence of foreign intervention or an indigenous uprising, the army cannot continue to maintain an Islamic banana republic in South Asia for another decade or more. This grim prospect remains a distinct possibility. The situation on Pakistan's borders, however, is such that the survival of the military régime depends, to a certain extent, on a stabilization of politics in Iran and Afghanistan. This is unlikely. The nightmare that haunts the generals in Islamabad is that changes abroad could spark off dissent at home. The army is only too keenly aware of the fragility of the state over whose destiny it now presides. The corps commanders realize full well that they are not popular. They know their régime cannot survive simply on American military aid. Aware that meeting new challenges at home by renewed bouts of repression further weakens their hold, they do not see a serious alternative. Any civilian government would have to recognize the army as a permanent force in the political life of the country. Yet any political party which agreed to that would sign its own death-warrant.

Ironically, the survival of Pakistan as a state today does not depend on vested interests or the armed forces. Only a thoroughgoing social transformation and the institutionalization of democracy, together with the disbandment of the mercenary army, could offer Pakistan a future. That is the supreme paradox: those who have made religion into the organizing cement of the state are no longer capable of holding it together; those who, by changing its very character, could maintain it are weak, dispirited and demoralized. The controlled optimism of the subcontinent's greatest living poet, Faiz Ahmed Faiz, provides a suitable epitaph:

> Only a few days, dear one, a few days more.
> Here in oppression's shadows condemned to breathe,
> Still for a while we must suffer, and weep, and endure
> What our forefathers, not our own faults, bequeath –

Fettered limbs, our feelings held on a chain,
Minds in bondage, and words each watched and set down;
Courage still nerves us, or how should we still live on,
Now when existence is only a beggar's gown
Tattered and patched every hour with new rags of pain?

Yes, but to tyranny not many hours are left now;
Patience, few hours of complaint are left us to bear.[38]

7 Between the Hammer and the Anvil: Geopolitics and the Super-Powers

The triune influence of military dictatorships, failed populism and rural conservatism on the political development of Pakistan has reduced the country to a state of permanent crisis. To its internal difficulties must now be added the unpredictable and unstable situation that has developed on its frontiers. Since the fateful years of 1971–2, the élites that govern the country have been attempting to rediscover an identity which never existed in the first instance. The fact that there are now more Muslims in India than in Pakistan illustrates the scale of the dilemma that now confronts the self-appointed spokesmen of the subcontinent's Muslim populations. It is unlikely that any of its problems will be overcome by Pakistan's new status as a 'front-line state'. The fact that the State Department in Washington and the Foreign Office in London have sought to transform a sordid military dictatorship into a plucky defender of the frontiers of the 'free world' may have had some impact on leader-writers and politicians in the West. Inside Pakistan and elsewhere in the subcontinent, however, it has only heightened the widespread cynicism towards the West. The shift in Western attitudes towards the military dictatorship has given the régime in Islamabad a renewed lease of life, but not even the United States has the capacity to extend this lease indefinitely. Geopolitical realities will be far more crucial in re-shaping Pakistan than either Washington or London.

The left-wing coup in Kabul in April 1978, followed by the overthrow of the Shah of Iran in February 1979 and the re-emergence of Mrs Gandhi at the head of a victorious Congress Party in India, created a new situation on Pakistan's frontiers. Not long after came the election of Ronald Reagan to the White House in November 1980, an event which came as a sorely needed relief for military dictators throughout the world. Merely tangential reference to these events (especially those in Iran and Afghanistan) would be insufficient. It is not simply that Teheran and Kabul are occupied by governments which have become the focus of worldwide attention. It is that the dramatic changes in these two capitals have determined the global and regional priorities of the military rulers of Pakistan. Only through an analysis of these developments can we come to grasp the predicament of the clerico-military dictatorship in Islamabad.

Afghanistan and the Consequences of Soviet Intervention

Afghanistan emerged in the middle of the eighteenth century as a tribal confederacy with a strong king at its head. Geography and history played a crucial role in preventing modernization of the state. Afghanistan was never occupied by a colonial power: the expanding Tsarist empire and British Raj ultimately settled for the survival of a tribal buffer-state between them (after two British invasions had been repelled). In the first decades of the twentieth century, the country was still not much different from what it had been a hundred years earlier. A mosaic of competing tribes and nationalities – ranging from the dominant Pushtuns or Pathans (themselves bitterly divided), the Tadjiks and the Uzbeks, to Hazaras (of Mongol descent), Nuristanis and Baluch – ensured that no strong central authority maintained its power for too long. The gulf between Kabul and the countryside was rarely, if ever, breached.

In 1917, however, the overthrow of the Tsar and the subsequent victory of the October Revolution transformed world politics. The decision of the infant Soviet Republic to renounce the former imperial treaties and protocols had a profound effect in the colonial world. The first serious attempt to modernize Afghanistan coincided with the early years of the Russian Revolution. For one long decade (1919–29), King Amanullah attempted to bring Afghanistan into the twentieth century. In the context of Afghan society, with its rural traditions and tribal mode of life, the young monarch's plans, inspired by liberal-democracy, appeared as a veritable revolution. The Afghan régime also adopted an intransigent hostility to the British empire on its eastern borders. It succeeded in inflicting a military defeat on the British in 1919, thus winning the right to determine Afghanistan's policies on both the domestic and the external levels. The Amanullah Decade is of continuing relevance to contemporary Afghanistan. The Reform Programme of 1919, inspired alike by the Bolshevik success and by Kemal Ataturk's triumph in Turkey, was far-reaching in its effects and, if successful, would have transformed the country's future.

Amanullah, with the advice of reformist intellectuals, wanted a secular and modern state. His political reforms visualized an elected lower chamber on the basis of universal adult franchise: women were to be allowed the vote. Thus Amanullah was in favour of a franchise still denied at that time by his British opponents not just in India, but in the metropolitan power itself. The reforms favoured co-education; rights for women; free elections; Turkish-style changes in dress; limited plans for import substitution through developing light industry; reorganization of the tax structure; the formation of a national bank; development of roads and a communications network.

However, Amanullah's plans for social and economic reforms were resisted by the clergy, since they would have effectively destroyed the corrupt privileges enjoyed by the mullahs and tribal chiefs. His audacious attempts to renovate the Afghan army caused an irreconcilable rift within his government, and led to the defection of the Nadir Khan faction which was hostile to all attempts to transform the army. The third and crucial obstacle to the King's plans was the hostility of British political agents based on the other side of the border. In this crucial phase of Afghani history, Amanullah might have benefited by an influx of Soviet aid; but by the late twenties the Russian state was much more concerned with restoring vital trade and diplomatic links with the British government.[1] In 1928–9, it chose not to assist the reformist King when he was threatened by a British-sponsored tribal revolt. The Afghan ruler, meanwhile, instead of organizing his support, which was not inconsiderable, retreated on every front and finally abdicated his throne. He went into exile in Italy, where he stayed until his death in 1960.

The first serious attempt to transform the country from above had thus ended in failure. Amanullah had not created a political party to extend his backing, and had become personally demoralized by the dissension existing within the ranks of those who supported him. He was no Garibaldi, but a King, albeit one with fairly advanced ideas. As such, he could hardly have been expected to conduct a guerrilla war against those who replaced him. None the less, Amanullah's decade in power was rich in lessons for all future modernizers.

In the event, there were to be none until 1978. Amanullah's successors merely institutionalized the social and economic status quo. A period of limited and self-restrained democratization in the post-war period produced an appetite in the urban middle class for more reforms; but King Zahir Shah and his cousin Prince Daud withdrew all progressive measures when they perceived that the political stability of the country might be disturbed. A palace coup organized by Daud on 17 July 1973 led to the overthrow of the King and the proclamation of a Republic: Daud pledged substantial reform of the political structures, winning the support of the *Parcham* (Flag) faction of Afghan communists. However, four years after Daud's coup, the level of illiteracy remained 90 per cent for men and 98 per cent for women; 5 per cent of landowners (in many cases also tribal chiefs) held 45 per cent of cultivable land; and Afghanistan possessed the lowest per capita income of any Asian country. In July 1977, *Parcham* reunited its forces with the other main communist faction (*Khalq* – the People), withdrew all support from the Daud régime and formed the People's Democratic Party of Afghanistan.[2]

There had been another dimension to the Daud coup, which concerns us more directly. Daud had always been a 'hardliner' on the question of Pushtunistan: the demand for a separate Pushtun (Pathan) state, with implicit rights to self-determination, in the Pushtun-inhabited areas of Pakistan's North-West Frontier Province. Afghanistan is one of the few countries in the world whose every frontier divides peoples speaking the same language and belonging to the same ethnic group or tribe. The question of Pushtunistan became a matter of dispute soon after the British civil servant Durand drew a line through the Pushtun populations of the region in 1893, and it has remained a bitterly contested issue ever since. Afghanistan was the only member of the United Nations to vote against accepting Pakistan, because of the unresolved dispute on its frontiers. Relations between the two countries have, on occasion, verged on open declarations of war. The situation was further exacerbated by the fact that the dominant political party on the Pakistani side of the Durand Line was the staunchly pro-autonomy National Awami Party, a successor of the Khudai Khidmatgars ('Servants of God') organized by Khan Abdul Ghaffar Khan in the thirties, one of the few Muslim organizations which campaigned and fought against imperialism. NAP leaders have always enjoyed friendly relations with successive Afghan governments. The legendary Ghaffar Khan was resident in Kabul for many years, in order to escape repression in Pakistan. His son Wali Khan too was a frequent visitor to the Afghan capital, and was welcomed as a friend by both Zahir Shah and Daud. In terms of language and culture, a Pakistani Pushtun had far more in common with a fellow-Pushtun across the border in Afghanistan than with a Punjabi or Sindhi. Till 1978 there was regular movement to and fro across the Durand Line by tribesmen, and passports and other formalities were usually ignored by officials on both sides.

Daud's rise to total power in 1973 worried Bhutto, who feared a re-enactment of East Bengal's secession. Instead of sanctioning maximum provincial autonomy, and reaching an accommodation with the NAP on a national level, Bhutto sought to imitate the Shah of Iran by effectively declaring war on any notion of meaningful autonomy. Instead he embarked on a concerted offensive in the Pushtun territories. The Tribal Areas in the NWFP comprised a population of 2.5 million Pushtuns, spread over 10,500 square miles of the Pakistani side of the Durand Line. These regions had traditionally been regarded as a kind of no-man's land: even the laws of Pakistan did not apply in the tribal zone. Soon after independence, Jinnah, in a gesture of goodwill, had closed the army camps constructed by British colonialism to monitor and police the tribes, and for twenty-five years the latter were left alone. Then, in 1973, without apparent warning, a change took place. A perceptive political agent (a civil servant in the Curzon tradition), Akbar S. Ahmed, has described what took place:

Then in 1973 Prime Minister Bhutto launched one of the most successful and spectacular economic programmes framed for a tribal people. Suddenly schools and dispensaries were being constructed in areas which could not boast a single cement building. Suddenly tractors and bulldozers worked in areas that had never seen even a bicycle. Suddenly roads were pushing their way through hitherto inaccessible areas and tribes ... The high point of the present tribal policy was surely the reactivation of the Razmak camp, which was carried out in the face of misgivings and many gloomy predictions ... This was one of the most remarkable strategic moves in the Frontier, in that it was conducted from start to finish without a single shot being fired, a clear enough indication that for the tribes such moves were a matter of government policy and not a threat to their structure or existence.[3]

What is surprising in Ahmed's account is that it contains only two references to Afghanistan in eighty pages, a remarkable feat of bureaucratic amnesia even by Pakistani standards. Nor is it true that not 'a single shot' was fired: there was a serious attempt to dynamite Bhutto during one of his visits to the region in 1976; the prime minister survived by pure chance, while a civil servant accompanying him was killed.

It is odd that a civil servant of Ahmed's intelligence should fail to mention that the drive towards superficial modernization of the Tribal Areas was clearly prompted by the overthrow of the monarchy in neighbouring Afghanistan. It was part of a strategic military offensive designed to destabilize Daud. That is why the Razmak camp in South Waziristan was reactivated, and that also explains the desperate rush to construct new roads and improve communications. The high command in Islamabad was determined to forestall a 'Pathandesh' on its northern frontiers. Bhutto's 'forward policy' was designed, by putting maximum pressure on Kabul, to permanently foreclose the Pushtunistan issue. A tribal revolt which erupted on 21 July 1975 in the Panjsher valley north of Kabul was planned and executed by Afghan exiles financed and armed by Islamabad.[4] In the event, the operation was crushed by the Afghan army and there was no mass popular uprising; none the less, the threat jolted Daud into action. He agreed to a three-cornered deal involving himself, Bhutto and the Shah of Iran. It was agreed that, in return for Daud's approval of the Durand Line as a permanent frontier, Bhutto would release the Pushtun leaders of the NAP, while the Shah would provide up to 3 billion dollars in aid. If Daud were to renege on this agreement, Bhutto warned, then Pakistan might not be able to control the activities of Afghan exiles operating from the NWFP.

After Bhutto's ill-fated elections led to the July 1977 coup d'état,

Islamabad's Afghan policy was in ruins. The Shah, however, continued to show a keen interest in Afghanistan, and SAVAK agents were provided to help Daud deal with the left and with dissent in general. The Shah pressed Daud on both the internal and the external front: inside the country, the Iranian dictator favoured institutionalized repression on the Iranian model; externally, he wanted Daud to ease links with the USSR and 'tilt' towards the West. The first result of the Shah's influence was the assassination of a popular PDPA leader, on 18 April 1978. Mir Akbar Khyber was a university professor respected by both wings of the reunited PDPA. His funeral turned into a mass demonstration, and Daud embarked on full-scale repression. SAVAK advisers recommended that the PDPA leadership be physically eliminated. Arrests of PDPA leaders did not provoke any great urban unrest, but the organization implemented plans to utilize its base in the armed forces to topple the Daud dictatorship. This was achieved with remarkable ease on 27 April. Daud was executed. The mass celebrations that took place in Kabul the following day indicated that the coup was popular. Contrary to later Western mythology, the Soviet Union was caught complete'y unawares, as was Washington. This was hardly surprising, since the objective basis for the coup had been prepared by Teheran rather than Moscow.[5]

The two factions of Afghan communism comprising the PDPA were subsequently to falsify their own history. Noor Mohammed Taraki, who became Chairman of the Revolutionary Council, was to claim 50,000 members for the party. The real figure was more like 4,000, and consisted exclusively of the urban petty bourgeoisie: teachers, lawyers, government servants and army officers constituted the vast majority of members. Taraki and foreign minister Hafizullah Amin represented the *Khalq* faction, while vice-president Babrak Karmal was the main leader of *Parcham*. The central problem confronting the new régime was a consequence of the method whereby the PDPA had seized power. Bonapartism has long been regarded as a crime in the Marxist classics; yet what the PDPA insisted on christening the Saur (April) Revolution was nothing but a glorified military coup. A necessary defensive act against those plotting massive repression, certainly; a revolution, by no means. All social revolutions are the extreme manifestations of social and class conflicts, regardless of whether those who push them through are aware of the fact or not. Social classes provide the motor force for every revolution, even though the actions of political parties or movements at the head of these classes may determine its success. In refusing to acknowledge this basic fact, the *Khalq* faction which organized the coup deliberately sought to shield itself from reality. What was particularly repulsive was its attempt to portray a defensive military coup as a model for other backward countries. Amin's braggadocio reached absur

> Prior to our revolution, the working class everywhere wanted to
> the footprints of the Great October Revolution. However, after the Great
> Saur Revolution the toilers should know that there does exist a short-cut
> which can transfer the power from the feudal class to the working class –
> and our revolution proved it.[6]

The first six months of the new régime did arouse the hopes and expecta-
tions of the people in both town and countryside. The rhetoric of the
Revolutionary Council was couched in radical–democratic reformist phras-
eology. Taraki's insistence that the official media use the languages of the
minority nationalities did much to offset the grey jargon contained in the
Kabul Times. The political formation and ideological training of the PDPA,
however, soon emerged as a tremendous obstacle. The *Khalq* refused to
tolerate the rival *Parcham* faction, and a ferocious inner-party struggle
resulted in a giant purge. Babrak Karmal and his associates were removed
from all government positions and sent off as ambassadors to various
Eastern European states (Karmal himself was posted to Prague). The coup-
makers who had overthrown Daud had promised democracy and reforms
to the people. The purge inside the PDPA, however, was a sorry symbol of
the monolithism that was to envelop the entire country.

In our opinion, reforms were only possible within the framework of
political democracy, with all allowances made for local conditions. It had
been argued that the PDPA's use of brutality within its ranks was a reflection of Afghan backwardness and the predominance of a tribal culture.[7]
This is at least partly true. But communists or Marxists form political
organizations precisely in order to challenge existing reality, on every
level. The reasons for the failure were more complex: it was a combination of Stalinist ideology and Afghan backwardness which produced the
Khalq mutation. A distinguishing hallmark of Stalinism is its substitu-
tionist equation of party and class, which leads to an equation of the
central committee with the party, and subsequently of the general secretary with the central committee. The common people are essentially viewed
as objects to be manipulated: their role is to be the active and willing
instruments of authoritarian party decisions. Monolithism is, therefore,
not an irrationality, but a necessary concomitant of Stalinist political
practice.

The crucial weakness in the PDPA armoury was its total lack of equipment on the question of democratic institutions and democratic rights. The
régime lacked popular legitimacy, since it was the product not of a revolution, but of a coup d'état. Its first task was therefore on the political plane.
It needed a Constituent Assembly elected on the basis of universal adult

suffrage to prepare a new Constitution. It should have permitted the flowering of different political ideas and currents, and utilized this period for taking its plan for rural reforms to the overwhelming majority of the population in the countryside. The one political leader and theoretician within classical Marxism whose writings had discussed such problems was Trotsky; but he, of course, had been anathematized within the official communist movement. Trotsky had written some comments on China which were, in fact, more applicable to contemporary Afghanistan:

> The stage of democracy has a great importance in the evolution of the masses. Under definite conditions, the revolution can allow the proletariat to pass beyond this stage. But it is precisely to facilitate this future development, which is not at all easy and not at all guaranteed to be successful in advance, that it is necessary to utilize to the fullest the inter-revolutionary period to exhaust the democratic resources of the bourgeoisie. This can be done by developing democracy before the broad masses and by compelling the bourgeoisie to place itself in contradiction to them at each step.[8]

Afghanistan was in some ways fortunate. It did not possess an indigenous or comprador bourgeoisie comparable to those of either India or China. Reaction, as in Amanullah's time, was concentrated in the complex inter-related structures of tribalism and nomadism. A patient, protracted *political* struggle was required to win over the masses. Such a struggle necessitated an elected assembly. This would have provided both an approximation of the relationship of social forces, and an arena within which political debates could be conducted. Of course, there was every possibility that the clergy and tribal chiefs (many of whom doubled as landlords) would have resisted all attempts to establish an electoral register and organize an election. But in these circumstances the PDPA régime would have been much better placed to wage an armed struggle.

The *Khalq* leaders, however, gave no thought to this question. They pushed through a series of radical land reforms *without* any serious infrastructure to ensure local support (as was to be admitted by a strong partisan of the PDPA, after the fall of Amin[9]). Instead of a political strategy designed to awaken the rural masses and permit the urban dwellers to speak for themselves, Hafizullah Amin, the *Khalq* strongman, who became prime minister in March 1979, devised a plan which achieved the exact opposite. The slogan which defined the *Khalq*'s political orientation was simple: '98 per cent support our reforms, but 2 per cent [the exploiters] oppose them.' The solution was equally simple: the 2 per cent had to be physically eliminated. The method and manner of implementing reforms from above was thus bound to provoke an explosion from below.

It is true that the tribal leaders and clerics opposed to the reforms were receiving aid from Pakistan, China and Egypt. However, such aid was not decisive; hardly of the sort that could have tipped the internal balance in Afghanistan, in any event. What was crucial for Afghani reaction was the fact that it could depend on a growing pool of mass support in *both* town and countryside. In other words, the majority of Afghanistan's population refused to accept that it had any stake whatsoever in the reforms proposed by the PDPA régime. This, by itself, constituted an incredible indictment of a régime which claimed to have made a revolution. The Cuban revolution has demonstrated that outside intervention, economic blockades or assassination attempts against leaders can impede advance, but they cannot topple a popular leadership. Cuba was also disadvantaged in that its geographical location placed it off the shores of its mortal enemy, the United States of America. Despite all this, the régime of Castro could not be overthrown. Even more strikingly half a million American soldiers backed by horrendous fire-power failed to defeat the Vietnamese communists. The Afghan PDPA leaders had come to office through unorthodox methods, without a real popular base; but it was their unwillingness even to recognize this fact which made it so difficult for them to overcome their weaknesses and win mass support.

Amin's repression was felt first by the rival *Parcham* supporters, then by the Afghan people as a whole, and finally – as the situation worsened in early 1979, with mutinies inside the army and risings in a number of towns – by opponents within his own faction. A shoot-out at the presidential palace in September 1979 resulted in the elimination of President Taraki,[10] and the consolidation of Amin's position now as a virtual dictator. There can be little doubt that the Taraki–Amin shoot-out was provoked by a Soviet attempt to get rid of the latter. There were over 5,000 Soviet 'advisers' in Afghanistan at this stage, fighting with the Afghan army against the diverse insurgent forces, since Kabul itself was clearly incapable (politically or militarily) of defeating the rebellion. Soviet pilots assisted in often indiscriminate raids on numerous villages, in an attempt to demoralize and weaken the base of the opposition; but senior Soviet advisers undoubtedly recognized that the situation was hopeless on virtually every front. The decision to overthrow Amin was intended to reverse the process of repression and rebellion in Afghanistan: the plan, however, obviously backfired.

Amin was not unaware of Soviet machinations. He had a number of grudges against the Brezhnev leadership. Moscow had given asylum to Babrak Karmal, his main rival, following the *Parcham* leader's peremptory dismissal as Afghan ambassador in Prague. Amin had criticized the Soviet Union obliquely in May 1979 for giving 'shelter to the enemies of the working class in its territory'. He had refused to visit Moscow for direct talks, and had demanded that Moscow withdraw its ambassador, Alexander Puzanov, from Kabul.[11] It is possible that he was actually considering a break with Moscow, via a deal with China – and thus indirectly with the United States and the West. In fact, he had few alternatives, given that he was at the head of a hated and isolated régime internally and now also on the hit-list of the Soviet Politburo. Amin's only base was among a rapidly diminishing group of PDPA *Khalqi* cadres, and in the armed forces. His secret service was not as powerful as he had thought, since its personnel were adept at shifting allegiances (a characteristic of many intelligence agencies in the colonial and semi-colonial world).

The Soviet decision to intervene in Afghanistan was taken some time after a visit to the country in April 1979 by a top Soviet delegation led by General Alexei Yepishev, First Deputy Minister of Defence and President of Political Affairs of the Soviet army and navy.[12] Yepishev is a self-acknowledged Stalinist and architect of the invasion of Czechoslovakia in August 1968. His visit was designed to gain a first-hand assessment of the situation in the field, before preparing a detailed plan of action. Yepishev is well-known in Eastern Europe as the figure in the Stalinist Apocalypse who symbolizes death and destruction. He visited Prague prior to the entry of Soviet tanks, and was a guest of General Jaruzelski in Poland three months before the imposition of martial law. The Yepishev Plan was approved by the Politburo after a long debate: Brezhnev admitted that 'it was no easy decision', and was only taken after the Central Committee had taken into account 'all the relevant circumstances'.

On 27 December 1979, tens of thousands of Soviet combat troops crossed the Oxus River (Amu Darya), which forms the Soviet–Afghan border, and embarked on a military occupation of the country. The Soviet Union initially claimed that they had been invited by Amin and the PDPA; but Amin was reported dead soon after the Russian troops arrived (together with a KGB general, Victor Paputin). Within a few weeks, the new Afghan leader, Babrak Karmal, who together with the bulk of his cabinet had been transported to Kabul in Soviet planes, was to denounce Hafizullah Amin as an 'agent of the CIA'. Neither Karmal nor the Soviet press provided any details to substantiate this. If the charge was true, then it was necessary to ask how long Amin had worked for the CIA. This was not an unimportant question, given Amin's key role as the chief liaison between the PDPA and its military cells prior to the April 1978 coup. If Amin had been recruited before then, the implication would be that what Karmal still refers to as the 'April Revolution' was in fact a dastardly plot manufactured in Washington! But the allegation can best be treated as belonging to the characteristic bureaucratic code whereby opponents are denounced as agents of foreign powers – a procedure whose genealogy can be traced without difficulty to the Soviet purges and show-trials of the thirties.

A much more fundamental question was why the Soviet Union had intervened militarily outside Eastern Europe for the first time since the Second World War. The answer did not lie in the mountains of Afghanistan. It would be wrong to perceive the Soviet move as motivated by anything so trifling as the situation in that country. The top Soviet politicians, and in particular the Soviet generals, are extremely cautious men. A fundamental bureaucratic conservatism underlies their actions, internally and externally. The view, common among politicians and political columnists in North America and Western Europe, that the Soviet Union is an aggressive power, hell-bent on expansion, is far from the truth. In its essence, Soviet foreign policy since the late twenties and thirties has been dominated by one over-riding concern: the preservation of stability and the status quo inside the USSR. At the end of the Second World War, the Soviet leaders refrained from taking advantage of the break-down of the capitalist system in France, Italy and Greece. They adhered faithfully to the Yalta Agreement, which divided Europe into 'spheres of influence'. It is true that the Yugoslav partisans refused to accept any deal and pushed through a process of re-volution; but that was hardly the responsibility of Stalin.[13] The Cold War of the late forties and fifties was, in many ways, a response to the crisis of colonialism in Asia: Vietnam (1945), Korea (1945) and China (1949) saw the outbreak of social upheavals that threatened Western hegemony in the region. The United States responded by putting pressure on the USSR in the West. Then, in the sixties, a new 'spirit of détente' was generated, as a consequence of which the Soviet Union maintained friendly relations and did not embarrass the United States throughout the period of the latter's military intervention in Vietnam. There were both political and economic reasons for what the Brezhnev–Nixon joint communiqué referred to as a 'new era of collaboration'.

Post-war Soviet foreign policy has, in its own fashion, attempted to mimic the United States. In seeking to win over third-world states, the Soviet Union has provided military and economic aid to large numbers of régimes in Asia, Latin America and Africa whose social systems were far removed from any form of socialism. The difference between Soviet and US foreign policy, however, remains crucial. Washington is the policeman of the world, seeing its main function as to prevent social revolution anywhere. Its strategic war cry can be summed up by inverting a well-known formula: 'Permanent Counter-revolution'. This gives US policy a political coherence and concrete aims, which its Soviet counterpart lacks. Attempts to expand the influence of the USSR have been motivated by purely nationalist considera-tions. The Soviet foreign minister, veteran Politburo member Andrei Gromyko, once defined his country's policy in the following crisp sentences:

Our foreign policy is and will continue to be characterized by resoluteness in defending the state interests of the Soviet people, in safeguarding the inviolability of our land frontiers, maritime coasts and air space, and in protecting the dignity of the Soviet flag and the rights and security of Soviet citizens.[14]

This is a far cry indeed from the declarations of the early Comintern, or the aspirations of the delegates attending the anti-imperialist congress at Baku in 1920. It is, however, far closer to the truth than the fantasies advanced by the State Department in Washington. Gromyko's forthright declaration also exposes the vacuity of a new breed of Western fellow-travellers, many of them ex-Maoists, who attempt to provide a radical cover to Soviet foreign policy. Finally, it is a refreshing change from the vapid outpourings of Soviet foreign-policy experts seeking vainly to reconcile bureaucratic nationalism with lip-service to the traditions of Bolshevism.

This foray into basic Soviet aims is not irrelevant, if we are interested in unravelling the real reasons for the Kremlin's military intervention in Afghanistan. In our opinion, these can only be grasped within the overall context of the changes in world politics over the preceding two decades. It is, of course, impossible adequately to discuss these important changes and shifts in alliances and perceptions, in the course of this study on Pakistan. We can only refer here to the pivotal transformations, in order to develop our argument in relation to South Asia.

The fall of Saigon in 1975 signalled a politico-military humiliation unprecedented in the annals of US history. In that sense, it marked a turning-point in world politics. The impact of this victory, however, was blunted. The Sino-US *rapprochement* had helped to lessen the isolation of the United States in Asia (and also in Africa). The emergence of Pol Pot as a *sui generis* Stalinist chieftain in Kampuchea was an unmitigated disaster, both for the people of Kampuchea (who suffered the most) and for the hitherto powerful attraction exercised by the Indo-Chinese revolution. The Vietnamese intervention in Kampuchea and the Sino-Vietnamese war could only engender further confusion. The Peking–Washington axis became the central obsession of the Soviet leadership, which not surprisingly perceived it as directed against the Soviet Union.

The result was a shift in Soviet foreign policy. Without breaking from the general framework of détente, the Russian leaders sought to extend their influence (in traditional big-power terms) wherever and whenever they had the opportunity. However, it must not be forgotten that this was occasioned by Washington's determination to reverse the political repercussions of the defeat in Vietnam. The American counter-offensive led to non-ratification of the Salt 2 agreements, the decision to site Cruise missiles in Western Europe, and an undisguised relaunching of the arms race. This development was accelerated after the fall of the Shah. Within the span of five years, the United States had lost the use of two giant military machines in South Vietnam and Iran. The Sandinista victory in Nicaragua, in July 1979, only compounded the siege mentality that was beginning to develop in Washington. Reagan's election a year later was, in part, the fatal consequence of this mood.

In this context, the Soviet political and military leaders felt that not all that much was to be lost by a direct military intervention in Afghanistan. They saw no reason why they should not benefit from the weakness of the United States in the region, following the overthrow of the Shah. The decision to intervene was taken by Moscow and Moscow alone. It was designed to preserve a régime closely linked to the USSR and to prevent the emergence of a government more friendly to Peking or Washington. Though official Soviet propaganda explained the Kremlin's reasons for invading a sovereign state as a response to 'foreign interference', the actual purpose was to remove Amin and replace him with a more pliant politician. Babrak Karmal's first speech was characteristic: 'Today is the breaking of the machine of torture of Amin and his henchmen, wild butchers, usurpers and murderers of tens of thousands of our countrymen, fathers, mothers, brothers, sisters, sons and daughters, children and old people.'[15] The fact that some of the henchmen were included in Karmal's new government must have weakened the impact of the verbal assaults on his predecessor's crimes. Though the release of thousands of political prisoners was undoubtedly popular, all the old problems in fact remained. Karmal pledged not to practise socialism, to abolish all anti-democratic laws, to respect Islam and to permit political parties to function. From this, it would appear that the Russians hoped to establish a national coalition government and restore the *status quo ante*, though with an increased role for themselves. Such a view displayed complete naïvety. To imagine that the Afghan people would rush to welcome Karmal as a 'liberator', when he arrived with 100,000 Soviet troops, was a dangerous misreading of the real situation. In fact, the Soviet invasion was wrong on every count.

There can be little doubt that the Soviet intervention in Afghanistan was a gross violation of the right of the Afghan people to national self-determination. This right cannot be abrogated simply because the Afghan masses have stubbornly refused to support the PDPA. Moreover, it should be pointed out that the entry of Soviet troops was not even requested by a majority of the PDPA. There is thus no analogy with the military aid provided by the Cubans to Angola and Ethiopia.[16] Nor can it seriously be argued that the Kremlin's decision to occupy Afghanistan was a defensive measure, vital to the security of the Soviet state. The USSR has coexisted satisfactorily with virtually every government in Afghanistan since the twenties. It maintained friendly relations with the Shah, despite the fact that Iran under his rule was the largest US base in that region. The existence of NATO bases in Turkey has not led to a military invasion of that country.

In fact, the entry of Soviet troops further weakened the PDPA régime. Its political credibility reached an all-time low, and it resorted once again to repression. Karmal and his colleagues are regarded by the overwhelming majority of Afghans as 'quislings'. The result is hardly surprising. The Russian presence has united the vast majority of Afghanistan's citizens, despite political, religious or ethnic differences. Apart from the Karmal faction of the PDPA and its tiny network of supporters, almost everyone is hostile to the occupying forces, including even a layer of the *Khalq*. Those sectors of the population in the towns which were previously neutral, or even sympathetic to the PDPA, are now inclined to favour any resistance to the régime. The results of the invasion on the political front have thus been catastrophic for the Afghan left. Despite its total halting of the reforms and its cynical utilization of Islam,[17] the Karmal régime has not been able to establish any legitimacy.

The argument that the Soviet Union and its supporters regard as central to their case is the fact that the resistance is receiving outside backing. They point to the refugee camps in Pakistan, and insist that Zia's régime is training the guerrillas. This is true, but does not resolve the real problem, which is lack of support inside the country. If the PDPA, which comprises several thousand members and sympathizers at most, were an organization based on some degree of mass mobilization (like the South Yemenis in the early sixties, the Angolans and Ethiopians in the seventies, or the Nicaraguans and El Salvadorean FMLN today) it would be able to deal with the Peshawar-based reactionary groups. The key to the impasse does not lie in Peshawar, but in Kabul. The resistance which is active inside the country functions with its own rules, and is largely autonomous of the Peshawar organizations.

Since the Soviet invasion the Western press, following the lead of the government-controlled media in Pakistan, had published wildly exaggerated reports of rebel activity.[18] Most of these can easily be discounted, yet the reality remains different from that portrayed by propaganda handouts distributed in Kabul. What is beyond dispute is that there have been semi-uprisings in Kandahar and Herat; student demonstrations in Kabul; mutinies inside the Afghan army, followed by substantial desertions and the emergence of small but influential left-wing groupings inside the resistance. Within the country, those opposing the occupation acquire their weapons from the enemy. They have also found it necessary to resort to traditional guerrilla tactics, favoured by the terrain and by the fact that the cities are well patrolled. In June 1980, *Pravda* described the guerrilla methods as follows:

> The Afghan rebels have reduced the size of individual fighting units to 30–40 men, and they like to use ambushes at bridges and narrow places ... They blow up a bridge or create an avalanche, and then open fire from high terrain ... If a strong military column is passing, they let the reconnaissance and advance units through. Then they open fire suddenly and with close aim, and scatter quickly ... They mine roads, and then set up rifle and machine-gun cover of the mined area. One can feel the hand of professional foreign instructors.[19]

The last sentence quoted above is clearly designed to explain away the effectiveness of the resistance. The experience of guerrilla war throughout history reveals that, if a movement has real support, then the masses learn very quickly. Even if Pakistan sealed off its border with Afghanistan and prevented the Peshawar-based organizations from operating, the resistance inside the country would not disappear.

Moscow's political position is almost untenable. They have told friendly régimes that, once the Karmal government is able to secure its base and police the country on its own, then the Soviet Union will withdraw. This could only be an argument for a permanent occupation – which one doubts is a serious possibility for either the Politburo or the army chiefs, who between them dominate Soviet politics. In fact, the longer the Soviet soldiers remain, the greater the chances of a massive internal resistance developing and ultimately confronting the Russians with a hard choice: large-scale massacres (which have hitherto been avoided) or withdrawal. While the Western press has concentrated on the extreme right-wing Peshawar-based groups, those who had been following developments in South Asia for many years prior to the Russian invasion have concentrated on the resistance that has developed inside the country. Lawrence Lifschultz, a South Asian specialist for the *Far Eastern Economic Review*, has described the left-wing groups operating against the Russians:

> Among the various local internal fronts is woven another, more national, organization that links several resistance groups. It is called the Jebheye Mobarizin Mujahid-i-Afghanistan, which roughly translated means the National Front of Militant Combatants. It was this organization which staged the Bala Hisar mutiny in the Kabul garrison on 6 August 1979. Several leftist organizations are operating within this front and in individual capacities within various regional fronts. These are all organizations which took a critical attitude to the Soviet Union and the

Khalq (Masses) and Parcham (Flag) wings of the PDPA during the various debates on 'revisionism' which swirled through Afghani leftist intellectual circles in the late 1960s and 1970s. Another internal resistance group is the Sazman-e-Azadbaksh Mardom-e-Afghanistan (SAMA, Organization for the Liberation of the Peoples of Afghanistan) which is linked to a number of internal fronts. Still another is the Grohe-Inquilabi-Khalqaie Afghanistan (the Revolutionary Group of Afghanistan), which also remains extremely active in the anti-Soviet resistance, particularly in various rural areas. SAMA members appear to be most active in Kabul and other urban centres. Lastly, another Marxist tendency which never regarded itself as either pro-Peking or pro-Moscow, called Millat (The Nation), remains an active element in the present resistance. While a number of these anti-Soviet Marxist tendencies are active within the various internally based united fronts, none can be said to be taking an openly leading role. Given the reputation the Khalq, the Parcham, and the Soviet Army have collectively given the word socialism in Afghanistan over the past year, they recognize it will be quite some time before their concepts can again be discussed in anything like a positive context.[20]

The resistance, like most guerrilla formations during an early stage of development and clarification, is at its weakest during pitched frontal battles. One such clash, the battle of Panjshir Valley, which took place in March 1982, resulted in heavy casualties for the rebels as the Soviet army brought in its heavy artillery and air cavalry. Several hundred civilians and guerrillas were killed, and several hundred captured. But the Russians are perfectly well aware that they have to make decisive gains on the political field as well. Here they are reviving the time-honoured ruses and strategies of British imperialism. The government department to which the Russians pay the most attention is the Ministry of Tribes and Nationalities, where the key figure is Najibullah, the head of Afghan Intelligence, who works under the direction of his Soviet superiors. The main function of this ministry is to win tribal support. This is attempted by extending lavish financial aid and patronage on the old English model, while developing a youth volunteer corps to provide a network of informers in the countryside. The ministry has had some limited successes, but few believe that such methods can guarantee even a temporary stability.

While the Soviet Union is totally wrong to imagine that the internal resistance would disappear without external aid, it does have truth on its side when it maintains that the United States is not interested in a settlement in Afghanistan. Western interest in Afghanistan postdates the Soviet invasion. Prior to the crossing of the Oxus River by the Russians, no concern with the fate of the country or its people was expressed by Western leaders. Since December 1979, indeed, more books have been published and articles written about Afghanistan than in the entire two centuries and more since the country was first established. It would be difficult to claim that US interest in contemporary Afghanistan is motivated by anything other than a desire to see the Soviet army held down by tribal warriors and humiliated before the entire third world. In that sense, the Indian prime minister Indira Gandhi has been quite right to deny flatly that the United States was interested in an early settlement of the dispute. The Pentagon and State Department are not unaware of the fact that continued Soviet involvement in South Asia makes their own intervention in Central America much easier. The international situation, in that regard, makes a Soviet withdrawal much more difficult.

Some have argued that if Soviet forces returned to their country, there would be serious danger of a bloodbath of PDPA leaders and supporters. This danger can certainly not be discounted – though, given the relatively small number of party members and sympathizers, it would not be difficult for them to be given temporary exile in Soviet Central Asia, until conditions were ready for their return. But the more important aspect of the problem, in our opinion, has generally been ignored. It is by no means certain that, in the event of a Soviet withdrawal, it is the Peshawar-based fundamentalist groups which would form the government. What is equally possible is that the Afghan army would emerge as the immediate guarantor of stability and would aid the formation of a national government composed largely of ethnic and political groups based inside the country. The inability of the right-wing opposition to unite despite the Russian occupation is, in itself, an interesting reflection on the endemic political instability and inter-group rivalry that afflicts these organizations, with Iran and Saudi Arabia providing alternative poles of attraction. It is likely that whatever government comes to power in Kabul following a Soviet retreat would not win the support of progressive liberals, enlightened social-democrats or socialists anywhere in the world. This may be unpalatable to some, and quite unacceptable to others, but the lessons are still clear: there can be no short-cuts to socialism. Mass support has to be an essential ingredient. The Afghan people must be permitted to elect and choose their own government. Experience is the best educator of oppressed peoples.

Some writers have evoked another scenario. Fred Halliday, for instance, has written: 'In Afghanistan itself events alone will show whether Russia's gamble can in the long run succeed, producing the sort of social advance now seen in Mongolia, where the Communist régime was established in 1921 by comparably direct military intervention in support of a small revolutionary movement.' True, this is one possible option, but in our view it is far-fetched. There is very little comparison between Soviet policy towards Outer Mongolia in the twenties and today in Afghanistan. We might allude to several crucial differences:

– The Soviet régime in 1921 was qualitatively different from the present-day bureaucracy. Even the most hostile anti-Soviet scholars in the West admit that the Communist International was not just a Great Russian manoeuvre designed to facilitate world conquest, but rather an instrument for achieving social change on a global scale. Lenin's advice to the Mongolian revolutionaries was extremely sober and cautious: 'The revolutionaries will have to put in a good deal of work in developing state, economic and cultural activities before the herdsman elements become a proletarian mass ...' (*Collected Works*, vol. 42, Moscow, 1969, pp. 360–61)

– In 1921, the infant Soviet Republic was immersed in a civil war in which the counter-revolution had the active support of the major capitalist powers. Baron Roman von Ungern-Sternberg, a general of the White armies notorious for his sadism and cruelty, had taken his forces with him into Mongolia. The aim of the operation was to form an anti-Bolshevik alliance with Mongolia as a base. Mongolia itself was governed by a tribal autocrat, Bogd Khan, who was incapable of resisting the White invasion. To complicate matters further, there was a Chinese army also present in the region.

– Despite all this, the Soviet Union avoided military intervention in Mongolia until the very last. It first sought to reach an accommodation with the Chinese, and pledged to respect Mongolia's buffer status, provided the Chinese turned their fire on Ungern's crazed Cossacks and rid Mongolia of all forms of autocracy. It was only when the Chinese armies proved incapable of the task that Red Army units crossed into Mongolia in June 1921, in order to defeat the Whites and provide vital aid to the Mongolian partisans in their fight against the Chinese.[21] The troops stayed in the country for four years.

The analogy with Afghanistan in 1979 is, therefore, false on virtually every level. The political orientation of the Russians in Afghanistan today has far more in common with the attempt of a big power to preserve its influence in a semi-colonial country than it does with the Soviet response to events in Outer Mongolia in 1921. It is true that the Russians are militarily capable of assimilating Afghanistan into the Soviet bloc; but the price would be too high both inside the USSR and on a world scale. It would be a big risk for the Kremlin leaders, for they might thereby unwittingly import political instability into the very heart of the Union of Soviet Socialist Republics.

In Pakistan, the main impact of these events has been to strengthen the military régime of Zia-ul-Haq, and to aid those who are arguing for the army to have a semi-permanent Turkish-style presence in the political life of the country. The million or more Afghan refugees are being used by Islamabad to bolster its standing in the Gulf States and Washington. On a more fundamental level, however, the débâcle in Afghanistan has had extremely negative effects on mass consciousness in the North-West Frontier Province. While the Zia régime remains unpopular, and there is growing resentment against the more privileged sections of the Afghan refugees, the mood is one of resignation and despair. A different outcome in Afghanistan could have led to serious repercussions in the region: a slow movement towards socio-economic reform, coupled with political democracy and a meaningful autonomy for all ethnic minorities, would undoubtedly have aroused the hopes and aspirations of Pakistan's Pushtuns. The contrast with their own existence under a strongly centralist military régime would have been obvious to the inhabitants of every rural centre. This, however, was not to be. The disastrous experience of PDPA power was followed by direct Soviet intervention. This was hardly an inducement to self-activity by the Pushtuns of the NWFP. The results are visible: it is the army and its rule that has benefited from the misadventure in Afghanistan.

The Fall of the Shah, Islamic Despotism and the Future of Iran

The overthrow of the Pahlavi dynasty in Iran marked a watershed in world politics. In economic, military and political terms, the fall of the Shah was a devastating blow against imperialist strategy for the region. Economically, Iran was a major producer of oil; militarily, it was the strongest relay of the United States in a vital zone; politically, the fact that the régime had lasted for over three decades enabled it to influence events throughout the region. The combination of circumstances which led to the birth of a mass movement that ultimately toppled the Iranian monarch has been described and analysed in detail elsewhere.[22] The gigantic insurrection in Teheran in February 1979 was conclusive proof of the Marxist assertion that a conscious mass can defeat powerful armies. Indeed, the most remarkable feature of Iranian politics prior to the Shah's fall in February was the breadth of mass mobilizations, which exceeded *in numbers* the strength even of the movement in China prior to the 1949 social revolution. The courage, consistency and audacity of the ordinary people of Iran were the decisive factors in defeating a régime that had prided itself on its political stability and military strength. There can be no doubt that the United States and the West suffered a severe political shock.

The Shah's interference in the internal political life of Afghanistan and Pakistan had won him few friends in either country. His collapse was generally greeted as a victory by the people throughout the region. Despite his public relations façade, Pahlavi was a tyrant who exercised power on the basis of a torture machine which had no rival till the 1973 coup in Chile. The Shah's secret police, SAVAK, was known and feared by Iranians inside and outside the country. SAVAK also helped to train torturers from Pakistan and the Gulf states.[23] The lesson was obvious, both for the Pentagon and for those under the iron heel in other parts of the world. If the Iranians could get rid of their dictator, why not the Guatemalans or the Pakistanis, the masses in Zaïre or Chile? The Iranian upheaval thus came as an inspiration to oppressed peoples elsewhere in the world. It was different from previous revolts in that the social structure of the country had undergone a significant change: half the population was now based in the towns. Thus the urban character of the uprising left the autocracy with few safety-valves. Despite material aid from the West, tacit support from the Soviet Union and public endorsement by China (Hua Guo-feng visited Teheran at the height of the movement in August 1978), the Iranian monarchy could not resist the tidal wave of growing opposition to its rule. It fell, leaving in its wake a massive political vacuum.

The only force in the country capable of taking over was the Shi'ite clergy. The mosque rather than the factory had been the organizing centre of the popular movement. Once it had established its political hegemony over the movement, the workers in the factories accepted the leadership of the clergy. Internationally the left had tended seriously to underestimate the role and ideological importance of the clerical hierarchy. It was assumed that Ayatollah Khomeini, the acknowledged leader of the anti-Shah movement, was a figurehead who would soon be swept aside by the elemental force of class struggle. Analogies with the 1905 and 1917 revolutions in Russia became a commonplace: Khomeini was at best a Father Gapon, at worst a Kerensky (or possibly even a combination of the two). February 1979 was regarded as the 1905 of the Iranian revolution. The specificity of the revolt was ignored. The consequences of this misanalysis continue to haunt the Iranian left, which, with the exception of a few individuals inside and outside the country, proved quite unable to predict the direction in which the clergy would take the state. As a result, Khomeini was able to outwit, outmanoeuvre and outflank the groups on his left.

'Religion,' wrote Marx, 'is the sigh of the oppressed creature, the heart of a heartless world and the soul of soulless conditions.'[24] He went on to argue that it was utopian to expect the abolition of religion, unless new conditions were created in which the need for such illusions no longer existed. The fact that religion is far from extinguished is a terrible indictment of the failure of those who pledged to change the conditions under which human beings laboured. Only a vulgar Eurocentrist could fail to see that the reversion to Islamic archaism in Iran is not the only instance of the post-1975 religious revivalism. The reception accorded the Pope in post-capitalist Poland and the capitalist United States alike is the other side of the same debased coin. The mistake of the Iranian left and its supporters abroad was to imagine that the hold of the clergy could easily be broken. It has already been pointed out that the left's best chance was lost when it failed to break openly with the clergy and to seek to project an alternative pole, prior to the Shah's overthrow in February 1979. Once the ayatollahs were in power, it was already too late.[25]

The Iranian upheaval was a consequence of the socially disintegrating impact of a one-sided capitalist development, which threatened the small producers and distributors of the bazaar, combined with the desperation of the urban proletariat, fuelled by the demagogic religious rhetoric of Shi'ite agitators. Shi'ism has its origins in the early history of Islam, which was characterized by long periods of civil war. The founders of the Shi'a sect were opposed to a state structure which attempted to base itself on the material realities of the day: commerce and petty-commodity production. The Shi'ites preferred to maintain the old tribal structures and talk about 'heaven'. The military defeat of the sect provided it with martyrs and an ideology which claimed to defend the 'purity' of Islam against the tainted Sunnis. Throughout the two years of struggle that preceded the Shah's downfall, the Shi'ite clergy and their student supporters had dominated the opposition. The bourgeois-nationalist National Front and the pro-Moscow Tudeh Party were largely absent from the scene, unable to play a significant role because they lacked any real base. The Fedayeen and the Mojahideen, the two armed-struggle factions, had prestige and a presence; but they began to differentiate themselves from the clergy only several months after the formation of the 'Islamic government'.

Shi'ite Islam became a material force because it had gripped the masses. Islamic preachers and ideologues did not simply talk about the 'heaven on earth' which would come into existence after their advent to power. They constantly stressed the failure of the other two alternatives which had hitherto had a positive impact on popular consciousness: nationalism and communism. The respective examples of Egypt and Kampuchea were frequently cited as symbols of the ultimate degeneration of the two competing ideologies. So far as socialism was concerned, moreover, neither the Soviet Union nor China had in the decade prior to 1979 encouraged any popular movement against the Shah. The Soviet press had published paeans of praise during Pahlavi's visit to Moscow and when Podgorny returned the honour in Teheran. This cynical display of *Realpolitik* by the two states regarded by millions of people as outposts of socialism could not but indirectly aid the political project of Iran's clergy.

With respect to nationalism, in 1924 the victory of Kemal Ataturk in Turkey had ended the dreams of Pan-Islamism together with the Ottoman empire. In the decades that followed, a modernizing nationalism gained ground and, following the Second World War, achieved a number of victories: Nasser in Egypt, Ben Bella in Algeria, Bourguiba in Tunisia. Of these, Ben Bella's experience was the most illuminating. A struggle broke out between contending groups inside the Algerian National Liberation Front on the future of the revolution. Ben Bella's indecision led to a military coup, which embarked on a Nasserite course: the state would inaugurate reforms from above. No participation from below could be permitted, lest it threaten the new ruling castes. Nasserism undoubtedly pushed through a number of crucial social reforms, but its modernization was of a half-hearted and limited character. The fervent secularism of Ataturk was not institutionalized in Egypt, Algeria or Tunisia. The declarations of their leaders were, more often than not, larded with appeals to religion. Society remained 'a vale of tears of which religion is the halo'. The failure of nationalism fundamentally to alter the living conditions of the people, coupled with a disenchantment with the Stalinist model of socialism, helped to bring about the revival of religion as a political force.

Islam is regarded by its fanatics as a complete and total code of life: politics, economics and private existence are all subsumed under a rigid set of precepts. Shi'ism was defined by its most radical theorist, Ali Shariati, as a 'revolt against history', a movement against the present and the future. The past is glorified, and the early period of Islam regarded as a 'golden age' to be emulated by latter-day believers. There is no place for civil society in this scheme of things. Clearly, such a project is inherently unstable, as Khomeini's Iran has demonstrated in a vivid, if unpleasant, fashion. But it remains a tragedy that the Ayatollah was at first not taken seriously by some of his more capable left-wing opponents. Khomeini had made no secret of his anti-democratic beliefs, expounded in his book *Islamic Government*. It was easy to laugh at this book, and point out that the Imam's preoccupation with bestiality in rural Iran provided no solution to the problems of the masses; certainly, we can all agree that buggering donkeys is a sign of spiritual poverty or repressed sexuality. But Khomeini did not leave matters at that level. He explained his conception of Islamic rule in clear terms:

> Islamic government is the government of laws of God over people. This is the main difference between Islamic government and the constitutional monarchies or republics. That is, in the latter types of government the king or the representatives of the people engage in the act of legislation, while in Islam the legislative power belongs solely to God ... No one else has the right to legislate. No law other than the divine decree can be implemented. For this reason, in the Islamic government instead of a

legislative assembly . . . one has only a planning assembly that arranges the work of different ministries according to Islamic laws.[26]

The iron logic of this 'revolt against history' is thus clear. Only the religious experts, who have spent their entire adult lives interpreting holy laws, have any real place in the administration of society. The masses can only be mobilized to defend these laws and to crush all opposition. Islamic precepts, first formulated during the Middle Ages, have no conception of popular sovereignty. In this, of course, they are not fundamentally different from the doctrines of medieval Christianity, truculently reasserted by the Counter-Reformation (and continued in the theory of papal infallibility). The difference is one of historical time and socio-political evolution. The Catholic Inquisition was followed by the Enlightenment: the greatest of all bourgeois revolutions (France, 1789) was fiercely anti-clerical in character; the birth of the modern nation-state made religion a matter of individual freedom. The world of Islam, however, experienced no bourgeois revolutions. The collapse of the Ottoman empire led to occupation by French and British imperialism. Nationalist upheavals were partial in character. No Islamic state has experienced a social revolution, with the exception of the mountain fastness of Albania. In the age of imperialism, the Islamic countries have stagnated economically, politically and culturally.

The industrialization of Iran was both limited and cruel, increasing exploitation and creating the conditions for a major upheaval. Sixty thousand people died so that the Shah and his régime could be overthrown. Shi'ite ideologues stoked the revolt, but few of those who fought could have imagined that, within three years of the establishment of the Islamic Republic, they would be faced with four million unemployed, an inflation rate fluctuating between 55 and 80 per cent, public floggings for drinking alcohol, execution without trial for political offences, stoning to death for adultery, death for homosexuality, systematic and intensified oppression of women: in short, that a curtain of ignorance, superstition and repression would descend over the entire country. The national minorities too, in particular the Kurds, whose demand for regional autonomy was seen as a mortal threat by the theocracy in Teheran, have been at the receiving end of the Islamic whip since February 1979. Khomeini ordered a military assault on the Kurds, who resisted and fought back, temporarily holding the hounds of the new Inquisition at bay. The Turkomans and Baluch were warned that the Islamic Republic would tolerate no deviants. The hopes for democratic rights that had been aroused among the minorities were crushed within months of the clerical ascendancy to state power.

In August 1979, moreover, all newspapers and weeklies critical of the régime were banned. Fundamentalist Islam fears ideas more than anything else. Its own world is so heavily dominated by medieval ideology that it seeks to establish a monopoly of information, lest creative – and therefore subversive – thought begin to flourish. But of course, ideas never disappear. They go underground and bide their time, like the old mole. So now Khomeini launched a new offensive directed against dissidents and the organized left and anything else that was perceived as a hindrance to the Islamic project. He apologized to God and the people for not having acted earlier:

When we broke down the corrupt régime, and destroyed this very corrupt dam, had we acted in a revolutionary manner from the beginning, had we closed down this hired press, these corrupt magazines, these corrupt papers, had we put their editors on trial, had we banned all these corrupt parties and punished their leaders, had we erected scaffolds for hanging in all major squares, and had we chopped off all the corrupters and the corrupted, we would not have had these troubles today. I beg forgiveness from the almighty God and my dear people . . . Had we been revolutionary, we would not have allowed them to express their existence, we would have banned all parties, we would have banned all fronts, we would have formed only one party, of the *mustaz'afeen* [the oppressed]. I ask for repentance for my mistake, and I declare to these corrupt layers all over Iran, that if they do not sit in their place, we will deal with them in a revolutionary manner . . . like our master Ali . . . who would pull his sword against the *mustakbereen* [the oppressors] and the conspirators, and is said to have beheaded 700 in one day from the Jews of Bani Qarantia, who were like the Israelis and maybe these Israelis are their descendants . . . These conspirators are in the same category as the *kuffar* [infidels], these conspirators in Kurdistan and elsewhere are in the ranks of infidels, they should be dealt with harshly . . . The Prosecutor of the Revolution must close down all magazines which are against the popular will, and are conspirators, he must invite all their writers to court and put them on trial. He is obliged to call upon those who engage in conspiracies and call themselves parties, put the leaders of these parties on trial . . . Those layers of the army who disobey (in suppressing the corrupters and the conspirators) must know that I will deal with them in a revolutionary manner . . . I demand of all layers of the population, of all intellectuals and of all parties and groups, whose number unfortunately now exceeds 200, that they follow the popular path, the path of Islam . . . otherwise they will become the victims of their own wrongdoing . . . Other nations must learn from our movement . . . the people of Afghanistan must learn from Iran . . . We hope that the unity of the world of Muslims will solve the problems of Islam, the problems of Palestine, and those of Afghanistan.[27]

The anti-imperialist rhetoric of the Islamic régime was not based on any concrete measures. Previous revolutionary nationalist and anti-imperialist movements had had something to show in addition to their demagogy: the Bolivian MNR nationalized the tin mines in 1952; Nasser nationalized the Suez Canal in 1956; Nehru pushed through measures designed to safeguard Indian capital from Western encroachments; the Algerian FLN defeated the French colonialists. By contrast with these real encroachments on imperialist interests, we find a theatrical gesture, when one faction of Khomeini's followers sought to gain an advantage by seizing the American Embassy and taking its staff as hostages. The act was meaningless in itself, but served to legitimate the régime by providing it with a 'radical' cover. At the same time, its repercussions on the international level can hardly be described as beneficial for the anti-imperialist cause.

The clash with the United States did not, however, permit the régime to achieve any real stability. The embryonic discontent that was beginning to develop among the population of Teheran and other towns was reflected in conflicts at the top. Bazargan fell because of his critical stance on the hostage issue, and was replaced by Bani Sadr; the latter, however, failed to win the support of the dominant Islamic Republican Party, and was forced in June 1981 to flee the country and take refuge in Paris (where he has joined forces with the Mojahideen and issues calls to overthrow the repressive régime over which he formerly presided). The brunt of the struggle against confessional despotism has been borne by the Kurds, and by the Mojahideen, who have sought to resist the brutal rule of the theocracy. The Fedayeen for their part have split, with a majority adopting the political positions of their old rivals in the Stalinist Tudeh Party. The latter has remained loyal to Khomeini: in his own way, the old fox has after all established a dictatorship whose façade is not too different from its own preferred model. Some of its leaders are no doubt thinking: 'After Khomeini, our turn.' History, however, may have some nasty surprises in store for them.[28]

The clergy has developed its own semi-fascist, characteristically *lumpen*, armed gangs; but it has not been able seriously to dent the power of the army. The moment when the latter could have been disbanded, and a new force rebuilt from top to bottom, was soon after the insurrection of February 1979. The clergy, however, then consciously resisted all such attempts. Since that time, moreover, the relative success of the Iranian armed forces in the conflict unleashed by Iraqi dictator Saddam Hussein has enabled them to recover their former prestige. Most observers are agreed that, after Khomeini's death, the army could become the guarantor of a new stability on the Turkish model (though preserving the Islamic Republic in name).

Such an evolution is likely to be favoured by the United States, which has maintained a significant silence on Iran since the defusing of the hostage issue. Whether the army will in fact be able to hold the ring remains to be seen. Khomeini's rule has not been based just on coercion, but has retained considerable popular backing. A military dictatorship would not be able to count on any such mass support.

The question that remains open is whether the brief experience of a 'pure' Islamic government will have been sufficiently educative to impel the masses towards social-revolutionary goals. It is difficult to answer with certainty. Undoubtedly, the logic of Capital has not been displaced by the archaic revival of medieval laws on usury! Whether or not Iran will move to the left or succumb to a new form of despotism after Khomeini will ultimately depend on the political consciousness and the level of self-activity of the toilers in town and country. If political organizations emerge which are capable of winning support for socialism and democracy (plurality of parties, regular elections based on adult franchise, equal rights for women, full autonomy for the ethnic minorities), then everything could change. But neither the Iranian army nor its backers in the Pentagon should be underestimated.

The operative interests of the United States in Iran are economic, military-strategic and politico-ideological. It is unlikely that the State Department would permit a move to the left in Iran without a major struggle. The instability of contemporary Iran, therefore, betokens an unpredictable future. Whichever direction is finally embarked upon, the effect on Pakistan will be immediate. Shi'ite fundamentalism, by blocking the revolutionary aspirations and self-activity of the masses, has paved the way for the United States to reassert its influence in Iran. Washington will be determined to avoid any triumph of political 'subversion', and to limit the demonstration effect of any change upon Pakistan or the Gulf States. If Iran had avoided a theocracy and instead institutionalized democratic rights and institutions, the position of the Iranian Baluch would have become a magnet for their brethren in Pakistan. On this occasion, too, however, God was on the side of the ungodly. The military rulers in Islamabad must have been delighted that their theocratic counterparts in Teheran were taking a 'firm line' with minority nationalities. But time is not ultimately on the side either of Ayatollah Khalkali, 'butcher' of social, political, cultural and religious dissidents in Iran, or of his Pakistani military equivalents.

Pakistan, India and US Strategy

The strategic importance of South Asia for the West can be gauged by even a cursory look at the map. The area's proximity to the USSR, China and the oil-rich Arab Gulf means that if any of its component states were to 'fall', the resultant political instability in the whole region would be virtually uncontrollable. Soon after Independence, the two major states in the region, India and Pakistan, decided on their international priorities. India advanced the notion of 'positive neutralism' and refused to join the US-sponsored military alliances. Instead, the Indian leader Jawaharlal Nehru attempted to lay the basis for a 'third-world' nationalism that was both anti-imperialist and maintained a healthy distance from the orientations of the Soviet leadership. At the height of the cold war in the fifties, this was a courageous policy and represented something tangible.[29] The alliance of Nehru, Tito and Nasser against the super-powers won them the sympathy of many movements in the colonial and semi-colonial world.

Pakistan, for its part, chose to become a 'bastion of the free world against communism'. The military–bureaucratic complex and its favoured politicians sold their souls to the United States. Pakistan's active membership of SEATO and the Baghdad Pact (later CENTO) meant that it refused to support the Algerian war of independence, and refrained from backing Nasser's nationalization of the Suez Canal. When the Anglo-French-Israeli conspiracy resulted in the military invasion of Egypt in 1956, Pakistan, in effect, backed the old colonial power. (Nehru, by contrast, emerged as the most vociferous opponent of the invasion.) From 1954 to 1965, the United States armed Pakistan and openly infiltrated its armed forces. In response to Indian protests that Pakistan was being armed indiscriminately, the United States assured New Delhi that these arms would not be used in a war against India, but were intended to defend Pakistan against 'communist aggression'. In fact, however, the army has utilized these weapons not only against Baluch and Bengalis within Pakistan, but also on three separate occasions against India. After the 1965 Indo-Pakistan war, the United States did, it is true, cut off military aid. But during the 1970–72 crisis and the civil war in Bengal, Kissinger and Nixon decided that a 'tilt towards Pakistan' was necessary:[30] they preferred the Pakistan army, as a more reliable defender of US interests in the region, to the weak and sickly nationalism of the Awami League.

Not surprisingly, India has perceived Pakistan as, in effect, a large US base, designed to pressure it into itself becoming a pliable, client republic safeguarding Western interests. For there is no doubt that what the United States would really like is a total break between Moscow and New Delhi. In the past, American policy-makers have imagined that Pakistan could be used as a bargaining counter. However, since 1971 successive régimes in Islamabad have been too weak for this purpose, so Washington has devoted much more time and money to improving relations with India. Despite the 'tilt towards Pakistan', the more rational policy-makers in the State Department and serious political analysts have always been aware that India is *the* major state in the region.[31] Militarily, it is one of the strongest states in Asia and has nuclear capability; politically, it is one of the very few former colonial states that has evolved a relatively stable form of bourgeois democracy (which, despite all the economic and political strains, remains the chosen option of the ruling class); economically, it has the advantage of possessing an indigenous capitalist class, which has enabled it to undertake a semi-industrialization and build its own defence industries. India also produces one-third of the entire trained scientific manpower of the capitalist world and has the largest reservoir of skilled manpower outside the United States[32] – all this despite the fact that 50 per cent of the population live in conditions of semi-starvation.

The Afghanistan imbroglio, however, has now resulted in a cowboy administration in Washington throwing caution and State Department rationality to the winds. The decision to equip Pakistan with up-to-date weaponry and resume aid on a massive scale to the military régime is bound to lead to increasing tensions with India. The provision of F-16 aircraft is indeed an open provocation, since it just might encourage Islamabad to embark on an adventure vis-à-vis its powerful Eastern neighbour. The total aid now being earmarked for the rearmament of Pakistan's beleaguered and internally isolated military régime could well exceed the amount handed over during the halcyon years of 1954–65. The question that is posed most sharply is what the United States aims to get out of the new face-lift it is providing for the military junta in Islamabad.

While officialdom in Pakistan is remarkably coy on what has been agreed, American army and navy personnel have made it clear that what the US needs above all is a number of military bases for its Rapid Deployment Force (RDF). Admiral Thomas Moorer, for one, has even specified the name of the port where the US would like a base. In an article in the military magazine *Strategic Review*, Moorer argues for a US naval base to be constructed at the port of Gwadur in Baluchistan. This would replace the facilities which the Americans have lost in Iran, and would be utilized as a major station for policing the Gulf – as well as Pakistan itself. Moorer has also demanded the reopening of the Badaber base near Peshawar, which was used as an electronic surveillance centre in the fifties and sixties. Francis Fukuyama, a State Department strategist, has repeated Moorer's arguments, but suggested that Karachi should be the port utilized. He has also concluded: 'Furthermore, there is the possibility that the Pakistan army could serve as a proxy fighting force in the Gulf . . . provided once again that the United States undertakes to protect Pakistan from the consequences of such a decision.' Discussing the views of Moorer, Fukuyama and their like, Lawrence Lifschultz has analysed the aims of the US administration in an article which has been widely quoted in India. He has written:

> Military strategists within the US administration expect at least three specific operational objectives to be developed from the new agreements. These would all include military base facilities in one form or another. Highest and most immediate priority of all would involve the pre-positioning of vast stockpiles of military equipment and matériel for the US RDF, now the dominant concept for a last-resort style deployment of American power in the region.[33]

This is undoubtedly the desire of military strategists in the United States. However, as Harrison sagely comments, 'it is wishful thinking to assume that the generals now whispering promises to Washington will be in power when and if the anticipated Gulf crisis materializes'.[34]

Divisions in Washington thus appear to have been temporarily decided in favour of repeating all the old mistakes, and the faction in the State Department that would favour an effective confederation between India and Pakistan has suffered a defeat. Its supporters elsewhere, however, have begun to float the idea 'independently'. On 31 October 1981, *The Economist*, in a rare gesture, provided four entire pages to a former lieutenant of Bhutto, Mustafa Khar, now in exile in Britain. Khar advised the Pakistani régime against becoming a total satellite of the United States, stressed its crisis of legitimacy and suggested a long-term deal with India. Khar's article dismissed any reliance on the Muslim world as a utopian dream, attacked a pact with the USSR as unrealistic, and argued that only India could guarantee the present frontiers of Pakistan. These views, as Khar himself noted, were remarkable for a Punjabi politician. The point is, however, they did not fall from the sky. They represent the thinking of an important layer of policy-makers in the United States, and also inside the Pakistani civil service. Khar presented his option as a way of preventing total dependence on the United States, but this involved some sleight of hand, since there can be little doubt that the long-term interests of the USA dictate *one* strong state in South Asia rather than two. India is potentially a far more powerful defender of capitalist interests in the region than either the Shah's Iran was or a military-dominated Pakistan could ever be.

Contrary to the conventional mythology in Pakistan, India does not at all want to encourage a process of Balkanization in South Asia. It is perfectly well aware that a further disintegration of Pakistan would import instability into the Indian Federation itself. On the other hand, it is also aware that a Pakistan on the verge of achieving nuclear weapons is becoming a far more potent threat than hitherto. The temptation to embark on a quick Israeli-style pre-emptive raid to destroy Pakistan's nuclear reprocessing plant at Kahuta must be a serious one for Indian military planners. Khar's initiative could ultimately prove to be a compromise acceptable to all three sides, though it will confront two obstacles – the army and the people – of which the latter at least appears insuperable. For it is possible that Washington, in order to facilitate a larger design, could tame the generals in Islamabad. After all, General Zia has stated:

> We would, of course, dearly love to see a more active participation by the US. But history has taught us not to harbour any illusions on this score. Is America still the leader of the free world? In what respect? I hope it will soon restore its countervailing role, abandoned after Vietnam. There are signs that it is waking up. But so far it's mostly words.[35]

But the intractable problem confronting Pakistan's rulers is that presented by the citizens of the country. If a future civilian government were to push towards confederation, reduce the size of the army and abandon the nuclear project, the old problems of land, bread and freedom would still remain. Who will sustain the country's crisis-ridden economy, defend its antiquated social order and preserve its crumbling political structures? Khar's proposal, in essence, involves replacing the Pakistan army with the Indian army as the guarantor of the status quo in Pakistan itself. The Baluch, Sindhis and Pathans are not likely to tug at the bait: they will clearly reject any solution which institutionalizes their national oppression. None the less, it must be admitted that this remains the only serious bourgeois alternative to an ultimate Balkanization. The very fact that Khar makes the proposal is symbolic: that it is regarded as a serious option in the Pakistani Foreign Office only indicates how deep the crisis of identity has become, and how hard it has hit the ruling élites.[36]

On the other hand, blurred vision and a loss of perspectives could equally well lead to a primordial response to the crisis. There is an important layer within the officer corps which regards Zia-ul-Haq as 'soft': incapable of achieving a final solution of Pakistan's 'fifth column' of intellectuals, poets, professors, teachers, Marxists, trade-unionists and politicians. These officers are admirers of General Pinochet and the Saudi monarchy. A bloodbath on the Chilean model would, in their view, soon 'cleanse' the country of 'impurities'. American military and economic aid is seen as the instrument which could restore discipline and stability, thus providing the army with an extended breathing space. The fools! They are obviously not aware that a decision to reinforce the iron heel of repression would sound the tocsin for Pakistan, which would then move rapidly towards disintegration. The nuclear capability which the generals want, moreover, would only result in a dangerous exacerbation of the crisis.

The Reagan administration (guided by Haig during his period as Secretary of State) has strengthened the most revanchist elements inside the army, with a political short-sightedness that borders on suicide. The CIA has prepared many plans for destabilizing left-wing régimes (some of which have backfired), but the form of destabilization now being introduced in Pakistan is not conscious – in fact, the aim of the operation is the exact opposite, to strengthen the régime and the army which sustains it. But the objective results of so many previous endeavours stares us in the face. Think of the number of indigenous despots who have been choked with American weaponry and money: Thieu in Vietnam, Batista in Cuba, Pahlavi in Iran, Somoza in Nicaragua. The same thing is happening today in El Salvador, and tomorrow we could well see Thailand, Pakistan, Saudi Arabia or Indonesia added to the list of imperialist failures. Now, however, a new and horrifying prospect has emerged with the spread of nuclear weapons to the third world. The colonial and semi-colonial world has been subjected to pillage and plunder for centuries, its inhabitants regularly dehumanized and treated as commodities in the world market. But could it be that History has something still worse in store? Will nuclear weapons be used first in Africa or the Middle East, by the recalcitrant offspring of Western capitalism: Israel or South Africa? Or will the antediluvian generals of South Asia, bedecked with former imperialist medals, try to beat each other to the nuclear draw? These are not abstract questions. Those who arm the military dictators of Pakistan will bear a heavy responsibility for any future political or military catastrophe.

External disaster and internal change have gone hand in hand in Pakistan's short but tortuous history. One military dictator was destroyed by a war with India, a second brought down by a civil war which developed into another war with India. Islamabad is aware of this dialectic. Yet it accepts US aid in the hope of achieving parity with India, at least in the air, and so improving its negotiating position vis-à-vis New Delhi. So when the dictatorship sent its unofficial ambassador, A. K. Brohi, to India to reassure all concerned that Pakistan desired only peace, the envoy's bland assurances did not convince his audience. Moreover, a few sentences uttered by the constitutional lawyer turned Islamic fundamentalist send a real chill down the spine: 'Because of their special relationship, India and Pakistan shall either live together or perish together ... They have to choose between coexistence or no existence.'[37] This may simply be a thoughtless rhetorical flourish, which can safely be ignored. But it may also be a scarcely veiled threat, which conjures up the spectre of mutual nuclear destruction.

Of course, the United States is not actively preparing Pakistan for a quick war against India. On the contrary, it is likely that secret protocols contain assurances by the Pakistani generals to Washington in this regard. Nevertheless, whatever guarantee the United States may have obtained in private, the lessons of the past remain unambiguous: once a state receives technologically advanced military equipment from a super-power, it will use these weapons whenever it sees fit. The donor state cannot in the event determine the conditions under which these weapons will be used. India is naturally not unaware of this fact.

The overriding regional obsession of Washington is not, of course, Afghanistan, but the situation in Iran and the Gulf. The Pentagon's refashioned strategy envisages Pakistan, Turkey, Saudi Arabia and Egypt constituting a powerful safety net of reliable states to maintain the status quo in the Gulf. Zia, Evren, Fahd and Mubarak have been awarded the dubious privilege of serving as the main US gendarmes for the region. But who will police the policemen? Who will protect the dictatorial states which the gendarmes themselves rule? Few serious observers believe that any of these régimes will last out the decade.[38] The problem is a perennial one, and arises from the very nature of US foreign policy, which is based on maintaining the rule of corrupt dictators and landed élites over populations living in penury.

The real tragedy of the situation, as we have indicated earlier, lies in the absence of any countervailing force. The USSR does, it is true, provide aid to many liberation movements, but the conditions it imposes are strict, self-seeking and dependent on the state of US–Soviet relations. China has cynically emulated the USSR, to the point where its foreign policy is now a grim parody of Moscow's. The rulers of both the world's non-capitalist big powers have thus subordinated the internationalist needs of the workers' movements to their own narrow, national caste interests. How the complex pattern of global relationships will unravel in the future cannot be predicted with certainty. While the overall effect of the Sino-Soviet split, and the further degeneration of the bureaucratic apparatuses in Moscow and Peking, have not been beneficial for those struggling against capitalist oppression in the third world, they might have at least one positive outcome. If the new movements emerging in Latin America and South or South-West Asia learn to be self-reliant in politics and theory, we could soon see more creative and inventive paths opening up towards socialism. The history of social change in this century has taught us to be patient.

Towards a Long View of History

Where does all this leave us, in relation to the subject of our study? The old question is becoming more and more persistent: can Pakistan survive? There are some, victims of exhaustion and despair, who have already answered 'No', and who are waiting impatiently for outside intervention. It is true that the break-up of 1971–2 came as a terrible shock for many people in

West Pakistan, and that Pakistan's benighted citizens are psychologically prepared for almost any eventuality. But we must warn all fatalists: this is not an epoch in which new states are born and old ones disappear at regular intervals. Modern states, even the most dilapidated of banana republics, are far more powerful than their predecessors, and are characterized by a marriage of new technology to coercive structures and ideological manipulation that has had unhappy consequences for the majority of the third world's inhabitants. No spontaneous collapse of Pakistan will take place: however irrational the process of its birth, a Pakistani state now exists, albeit in a gnarled and deformed shape. Though its foundations may have crumbled, it is held together by uniformed scaffolders, who are in a desperate mood.

It is true that a military adventure abroad could lead to the Balkanization of present-day Pakistan: that certainly remains a possibility. On the other hand, a successful internal rebellion could have the opposite result – provided it did not stop half-way. A long future for Pakistan is now only likely if society is reshaped from top to bottom. That is the irony of the situation today, unpalatable to general, bureaucrat and mullah alike. They have tried since 1947 to preserve the state on behalf of the rural gentry and nouveau-riche urban entrepreneurs. But history's verdict on their efforts is unmistakable: the spectres of Bangladesh and an executed Bhutto continue to haunt the traditional rulers of the country. Military dictatorships have lost their novelty, and the dominant classes cannot carry on in the same old way indefinitely. They have strengthened the state militarily, and a competing network of intelligence agencies provides detailed and regular reports on the state of the nation to the generals running the country, but – as Iran has demonstrated – not even the most powerful armed force can resist a popular revolt. Such an assault from below is not likely to be long in erupting. It should have the advantage, moreover, of not being confessional in character – since, in Pakistan, Islam has been a preserve of the army and the Jamaat-i-Islami. It would be futile indeed if their opponents were to entrap themselves by fighting on the same battlefield.

The political temperature is beginning to rise again in Pakistan. The Baluch guerrillas of the BPLF are no spent force. They represent the most advanced core of socialists in the country. In a remarkable interview (part of which may be found in Appendix Two), a BPLF leader, Murad Khan, has explained how, though the Pakistani state is the main enemy, geopolitical realities cannot be ignored.[39] It is a striking fact that backward, nomadic Baluchistan should have produced a dedicated and internationalist cadre without equal in contemporary Pakistan. The creative approach of the BPLF and the self-education of its cadres are in polar contrast to the stale and bankrupt Stalinism of the Afghan PDPA (a political organization which grew in roughly similar socio-political conditions). Many BPLF fighters are living in camps near Kandahar in Afghanistan, where their life is difficult since they are maintaining a strict neutrality on Afghan affairs. But it would be instructive for those Western dignitaries impelled by domestic political considerations to pay a call at the camps outside Peshawar, if they were to compare living conditions and morale there with those prevailing among the Baluch fighters as they bide their time.

In Baluchistan itself, meanwhile, the Chief Justice of the High Court has resigned in protest against the hanging of a young Baluch leader, Hamid Baluch, sentenced for a murder he could not have committed – since apart from anything else the man supposedly murdered was still alive – and killed by the army, presumably to remind the Baluch that they are still under colonial-style occupation.[40] Tension is mounting, too, in the North-West Frontier Province. A veteran nationalist, Arbab Sikander, a close associate of Wali Khan, was shot dead by a Muslim fanatic on 7 March 1982. At the same time there were street clashes between striking teachers and the police. In Sind, the influence of nationalism is increasing among the youth in the rural areas. The death in prison of a student leader, Nazir Abbasi, has sent a wave of anger through colleges and universities in the province. In Punjab, finally, Jamaat-i-Islami students on the campuses are meeting with increasing opposition, despite the support they receive from the army and bureaucracy.

True, all these are only symptoms. But what they reflect is a perceptible change in consciousness. What the state fears most is an eruption onto the streets of masses who confront its authority and will not be cowed. Last-minute reforms may now be offered to prevent a political explosion. However, the situation in Pakistan is such that, even though reforms (a free election, for example), will be welcomed, they will not satisfy everyone. The suffering of the last decade has been so great that any opening which permits the re-entry of the masses into the political life of the country will be exploited to the full.

These are questions of contemporary politics, but what of the future? Even if, by some miracle, Pakistan were transformed into its opposite, would it be able to exist in isolation from its neighbours, or from China and the USSR? The answer we would give may appear utopian, yet we are convinced it provides the only long-term solution to the problems bequeathed by British imperialism to the peoples of South Asia. Orthodox communist parties (regardless of whether they were loyal to Moscow or Peking) have all fallen prey to a specific form of nationalism. (The most repulsive and extreme example of this degeneration of Marxism was seen in Kampuchea under Pol Pot, with extremely negative results in many parts of the world.) But in our opinion, it is precisely the old frontiers which will have to be abolished one day, the laws of revolution overriding both geography and history.

A voluntary Federation of South Asian Republics must remain the goal not only of socialists, but also of democrats, who should not accept the cruel and arbitrary lines drawn by past British rulers to divide nationalities and tribes from each other. We are a long way from realization of this goal, but it alone can be the long-term aim of the South Asian left. The separation of 1947 was a tragedy, and its consequences have proved an unmitigated disaster; but it cannot be ended except on a voluntary basis. Only a gigantic social transformation could create the conditions for transcending the existing frontiers, but that does not mean we should become worshippers of accomplished facts and regard the existing borders as immutable. Such fatalism creates a myopic political vision, and must be discarded, exorcized, banished if advance is to be possible.

Pakistan has not been fortunate in its politicians, whether of the right or the left. It has been singularly unlucky in its communist party. As a result, the country has been run by the representatives of two institutions bequeathed by the former colonial power: the civil service and the army.[41] Where Pakistan has, however, been blessed is in its poets. Poetry has retained its vigour and critical independence, when these qualities have disappeared in every other field of socio-political or cultural life. The poets have not only proved more perceptive than the politicians. They have also intellectually outdistanced the 'theoreticians' of the traditional left. Habib Jalib's popular verses against oppression are chanted in street cafés and city slums. Ahmed Salim's Punjabi poems defending the Bengalis against a Punjabi army in 1971 appeared as the only sign of sanity in a province distorted by ugly chauvinism. But Faiz Ahmed Faiz, one of the greatest of twentieth-century poets, remains peerless in South Asia. His voice has risen above the gloom of a persecuted and crushed intelligentsia. It is, therefore, only right that we end this extended essay on Pakistan with a few verses from 'Dawn of Freedom', the first poem Faiz wrote after Independence in August 1947. Their message remains apposite:

> This leprous daybreak, dawn night's fangs have mangled –
> This is not that long-looked-for break of day,
> Not that clear dawn in quest of which those comrades
> Set out, believing that in heaven's wide void
> Somewhere must be the star's last halting-place,
> Somewhere the verge of night's slow-washing tide,
> Somewhere an anchorage for the ship of heartache.
>
> But now, word goes, the birth of day from darkness
> Is finished, wandering feet stand at their goal;

Our leaders' ways are altering, festive looks
Are all the fashion, discontent reproved;
And yet this physic still on unslaked eye
Or heart fevered by severance works no cure.
Where did that fine breeze, that the wayside lamp
Has not once felt, blow from – where has it fled?
Night's heaviness is unlessened still, the hour
Of mind and spirit's ransom has not struck;
Let us go on, our goal is not reached yet.[42]

APPENDIX ONE

Poem
For Dali, Who Dared to Struggle and Die

dear comrade,
your eyes were like flaming stars at night,
bloodshot flags fluttering in the face
of a stormy land, your marri beard like a
young lion's mane, gust of blackbirds swirling
in the face of a tender land, and your voice
like a hypnotic flute echoing from mountains
to men in the face of a bloody land –

dear comrade, sweet jay
all my nights
are lit bright
by the sunshine
of your quiet smile
glancing off gun-sights
as you take aim to kill
the cracking of your gun
ricocheting in my orphaned heart
victory freedom victory freedom . . .

but one big fresh day
in a big red square
the sky will kneel at your feet
under a multicoloured arch
and swallows will come back
and doves perch on your shoulders
to eat out of your hand
while lovers lean over under the finger of your
shadow and bright-eyed children play with you
once again . . .

Reprinted from *Jabal*, a publication of the Baluchistan People's Liberation Front

Interview
Murad Khan,
a representative of the Baluchistan People's Liberation Front,
speaking to Raymond Noat

Raymond Noat But, in the case of Pakistan, the B P L F as a movement is not demanding independence. How then are the struggle against the Pakistani state and the objective requirements for self-determination in Baluchistan to occur?

Murad Khan We in the Baluchistan Liberation Front have voluntarily decided not to exercise our right of national self-determination. This is a free choice. But that does not necessarily apply to other situations, and it does not necessarily mean that we do not have this option. As a right it continues to be an inalienable right. We have merely decided to merge our national struggle with the class struggle of Baluchistan, on the one hand, and also to merge our national struggle with the struggle of other oppressed nationalities in Pakistan. Since both the class and the national contradiction in Pakistan stand directly opposed to the Pakistani state – and our struggle is principally against the Pakistani state – we find that there is a coincidence of interests, that there is an objective platform for a very broad united front, bringing together oppressed nationalities and oppressed classes within a common revolutionary framework. It is in pursuit of the broadest revolutionary goal that we have temporarily abdicated or denied ourselves the right to independence.

Raymond Noat However, this is more than a temporary abdication. Is it not a strategic view on how to realize full national rights and liberation in the region as a whole?

Murad Khan Yes, you are correct, because our dilemma is part of the dilemma of the general revolutionary movement in the area. We are today directly confronted with US imperialism. The Pakistani state is in our opinion a client state and completely subservient to US regional interests. We take recognition of this reality. In relation to our anti-imperialist struggle, we find it absolutely necessary for the Baluch national liberation movement to forge a united front as broad as possible against imperialism in the entire region. In particular, it means that the United Front in Pakistan has to be very extensive. After all, what is the revolution? The revolution is a concrete analysis of the concrete conditions that prevail. What are our concrete conditions? We are in a situation where we are oppressed by a state which is completely artificial in its composition, whose ideology is completely reactionary, and which stands in contradiction to the oppressed classes and the oppressed nations within the territory of our people. Therefore, it is in our revolutionary interest to unite with all of those elements that stand in contradiction with this state. If for the purpose of unity with other revolutionary forces, we have to sacrifice the policy of independence, we are willing to do so, because in our understanding of the Baluch revolution, the revolution's objective is not independence, but rather the complete transformation of the existing social and economic order.

The oppressed nationalities in Pakistan are oppressed by a common order. The colonies of Sindh, Pushtunistan and Baluchistan have been integrated into a common cause. Therefore, there is absolutely no reason why we should isolate ourselves from the rest of the oppressed forces in the country. It would be absurd. Furthermore, the whole notion of independence, if it is related to the complete social and economic transformation of the existing societies, can only come about through a total revolution. If there is to be a total revolution in Baluchistan, this revolution will have to be a total revolution against the existing structures of Baluchistan and against the existing socio-economic conditions prevailing in Pakistan as a whole. We cannot conceive of a situation where a Pakistani state would exist side by side with an independent Baluchistan.

If we identify our dilemma as existing within the anti-imperialist context, as part of the regional problem, it would not work to our own interest to fight for independence. We would be fighting to achieve an independence that would be denied to us the moment we had achieved it. It should still be noted that as a national liberation movement we preserve our political independence. We preserve our organizational independence, and therefore, we preserve the right to independence, if and when that might become a necessity.

However, there are clearly long-term strategic, military, political and economic factors that come into consideration. What type of revolution are we fighting for? What type of social and economic transformation are we involved in? Our vision of the revolution is based, to a large extent, on a Marxist understanding of a socio-economic transformation. The Pakistani state is a feudal-capitalist state which is completely tied to international imperialism. Therefore, we must destroy this state. On the military plane alone, Baluch independence is inconceivable until and unless the military institutions of Pakistan are totally destroyed. The balance of forces is very much against us on the military plane. If we therefore support the guerilla movement, our only option is the strategy of long-term people's war. There is no denial of the fact that the strategy of long-term people's war can create conditions favourable to the revolutionary movement and bring about a fundamental change in the balance of forces. Given the factor of time, given the factor of sacrifice, determination and struggle that we would have to put in to bring about this change, it is ridiculous on our part to do so independently of a number of tools and instruments which are favourable to bringing about that change – such as the other oppressed nationalities and classes in Pakistan. Even if the Baluch revolution were not a revolutionary movement in the sense that it were not an anti-imperialist movement, even if it were simply a national chauvinistic movement with the simple objective of an independent Baluch state without the demand for fundamental socio-economic changes, this objective could never be realized without the defeat of the Pakistani army.

In the case of Baluchistan, we do not deny the possibility, for example, that the Baluch national struggle could, under certain conditions, serve as a pro-imperialist regional scheme. Bangladesh is a classic example in that the communist movement as a whole stood in opposition to the national liberation movement. This opposition in no way restricted the development of the national liberation movement in Bangladesh – this was an inevitable course related to the laws of social development. But it did push the petty bourgeoisie and the bourgeois leadership in Bangladesh to a point of exercising complete control over the national liberation struggle. Here you have an instance where the progressive movement is responsible for driving the national question into the hands of imperialism. The problem has to be grasped at another level. We believe that the success or the defeat of the revolution is basically the responsibility of the revolutionary movement. We do not work on the principle that it is the strength or weakness of the counter-revolution that determines the success or defeat of the revolution. Therefore, we believe that every contradiction which has the potential of serving the revolution has got to be utilized by the revolutionary forces themselves and used for the anti-imperialistic struggle. The revolutionaries themselves are responsible for the failure of that struggle.

Raymond Noat Having raised this issue, could we talk about some of the other national minority movements which may not have taken on broader revolutionary objectives in all instances? What have the experiences of the Kurds, the Eritreans and the Biafrans meant for your own movement and struggle?

Murad Khan Here again the question is really a more fundamental one than each specific example. We return to the same problem of the Leninist conception of the right to national self-determination. We have said, on the one hand, that this concept is arbitrary, and on the other hand, that the arbitrary nature of this concept permits a dualism to exist in the application of this policy. Again the distinction must be made with Lenin's own complete commitment to the right of self-determination of oppressed nationalities and the practice of various states and parties regarding themselves as socialist. According to certain of these states, national struggles may be conceived of as part of the world socialist movement, if they directly serve the global strategic interests of the principal socialist power. Or a national struggle may be opposed by the world socialist movement, if the political character of a national struggle does not conform to certain criteria, according to which the world socialist movement can call its national leadership progressive.

On the part of the national liberation movements, a similar duality has functioned. In their attempt to exercise their right of national self-determination, there have been certain movements which have tried to apply this principle in a very dogmatic way – as for example in Eritrea. They were not willing to concede the 'right to independence' for the 'right of a socio-economic revolution'. In our opinion the principal aim of the revolution is the social and economic transformation of society. If one particular nationality's fate and socio-economic advancement is related to a number of other nationalities or classes, and if objective conditions are favourable for all these nationalities and classes to achieve the desired social and economic objective via the revolution, then we feel that it is progressive on the part of the national liberation movements to give up the 'right of independence' in order to become integrated with the broader socio-economic goals of the revolutionary process. In the case of Eritrea, without fundamental changes taking place within the Ethiopian régime itself, those conditions would not be there. Thus, the Eritreans during the Haile Selassie period were absolutely justified to fight for total independence.

Raymond Noat   Do you say then that with the overthrow of Haile Selassie in Addis Ababa, the objective conditions of the Eritrea struggle changes?

Murad Khan   In our opinion, it was no longer a pro-imperialist régime that they were fighting. Obviously, there are problems – ideological problems. The unity of one nation with another is going to be based on ideological formulations. The social and economic revolution would obviously require a united front where the socio-economic objectives are to be the same. Here problems can definitely arise. There are definitely problems regarding the specificity of the Eritrean movement and the specificity of the Ethiopian situation.

Raymond Noat   Do you feel that the reason that the Eritrean movement is in the situation it is today is because a decade ago it precluded the possibility of establishing links with other nationalities within Ethiopia?

Murad Khan Yes, the Eritrean movement completely isolated itself from the class struggle within Ethiopia itself, which is why the movement is having problems today. In any case, even under the old régime of Haile Selassie, it was imperative for the genuine success of the national liberation movement in Eritrea to be part and parcel of the class struggle within Ethiopia itself. If there had been an independent Eritrea, as a result of the defeat of the reactionary forces led by Haile Selassie, it would not have brought about a revolutionary Eritrea but simply another Third World state. The notion of independence on its own is not in itself a revolution. Revolution in isolation from the class struggle in the oppressor country does not in itself satisfy the fundamental requirements of a revolutionary régime.

After all what is happening in Eritrea and Ethiopia is basically the continuation of what happened after the victory of the revolution in the Soviet Union with its policy of consolidating 'socialism in one country'. It is the same problem. The difference here is that the question is located at a regional level. We have experienced the construction of 'socialism in one country' at the cost of abandoning the socialist revolution itself. We have witnessed a situation where certain revolutionary blocs of struggle have succeeded in these specific regions, but were then completely surrounded by reactionary forces. The difficulties that the revolutionaries experienced after the seizure of state power in consolidating the revolution, in developing the revolution, the number of counter-revolutionary attacks – all this constitutes an important experience earned at the expense of the revolutionary struggle at the world level. There is no reason why we in the 1980s should not learn from that experience. If we have the objective possibility of bringing about a socio-economic revolution, which is the principal objective of the Baluch movement, through linking the national liberation movement in Baluchistan with the national liberation movements of the other oppressed nationalities and classes in Pakistan, then why should we deny ourselves that possibility? Just for the sake of independence?

Raymond Noat In the context of your general remarks, where do you place the struggle of the Kurdish people?

Murad Khan One of the problems of small nations, and particularly nations that find themselves within the new states (the so-called post-colonial states which compose a large number of present-day Third World countries), has been the problem of exercising their right of national self-determination on the one hand, and identifying themselves with the general progressive or Marxist movements within the state as a whole. Here, sometimes, as in the case of Eritrea, the national liberation movement denied itself the possibility of uniting with the oppressed nationalities of Ethiopia, and other oppressed classes. On the other hand, there have been certain instances where the other oppressed classes or nations, and the leadership of these revolutionary forces, have isolated themselves from the struggle of the oppressed nationalities. We have this instance in the case of Kurdistan; we have it very classically in the case of Bangladesh. Here the so-called progressive movement itself denied the existence of the national struggle and therefore isolated itself from the national liberation movement.

But we in the Baluch movement have learned something else from the history of the Kurdish struggle. In this regard I refer to what occurred during the period of the Shah. The Shah once said that in his role as the gendarme of the region he had two main weapons for dealing with the revolutionary threat which existed in the region. First, was direct intervention. This was applied in the case of Oman in 1973, and also in the case of Baluchistan when the Shah provided armaments and military finance for the Pakistani state's repression in the area. The second weapon was internal subversion of the national liberation movements among the various nationalities. This method was applied in Kurdistan. The goal, of course, was to allow the national movement to grow in a particular direction in order to defeat it. The case of Kurdistan was classic. The Shah said openly that the Kurdistan operation was relatively cheap for him. With 30 million dollars the job was done. He simply supported Kurdistan in order to destroy it. Such a possibility always exists in Baluchistan. What is the best way of destroying the Baluch movement? The answer is clear: allowing the development of the national movement under a reactionary leadership who would then be willing to sell the national resources and the strategic value of Baluchistan to the highest bidder. It is also clear that it is only the revolution which can defend the natural resources and the strategic value of Baluchistan from all foreign control.

Raymond Noat We are touching on many issues and situations tonight. But the reason I keep extending our conversation is that in many respects the Baluch movement and the B P L F, although almost completely unknown internationally, seem to have given more thought and consideration to the 'national question' in its modern context than many better known groups that I am familiar with. Possibly the most outstanding and intractable crisis surrounding the 'national' issue, and the right to national self-determination, is the Palestine question and the existence of Israel. What is your own understanding of this situation? What parallels may or may not exist between the founding of Pakistan and Israel, with both states being established on religious theocratic principles, and both denying the existence of any other nationality in their midst?

Murad Khan In my view the Palestinian national question can only be resolved by the Palestinians asserting their national rights in a manner completely independent from all other political forces in the region. The weakness of the Palestinian national movement and its inability up to the present to have delivered the goods in relation to the Palestinian question has in our opinion been directly related to its total dependence on the dual politics of the region. Its misdirected effort to integrate itself with the superficial Arab national movement has in our view led to the Palestinians paying a very heavy political price.

The pre-eminent lesson of the Palestinian experience for us in Baluchistan is the notion that the national independence struggle of any national movement must be based on an absolutely independent programme. By an independent programme we mean one representing exclusively the rights of the fighting nation concerned. The Palestinian leadership has deviated historically on a number of different occasions from representing the exclusive interests of the Palestinian people as such. Most unfortunately they have confused the interests of the Palestinian people with the grand strategy of Arab nationalism. In our opinion there is no such thing as the 'Arab nation'. They have, therefore, made themselves dependent on the vicissitudes of so-called Arab nationalism, ranging from the extreme right to the extreme left. They have paid a very bitter and difficult price as a result of these deviations.

Furthermore, these deviations in the Palestinian movement have led it to completely neglect the fundamental question of concern. By this we mean the status of the Israeli state. We may talk of destroying the Israeli state as an oppressor state, but this does not mean the destruction of the Israeli people. The failure to be clear on this has only accentuated the difficulties of the Palestinian movement. It has provided opportunities for imperialism at different times and under different circumstances to constantly suppress the Palestinian movement. It has kept the Palestinian movement on the run and constantly worked to isolate the movement from possible liquidation.

Raymond Noat What would be a correct attitude in your view towards Israel?

Murad Khan It is the same problem we have in Pakistan. As a result of the creation of the Pakistani state about 10 million people crossed over from different parts of India. These 10 million people have no ethnic, cultural or linguistic roots in any part of the present geographic area called Pakistan. Therefore, they are, in essence, alien to the existing territory that we call Pakistan. It is this same 10 million who, owing to their psycho-political dilemma, end up supporting the artificial form of Pakistani state most fervently. To them to do so is synonymous with their own security as aliens in the territory of another nationality.

A certain historic process has taken place in the Indian subcontinent. Obviously, there are reasons that explain this process. But we have now lived with the consequences of this process for the last thirty years. We cannot undo this consequence by sheer sloganizing. We cannot undo the process by throwing out the 10 million aliens who have entered the present areas from Sindh, Punjab, Pakhtoonistan or Baluchistan from different parts of India, even though they have no ethnic, cultural or linguistic roots in the territory of present-day Pakistan. We cannot throw them into the sea as such. Therefore, we have to express our political maturity and take on the responsibility as a national liberation movement to fight the essence of the problem. In our view this is the artificial quality of the Pakistani state. Our object is to bring about the destruction of the Pakistani state in its present form: that is its feudal, its capitalist, and its repressive undemocratic form. We have to replace it by a new state that would bring together the different nationalities that make up the present state of Pakistan – including the 10 million aliens that entered the present territory as a result of certain historical circumstances.

Raymond Noat What then does this parallel represent for the Palestinian/Israeli dilemma?

Murad Khan It means that you have to take cognizance of the people and the historical consequences. If there are 3 million people in Israel today, you have to take cognizance of the future political, social and economic role these three million people of Israel will have in a future Palestinian state. In our movement we are basing our strategy for a United Front of the different oppressed minorities of Pakistan and the oppressed classes as a whole in a struggle towards a confederation of the different nationalities and oppressed classes in a socialist democratic state. Within this context, it means that we have to clearly identify who are our friends and who are our enemies within the 10 million of the aliens that are there.

The failure of the Palestinian movement is that while it has intellectually and theoretically recognized the rights of the 3 million people that live within the present artificial state of Israel, in practical terms it has not manifested this recognition in any form as yet. The inability of the Palestinian movement to mobilize sections of the population in Israel today on its side is, I think, symptomatic of its neglect of the problem. Obviously, in the case of Israel there exists a tremendous hostility to the Palestinian movement and we cannot deny the fact that the majority of the population in Israel, owing to the accumulated effect of much history, does support the present state of Israel. Thus, it is obviously very difficult to work out a United Front between the population in Israel and the Palestinian people. It requires a determined effort not only from the

Palestinian revolution, but also from within the Israeli population itself.

We face the same situation in the relationship between the Punjab and Baluchistan. What we would like to really emphasize is that this emphasis of working out a United Front between the oppressor nation and the oppressed nations has to be a very determined and concentrated effort. This kind of determination and concentration is not possible when, for reasons of political expediency, the national movement is deflected. The problem of the Palestinian movement is not so much the mobilization of the different Arab peoples into a common United Front, as it is one of concentrating on the development of a United Front between the Palestinian people and the majority of the population within the state of Israel.

Raymond Noat   What you described in the case of the Palestinian situation, where the contending nationalisms of the Arab states have immobilized and cornered the Palestinians, evokes another type of parallel. In the Bangladesh experience we saw elements from the socialist bloc in an antagonistic situation to each other, with the Soviet Union supporting the national independence struggle in Bangladesh and the Chinese opposed to it. It seems that the national movements in the post-colonial states are facing not only the problem of being crushed by the USA, but also the dilemma of finding themselves caught between antagonisms within the socialist bloc. What is your view of these circumstances?

Murad Khan   We are in the heart of that dilemma in Baluchistan because of the country's strategic position and because of the vast unexploited economic reserves that exist, particularly in gas, oil and copper. We are at the crossroads of the three principal global powers. The policies of two of these powers – China and the US – coincide in their support of the Pakistani state and therefore in their direct opposition to the national liberation movement in Baluchistan. As far as China and the US are concerned, we count for nothing on our own.

We only matter in relation to our strategic importance. Therefore, it is obvious that the Soviet Union constitutes a potential ally for the Baluch liberation movement against the US and China, but not necessarily for the revolution in Baluchistan itself. We are in the heart of this dilemma because the liberation movement in Baluchistan has evolved completely independently from the international communist movement, and part of this independence stems from the fact that it is an outgrowth of a struggle against international central control over the world revolutionary movement. As a result, we obviously do not constitute a very favourable force to be supported by interested global forces. Thus, even the political ally that we have in the Soviet Union is not necessarily willing to lend its support to us on our own terms. The Soviet Union is only a potential ally, and as I said earlier, only an ally against the US and China. Therefore, its support to the movement in Baluchistan is going to be determined by when and how it feels threatened by US or Chinese strategy in the region. The Baluch national liberation movement on its own is not of any credible value to the Soviet Union. So we are basically left to fight the Pakistani state on our own.

As a result of our total ideological independence from all the world centres of revolution, we find that the only potential ally which exists in the region will withhold its support to us, except for those times when for its own interests it becomes absolutely necessary to do so, and not in the interest of the Baluch national liberation movement as such. Thus, we have a very isolated future ahead of us. But, this is where the specific characteristics of the Baluchistan liberation front's strategy come into play. We have always been conscious of the fact that we are at the very heart of this dilemma.

It is precisely to shift the balance of forces in our favour that we have opted for an all-Pakistan state. By forming a United Front with all the oppressed nationalities and classes in Pakistan, we are converting Pakistani society as a whole into an anti-imperialist front. We remove ourselves from an isolated position of national liberation and become an integrated part of the concrete revolutionary movement that extends throughout Pakistan as a whole. In this context, we do not think that the alliance of China and the US with the Pakistani state constitutes a deep threat to our future.

These extracts are reproduced by courtesy of *Pakistan Progressive*, Journal of the Organization of Progressive Pakistanis, P.O. Box 11528, Costa Mesa, CA 92627, USA.

APPENDIX THREE

How the Landlords Won in Sind
Feroz Ahmed

Allegations have been made of large-scale rigging in the National Assembly elections. Just what rigging means is illustrated by the following account about the Provincial Assembly contest in Constituency No. 5 in Thatta district (Bathoro Taluka) of Sind.

Mohammad Ismail Soho, a 28-year-old charismatic peasant organizer, was busy making final preparations for the convention of the Sindhi Hari Committee when Prime Minister Bhutto announced on 7 January that general elections would be held in Pakistan two months later.

During the 1970 elections, Ismail was the backbone of the PPP organization in Thatta district and a local hero of the people of Bathoro Taluka. He was flogged in the Hyderabad Central Jail on the orders of the former dictator Yahya Khan for having raised Bhutto's banner. The PPP was then an underdog and Mr Bhutto was viewed as the champion of the downtrodden workers and peasants. Ismail, like many other young people, had rallied to Bhutto's call for setting up a socialist system in Pakistan.

Disenchanted

By the end of 1975, Ismail was disenchanted and had left the PPP. The Government arrested him under the Defence of Pakistan Rules. No sooner had he been granted bail than he was rearrested and charged with a new offence under the DPR. He was again released on bail after long, agonizing legal proceedings in the Special Tribunal.

Immediately after the announcement of general elections, the Sind Government arrested a number of potential Sindhi Opposition candidates. Earlier, the Government had already arrested the well-known Leftist leader Rasul Bux Palijo, and popular local leaders like Fazil Rahu, Saleh Buwo and Hot Khan Buwo.

In the new wave of arrests, the Government arrested the President of the Peasants Committee, Sher Khan Lund, along with three other peasant cadres, but could not apprehend Ismail Soho who had gone underground and was waiting for an opportunity to file his nomination papers for the Provincial

Assembly seat from Bathoro Taluka and Belo circle of Sajawal Taluka.

On 19 January, Ismail's three-year-old daughter died. A police party accompanied her funeral procession up to the graveyard, hoping that Ismail would appear for the burial and they would arrest him there. However, Ismail made the difficult decision of not joining his daughter's funeral rites.

Daring attempt

22 January was the last date for filing nomination papers for Provincial Assembly seats. The Government had posted a large police force in front of the returning office in Thatta town. Many candidates, intimidated by the police presence, gave up the idea of contesting elections. But Ismail Soho, in a daring attempt, drove his motor bike through the police cordon, pushed aside the cops trying to grab him, ran up to the seat of the returning officer and submitted his nomination papers. Three police officers entered the office and arrested Ismail after a brief scuffle. The returning officer, a judicial magistrate, refused to take Ismail's papers.

The following day, the PPP nominee, Wazir Memon, along with 43 others in Sind, was declared elected unopposed to the Sind Provincial Assembly.

With Ismail Soho himself, his lawyer Rasul Bux Palijo and all the leading cadres of the Peasants Committee held under the DPR, it seemed that the peasants' challenge to the landlord power in Bathoro county was all over. But thanks to the determination of the rank and file of the Peasants Committee and the services rendered by the former Advocate-General Khalid Ishaque, the legal battle for Ismail's candidacy continued before the Election Commission. Not until a month had been wasted, and only 10 days for campaigning remained, that the Election Commission accepted Ismail's appeal on 23 February.

Ismail Soho's nomination papers were filed on 24 February. On the very next day, his chief polling agent and five other campaign-workers were beaten and arrested by the police while attempting to arrange an election rally. The following day, 16 members of Ismail's campaign team were picked up by the police, and arrest warrants were issued against another 23. Three of the detained persons were released and the remaining were sent off to Sukkur prison, where they remained till 5 March, the last day for election campaigning.

Between 27 February and 5 March, the rank and file militants of the Peasants Committee and other supporters of Ismail Soho, devoid of any funds, vehicles or other election paraphernalia, fanned out in the villages on foot and tried to reach every individual in the constituency with just one handbill and a long verbal story about the landlord terror. Only one campaign rally was held in the Mirpur Bathoro town and a few posters were posted on the walls.

While loudspeakers fitted on jeeps and pick-up trucks were haranguing the electorate to vote for the PPP candidate, it had become all too clear that given a fair contest, Ismail Soho would poll as many as 90 per cent of the votes.

Instructions

The DC is said to have called a meeting of all election presiding officers and assistant presiding officers on 2 March, and instructed them to make it sure that Ismail did not win in a single polling station. As an additional measure, the landlords of lower Sind who had already been declared elected unopposed as MNAs or MPAs were rushed to the Bathoro constituency and the nearby Golarchi constituency in the Badin district where another imprisoned popular leader, Fazil Rahu, was expected to win. With local landlords, they started pressurizing the various village community chiefs into voting for the PPP candidate and to prevent their young men from acting as polling agents for Ismail Soho.

On 7 March, the results of the National Assembly election showed a landslide victory for the ruling PPP. The following day, the PNA announced its intention to boycott the provincial polls scheduled for 10 March. However, the campaign team of Ismail Soho decided to go on with the contest, and test the peasants' will to resist the landlord terror.

Political observers believed that in order to render legitimacy to the provincial polls, the Government would ensure fair polls for the handful of Opposition candidates still remaining in the field. Their analysis proved to be largely correct in so far as the other three provinces were concerned. In Baluchistan, even a non-contesting candidate, Ahmed Nawaz Bugti, was declared elected. But not so in Sind. Here every landlord had to show his prowess, and there was a battle for obtaining 100 per cent votes at all polling stations. The Sind Chief Minister, Mr Jatoi, who was still licking his wounds after the defeat in Karachi, was determined to secure victory for his hand-picked candidates for the PA election.

Boycott

Bathoro and Golarchi were the only constituencies in Sind where a serious contest was taking place. Yet the landlords, the police and the bureaucrats vowed not to yield a single polling booth, let alone a constituency. Within a couple of hours of polling, it became evident that they had no intention of allowing people to exercise their franchise. By noon, representatives of both candidates had to boycott the elections and withdraw their polling agents.

In the Bathoro constituency, this is how it happened. The story of a few polling stations given below is applicable to nearly all:

1. *Daro High School* (for urban males): An Assistant Sub-Inspector of Police was snatching ballot papers from the voters, affixing the voting stamp on the symbol of the PPP candidate and handing them over to the Bathoro county clerk, who kept stuffing the ballot box. At least six other officials, including Assistant Presiding Officer and general PPP workers, were engaged in ballot stuffing. The Presiding Officer had shut his eyes to the gross malpractices taking place under his nose. The voters were turned away, being either told that they had no votes or that their votes had already been cast. Sind Constabulary was rushed in to ensure that there was no protest against the rigging. The DC and the Superintendent of Police also came to supervise the 'poll'.

Deaf ear

2. *Daro Primary School* (for rural males): The Assistant Presiding Officer, the Polling Officer and others were engaged in ballot stuffing, while the PPP workers turned away the genuine voters on false pretexts. The Presiding Officer turned a deaf ear to the complaints of Ismail Soho's polling agents.

3. *Daro Primary School* (for women): the polling staff and the goons of the PPP threw out Ismail's polling agents and cast all the bogus votes they wanted.

4. *Dari:* Local landlord, Jamal Khan Laghari, and five of his henchmen beat up Ismail's polling agent Loang Detho and threw him out of the polling station, saying: 'You bastard! You call yourself a polling agent. Has a peasant ever been a polling agent?' The same persons beat up another polling agent, Ali Bux Mundhiar, so much that he became unconscious. Afraid that Mundhiar might die, Jamal Khan's henchmen rushed him to Mirpur Bathoro town, where he was kept in wrongful confinement till the counting of ballots. The remaining two polling agents of Ismail Soho were also abducted, detained the whole day and forced to sign the results of the rigged elections.

5. *Soban Gado:* Landlord Shahnawaz Laghari was in charge of rigging elections. Because of the terror of his henchmen and blatant partiality of the polling staff, Ismail's polling agents were compelled to stage a walk out very early in the day. Then the ballot stuffing proceeded unprotested.

6. *Ghel:* Babu Shah and Aftab Shah, sons of local landlord Sher Ali Shah, stood in the polling booths armed with pistols, prevented the genuine

voters from casting their ballots and threatened to shoot down Ismail's polling agents who were protesting against bogus voting by hired persons bused-in from elsewhere. Ismail's polling agent, Ahmed Buwo, was beaten by police and goondas and thrown out of the polling station.

The election in Thatta-5 was fair in one respect: there was not even a pretension of fair polls by the ruling class. They committed all the bungling quite self-righteously and with unabashed intent. There was no bar on the identification, age, sex or residence of the PPP bogus voters. Under-teenage kids voted for adults, youths voted on behalf of the senior citizens, men voted in place of women, residents of Hyderabad district voted in Jhok, Laiqpur and Buno, Karo voted for Bachayo.

By noon it had become known throughout the constituency that the people of Bathoro Taluka and Belo circle (of Sujawal Taluka) had once again been disenfranchised and the game of balloting still remained a pre-serve of the landlord class. Fifteen thousand people had been turned away from scattered polling stations, without being allowed to vote. There was no longer any need for the other voters to make the long trek from their villages to the polling stations. Ismail Soho's staff had already boycotted the polls in protest.

The next day's newspapers announced that the PPP candidate had won a landslide victory by securing 30,000 votes against Ismail's 4,000. Similar results were announced in the Badin and Tharparkar constituencies. The ruling People's Party captured 100 out of 100 Provincial Assembly seats. The Sindhi landlords had no use even for a nominal Opposition.

Reprinted by Courtesy of *Viewpoint*, Lahore

NOTES

1. Origins

1. *Speech (in Urdu) at Patna, 26 May 1873.* P. Hardy, *The Muslims of British India*, Cambridge, 1972, contains the most useful account of the development of Muslim communalism in India.

2. Quoted in Aziz Ahmed, *Islamic Modernism in India and Pakistan*, Oxford, 1967, p. 64.

3. Quoted in Khalid Bin Sayeed, *The Political System of Pakistan*, Oxford, 1967, p. 28.

4. See Angus Maddison, *Class Structure and Economic Growth: India and Pakistan since the Moghuls*, London, 1971.

5. While there are a number of articles and books which discuss this aspect of British policy, none has succeeded in depicting the nuances of imperialist strategy as well as the late Paul Scott in his series of historical novels known as the Raj Quartet. Scott portrays the marriage between the colonial administration and the indigenous landed gentry with a subtle sensitivity absent from the writings of other English novelists. It is true that the novels concentrate almost exclusively on ruling-class life and politics, but this is precisely where their strength lies as works of historical fiction.

6. Irfan Habib, *Agrarian System of Mughal India*, London, 1963. This work by a Marxist historian has now achieved the status of a classic and remains the most scientific study on the subject. Habib is Reader in History at the University of Aligarh, where he has recently been the target of a series of sharp attacks from both Hindu and Muslim communalists: a unique tribute to his scholarship.

7. G. K. Shirokov, Moscow, 1973, p. 25.

8. In an extremely informative article, Kathleen Gough has written: 'Considering the violent enmity of the Hindu landlords, the wavering of the (largely Hindu) Indian National Congress and the terror instituted by the British, the rebel leaders' conduct must be considered moderate and the rebels' communal reprisals a minor part of the revolt, which was essentially a peasants' insurrection. The Moplah rebellion illustrates the fact that in India as elsewhere, agrarian classes usually have a partial isomorphism with major ethnic categories, whether these are Hindu and Muslim or culturally distinct blocks of Hindu castes, or even, in some areas, co-resident linguistic groups. What is labelled inter-religious or inter-communal strife is often, perhaps usually, initially a class struggle, but unity in the class struggle is all too often broken by the upper classes' appeal to and manipulation of cultural differences, and under duress those most oppressed may turn on all the co-religionists of their oppressors.' Kathleen Gough, 'Indian Peasant Uprisings' in *Economic and Political Weekly*, Bombay, Special Number, August 1974.

9. Saumyendranath Tagore, *Peasant Revolt in Malabar*, Calcutta, 1937.

10. Quoted in *Documents of the History of the Communist Party of India*, Vol. 1, ed. G. Adhikari, New Delhi, 1971.

11. Sir John Cumming (ed.), *Political India*, Oxford, 1932.

12. Ishtiaq Husain Qureshi, *The Struggle For Pakistan*, Karachi, 1974. According to Qureshi, a 'Muslim nation' came into existence when Sir Syed put forward the demand for Muslims not to join the Congress and when the Muslim League put forward the demand for separate electorates. Leaving aside the arcane, idealist character of such a supposition, it does give the game away. Neither Sir Syed nor the early League made a serious political move without consulting their 'English friends'. Are we to take it that Qureshi would agree with the view that it was the British who were instrumental in creating the 'Muslim nation'?

13. Hardy, op. cit.

14. ibid.

15. The Unionist Party, created by the two knights Fazle Hussain and Sikandar Hyat Khan, crossed communal boundaries with ease, uniting Hindu, Muslim and Sikh landlords. As premier of the Punjab, Sikandar Hyat was fairly crucial if Jinnah was to win over Punjabi Muslims to the idea of Pakistan. Sir Sikandar was initially hostile to separatism and proposed a federal solution for the entire subcontinent. The growth of communalism brought him into the League, but his sudden death in 1942 removed him from the scene. Whether or not he would have accepted the partition of the Punjab remains an open question. The Muslim families in the Unionist Party have played a crucial role in Pakistani politics. Shaukat Hyat Khan and Mian Mumtaz Daultana (sons of Sir Sikandar and Ahmed Yar Daultana, both Unionist chiefs) have proved to be the most durable and mobile commodities on the political scene. They have regularly changed parties and have tended to support most governments. The feudal legacy has never been seriously challenged by any régime.

16. M. Mujeeb, *The Indian Muslims*, London, 1967, contains the most balanced account of the poet's evolution, with especial emphasis on his early philosophy. Mujeeb, himself an Indian Muslim, can write with a freedom which is denied to most Pakistani writers and critics. In Pakistan any criticism of Iqbal is regarded as ritual high treason. Such an attitude not only encourages philistinism of the worst order, but also reflects the ideological insecurity of successive Pakistani governments.

17. Both passages quoted in Bipan Chandra, 'Jawaharlal Nehru and the Capitalist Class, 1936', a paper presented to the Indian History Congress in December 1974.

18. ibid.

19. This point is developed in detail by Iftikhar Ahmed, 'Pakistan: Class and State Formation', *Race and Class*, London, 1981.

20. G. Adhikari, *Resurgent India: 1946 in Review*, Bombay, 1947. In this pamphlet, Adhikari gives a useful round-up of struggles in the armed forces (there were airforce strikes in solidarity with the navy and embryonic mutinies in the army) as well as the class polarization which shook the country.

21. B. C. Dutt, *The Mutiny of the Innocents*, Bombay, 1971, p. 161.

22. A critical survey of the Comintern's analysis of Indian nationalism is contained in Jairus Banaji, 'The Comintern and Indian Nationalism', *International*, vol. 3, no. 4, London, 1977.

23. In the wake of the 'Quit India' movement, it was revealed that 60,000 had been arrested, 18,000 detained without trial, 940 killed and 1,630 injured in clashes.

24. K. Damodaran, 'Memoirs of Indian Communism', *New Left Review*, no. 93, London, 1975. Damodaran was, for a period, a member of the CPI's National Council.

25. *Pakistan and National Unity*, Bombay, 1944.

26. A. K. Bagchi, *Private Investments in India, 1900–39*, Cambridge, 1972.

27. Hardy, op. cit.

28. This poem by Amrita Pritam was written in Punjabi; I trust that experts will excuse my rough translation. Pritam is today one of the leading poetesses in India. Warith Shah belonged to a family of *sufis* and is one of the greatest of Punjabi poets. His epic *Hir and Ranjha* was written in 1766 and is the story of two young lovers, their forced separation and ultimate death. M. Mujeeb (op. cit.) writes: 'His [Warith Shah's] work transcends all barriers. It is not Muslim or Hindu or Sikh. It is the most perfect image of the Punjab, an image such as even the *sufi* could not create anywhere else in India.'

2. Post-Independence Realities: The First Decade 1947–58

1. In an extremely astute letter to Jinnah on 28 May 1937, the poet Iqbal drew attention to the political problems confronting the League: 'I have no doubt that you fully realize the gravity of the situation as far as Muslim India is concerned. The League will have to finally decide whether it will remain a body representing the upper classes of Indian Muslims or the Muslim masses, who have so far, with good reason, taken no interest in it. Personally, I believe that a political organization which gives no promise of improving the lot of the average Muslim cannot attract our masses. Under the new constitution the higher posts go to the sons of upper classes; the smaller ones go to the friends or relatives of Ministers. Our political institutions have never thought of improving the lot of Muslims generally. The problem of bread is becoming more and more acute.' *Letters of Iqbal to Jinnah*, Lahore, 1942.

2. Baluchi leaders today claim that, since they were never asked whether or not they wanted to be part of Pakistan, they feel no sense of loyalty to the existing state.

3. The creation of Pakistan in 1947 in no way solved the 'Muslim question'. There were 40 million Muslims left behind in India and increasingly regarded by Indian officialdom as a Pakistani 'fifth column'. The dilemma of Indian Muslims who decided to stay in India has been portrayed with sensitivity and skill in the last film made by the great Indian actor Balraj Sahni, *Garam Hava* ('Hot Winds'). This so antagonized Hindu chauvinists that it took the personal intervention of the then

information minister, Inder Gujral, to ensure that it was shown all over India. The film has yet to be seen in Pakistan!

4. Hamza Alavi's seminal text 'The Army and the Bureaucracy in Pakistan', *International Socialist Journal*, March–April 1966, was the first serious Marxist attempt to analyse the specificity of the new state. It was widely read in Pakistan, though whether its meaning was properly understood is a separate question.

5. The most useful survey of Pakistan's economic condition at the time of Partition is contained in Gankovsky and Polonskaya, *A History of Pakistan*, Moscow, 1964.

6. G. M. Sayed, *Struggle for New Sind*, Karachi, 1949.

7. A detailed description of this important episode in Pakistan's early history is contained in Kamrudin Ahmad, *The Social History of East Pakistan*, Dacca, 1967. This otherwise useful study of Bengali politics is marred by an adulatory and uncritical evaluation of H. S. Suhrawardy. Thus Ahmed ignores Suhrawardy's role during the Suez crisis, and underplays his refusal to back regional autonomy while prime minister.

8. ibid.

9. Quoted in Keith Callard, *Pakistan: A Political Study*, London, 1957.

10. Feroz Ahmed, 'Dictatorship and Imperialist Intervention in Pakistan', *Pakistan Forum*, April 1976, Karachi (in Urdu).

11. Mohammed Ayub Khan, *Friends Not Masters: A Political Autobiography*, Oxford, 1967.

12. *Pakistan Times*, 14 August 1956, editorial entitled 'How Far is Freedom Yet?'.

13. *Technical Assistance: Final Report of Committee on Foreign Relations*, Washington, 12 March 1957.

14. ibid.

15. A detailed account of the origins of NAP is contained in Tariq Ali, *Pakistan: Military Rule or People's Power?*, London and New York, 1970.

16. A well-researched analysis on the subject can be found in Bhagwan Josh, *Communist Movement in Punjab*, Delhi, 1979. It should be noted, however, that Josh's knowledge of the Punjabi 'Muslim' communists is largely dependent on reminiscences of Indian communists, which provide only a partial account.

17. Sajjad Zaheer, *Light on League–Unionist Conflict*, Bombay, 1944.

18. Talukder Maniruzzaman, 'Radical Politics and the Emergence of Bangladesh' in Brass and Franda (eds.), *Radical Politics in South Asia*, Cambridge, Mass., 1973.

19. *Pakistan Times*, 16 May 1958.

20. ibid., 22 March 1958.

21. Callard, op. cit. Callard's work concentrates on the political–constitutional wrangles that gripped Pakistan after Partition. Its crucial weaknesses are the absence of any social or economic analysis, and a propensity to underplay and ignore the evidence of totalitarianism in the countryside cited by the left press.

3. The Gun and the Hat: Military–Bureaucratic Dictatorship 1958–69

1. Hamza Alavi, 'Army and Bureaucracy in Pakistan', *International Socialist Journal*, Rome, 1966.

2. In his first address to the Pakistani Constituent Assembly on 11 August 1947, Jinnah said: 'Any idea of united India could never have worked and in my judgement it would have led us to a terrific disaster. *Maybe that view is correct; maybe it is not; that remains to be seen'* (my italics). In other words, Jinnah was assigning the ultimate judgement on the correctness or otherwise of creating Pakistan to the process of History. Only too aware what the results of an open debate and balance-sheet of the Partition movement might entail, Jinnah's civilian and military heirs ensured that there was *no* scientific debate or discussion. Any attempt to discuss the merits or demerits of what had taken place was denounced as a form of ideological treason. In such a stultifying atmosphere, it is hardly surprising that the Pakistani 'intelligentsia' was deformed from birth.

3. Angus Maddison, *Class Structure and Economic Growth: India and Pakistan since the Moghuls*, London, 1971.

4. Quoted in R. P. Dutt, *India Today*, London, 1940.

5. Fazle Muqeem Khan, *Story of the Pakistan Army*, Karachi, 1963. Another author, Hasan Askari Rizvi, attempted in *The Military and Politics in Pakistan*, Lahore, 1976, to take the story further, but was hampered by an apologetic approach: Rizvi's affiliation to the PPP, which was then in power, evidently determined his choice of facts and his political analysis; while the book contains useful empirical information, it thus lacks the critical analysis necessary for a coherent history of the subject.

6. The views of Punjabi bureaucrats (with honourable exceptions) and the army high command on the 'character' of Bengalis are well known. They were inherited from the ideologists of the Raj. In a memorandum on the country's political situation written in 1954, the army C.-in-C. General Ayub had this to say about the 'problem' of Bengal: 'they have been and are under considerable cultural and linguistic influence. As such they have all the inhibitions of downtrodden races and have not yet found it possible psychologically to adjust to the requirements of their newborn freedom. Their peculiar complexes, exclusiveness, suspicion and a sort of defensive aggressiveness probably emerge from this historical background.' This paternalism and racism was common to the military–bureaucratic complex that ruled the country.

7. Anouar Abdel-Malek, *Egypt: Military Society*, New York, 1968, provides a fascinating account of the rise of Nasser and military radicalism.

8. A detailed account of the take-over is available in Tariq Ali, *Pakistan: Military Rule or People's Power?*, London and New York, 1970.

9. *Pakistan Times*, Lahore, 26 January 1959.

10. Gustav F. Papanek, *Pakistan's Development*, Harvard, 1967.

11. *Underdeveloping the World: Harvard and Imperialism*, Harvard, 1969 (an *Old Mole* pamphlet).

12. Bhutto told me in 1969 that, soon after the military take-over in October 1958,

Ayub had told his new cabinet: 'There is only one embassy for us and that's the American Embassy.'

13. Ali, op. cit.

14. As a participant in and initiator of this demonstration, held in defiance of martial law regulations, I can testify that, while we had been deeply moved by Lumumba's murder, there were also numerous anti-Ayub slogans chanted on the streets. In East Pakistan, of course, there was a wave of unrest which went much further, with students openly marching against the dictatorship. The role of students in 'third-world' countries has often been remarkable. For example, in Pakistan, Thailand and South Korea – all dictatorships allied to the USA – students have utilized their strength to unleash frontal assaults on the régime; in the absence of organized politics, it was the campuses that became the organizing centres of opposition.

15. The failure of Pakistani academics to produce anything except apologetics on behalf of the government of the day is expressed most clearly in the field of foreign policy. In the important fields of history and politics, the very notion of encouraging creative debate is absent from the consciousness of the post-Partition academic. A case-study in the art of the banal apologia is Latif Ahmed Sherwani, *India, China and Pakistan*, Karachi, 1967. The two-page foreword by Dr I. H. Qureshi also provides a revealing glimpse of the thought-processes of one of the country's top academicians of that period.

16. *Pakistan Times*, Lahore, 30 March 1966.

17. Ali, op. cit.

18. The senior bureaucrat who ran the Ministry of Information was Mr Altaf Gauhar, widely regarded as a shrewd and skilful civil servant. His manipulation of the country's media led to universal disgust with the régime, and was a minor factor in aiding its fall. Journalism, during this period, became a profession analogous to prostitution. Journalists (with notable exceptions such as the staff of the Karachi journal *Outlook*) became ideological mercenaries. A classic case is that of Z. A. Suleri. As a leading apologist of the Ayub régime, he denounced Bhutto on a regular basis. Subsequently, he became the scourge of the Bengalis, and followed that by backing Bhutto to the hilt when the latter was in power. He is currently an ardent supporter of the Zia military régime and its favourite journalist. As for tomorrow . . .

19. Ali, op. cit.

20. In late 1966, J. A. Rahim arrived in London with a draft manifesto of the PPP and asked me to read it and become a founding member. I read the document, but rejected the kind invitation, on the grounds that as a socialist and secularist I could not belong to a party that was neither. In a long conversation with Bhutto at his Karachi residence in 1969, I realized that he had been informed of my views. He told me: 'You are too much of a purist. This is Pakistan and we cannot ignore Islam. There are only two ways to get rid of these bastards [the army]. Mine or that of Che Guevara. It's either me or the Baluchis in the mountains with their guns.' I suggested that there was a third way, but it required telling the masses the truth and not bringing religion into politics – something which would doom any radical organization.

21. Ali, op. cit.

22. ibid., Chapters 5, 6 and 7, provide the most detailed account of the uprising ever to be published. The book was banned in Pakistan.

23. Mian Mumtaz Daultana, the Muslim League veteran, in an interview with the author.

24. Throughout the five-month upsurge, the Chinese press remained silent about the struggle of the Pakistani people. What was, indeed, restressed during this period was China's support for the Ayub régime. The resulting collapse of Maoism in Pakistan revealed the weakness of a strategy that relied on one or the other of the big non-capitalist powers.

25. Karl Von Vorys, *Political Development in Pakistan*, Princeton, 1965.

4. The Break-Up of Pakistan 1969-71

1. 'Pakistan: After the December Election, What Next?', *Red Mole*, London, 1 January 1971.

2. See also Richard Nations, 'The Economic Structure of Pakistan and Bangladesh' in Robin Blackburn (ed.), *Explosion in a Subcontinent*, London, 1975. Another useful survey is Feroz Ahmed's 'The Struggle in Bangladesh', in a special number of *Bulletin of Concerned Asian Scholars* ('South Asia in Turmoil'), San Francisco, 1972.

3. A repeated argument of Awami League leaders was that the PPP had no fixed or clear position in relation to the country's future constitution.

4. Reported in *Le Monde*, Paris, 31 March 1971.

5. The most detailed report of the genocidal aspects of the war was published by Antony Mascarenhas: 'Genocide: Why the Refugees Fled', in the *Sunday Times*, 13 June 1971.

6. Ranajit Roy, *Hindustan Standard*, 20 May 1971.

7. That the prospect of a united Bengal displeased Washington may be inferred from the following editorial in the *New York Times*, entitled 'Bengal Is the Spark'. The occasion was apparently some stray reflections of mine reported from Calcutta: 'Mr Ali's radical vision of chaos on the Indian subcontinent cannot be taken lightly . . . A prolonged guerrilla conflict in East Pakistan would have profound repercussions in the neighbouring violence-prone Indian state of West Bengal, already shaken by the influx of more than three million refugees from the Pakistan Army's campaign of terror. Prime Minister Indira Gandhi is under mounting pressure to intervene to try and check this threat to India's own internal peace and integrity. It is obviously in no one's interest to allow the Bengali "spark" to explode into a major international conflict, one which might speedily involve the major powers. Nor is it wise to permit the situation in East Pakistan to continue to fester, inviting the gradual political disintegration of the entire subcontinent. To deprive Tariq Ali and his like of their "big opportunity" it is essential that Pakistan's President Yahya Khan come to terms speedily with the more moderate Sheikh Mujibur Rehman and his Awami League' (2

June 1971). My supposed 'radical vision of chaos' was to suggest that a unified and socialist Bengal would help Bengali peasants and workers more than the existing set-up, and could act as an inspiration for the propertyless in the rest of South Asia. I had also pointed out that such a development would be the best way to creating a genuine Federation of South Asian Republics in the distant future.

8. Published in the *Pakistan Times*, 13 April 1971. For a long time the more advanced Maoists in Europe, North America and Asia refused to believe that the Chinese could be guilty of such an act of betrayal. Those of us who strongly criticized the Chinese were denounced in the most crude fashion. The decomposition of Maoism in China and outside since those fateful years, however, has meant that few socialists today dispute the reactionary character of Chinese foreign policy.

5. The Populist Experiment: Bhutto in Power 1971–7

1. Fazal Muqeem Khan, *The Story of the Pakistan Army*, Karachi, 1963.

2. See Alain Lipietz, 'Towards Global Fordism?', *New Left Review*, no. 132, London, 1982.

3. Shahid Javed Burki, *Pakistan Under Bhutto 1971–77*, London, 1980, pp. 159–62.

4. I. A. Rehman, 'New Land Reforms: A Radical Step', and M. Masud, 'Bhutto's Land Reforms', *Viewpoint*, Lahore, 14 January 1977.

5. Dr Rashid Amjad, 'Pakistan's Economic Experience: Lessons for the Future', *Viewpoint*, Lahore, 17 August 1980.

6. Peron built up the Argentinian trade unions and established a strong base inside the working class, which still exists. Sukarno allied himself to the Indonesian Communist Party (PKI), which was the largest such party in the non-communist world until the coup of 1965.

7. This was done by favouring known PPP supporters, rather than by pushing through a structural transformation.

8. C. L. Sulzberger, 'Belief in Crude Reality', *New York Times*, 22 April 1973.

9. Selig S. Harrison, *In Afghanistan's Shadow: Baluch Nationalism and Soviet Temptations*, New York and Washington, 1981. Harrison's book is the first serious account of the political history of Baluchistan to be published. Accurate in its essentials, it deserves to be studied by all students of the region.

10. Wali Khan, Interview, *Outlook*, Karachi, 6 July 1974.

11. Quoted in Harrison, op. cit.

12. Interview with author, London, 1981.

13. Harrison, op. cit.

14. The first step on the road to emancipation was to permit male doctors to treat women patients. Once the first barriers were broken, women began to demand medical aid as an inalienable right and gradually men began to accept this. A BPLF leader, Osman, stated: 'The moment we are able to form an organization of women we will

do so. They must learn to resist the incredible amount of male domination. We cannot, however, confront this problem head on. It would give rise to violent antagonisms and that is not our objective. We hope that progressively the liberation of women will appear as a necessity, and that it will be undertaken by the women themselves.' *Jabal*, organ of the BPLF, 1976.

15. Fred Halliday, *Arabia Without Sultans*, London, 1974.

16. Interview with author. Bashir was disgusted with Zia for the amnesty releasing Baluch and Pathan detainees. He left the army, but was made chairman of the Ghee (clarified butter) Corporation, where he is stated to be prospering.

17. Harrison, op. cit.

18. See Appendix One for two examples of Baluch poetry.

19. Interview with author.

20. Feroz Ahmed, 'Pakistan: The New Dependence', *Race and Class*, XVIII, London, 1976.

21. The popular poet Habib Jalib, in his poem 'Adviser', penned a stanza which read something like this:

> China is our dearest friend,
> On it our life does depend,
> But the system that there prevails,
> Do not go too near it,
> Salute it from afar.

22. For details of Maoist policy in Pakistan, India, Bangladesh and Sri Lanka, see Tariq Ali, *Pakistan: Military Rule or People's Power?*, London, 1970, and Robin Blackburn (ed.), *Explosion in a Subcontinent*, London, 1975. Maoism as an ideology is now almost defunct, though Albanian and Lin Piaoist mutations survive in parts of South Asia. There can be little doubt that the Chinese turn towards the United States has had an incredibly damaging and demoralizing impact on the left throughout the region.

23. Zulfiqar Ali Bhutto, *If I Am Assassinated*, New Delhi, 1978.

24. 'The Democratic Path' (editorial), *Viewpoint*, Lahore, 14 January 1977.

25. See Appendix Three for a detailed report on the Soho case, which provides a number of insights into the peculiarities of Pakistani populism.

26. Leon Trotsky, *Writings (1938–39)*, New York, 1974, p. 326.

6. Crisis of Legitimacy: Martial Law with an Islamic Face 1977–?

1. Quoted in *The Economist*, 12 December 1981. When I first made the comparison between Israel and Pakistan in the first sentence of *Pakistan: Military Rule or People's Power?* in 1970, right-wing Pakistanis as well as many leftists were shocked. The contrast was supposedly outrageous. General Zia, of course, is well qualified to talk about Israel. In Jordan on active service for the Hashemite monarch, he played an

active role in massacring the Palestinians in September 1970. For his 'services' he was decorated by King Hussein. The crushing of the Palestinians marked a turning-point in the Middle East, and paved the way of the ultimate Israeli occupation of the West Bank.

2. The main influence was the Jamaat-i-Islami.

3. Zia-ul-Haq, 'Address to the Nation', 5 July 1977. These blandishments were part and parcel of a psychological war designed to confuse the masses.

4. Bhutto's rejoinder to Zia's allegations was made in a statement to the Supreme Court in 1977.

5. Information obtained from serving officers at the time, who do not wish to be named.

6. Leslie Wolf-Phillips, *Constitutional Legitimacy: A Study of the Doctrine of Necessity*, London, 1979. We do not intend to suggest that all Pakistan's judges were willing tools of successive régimes. There were honourable exceptions throughout Pakistan's history.

7. The most balanced assessment is provided by Leslie Wolf-Phillips, 'Comment', in *Public Law*, London, Summer 1979. The most detailed description is contained in Victoria Schofield, *Bhutto: Trial and Execution*, London, 1979.

8. Bhutto made the fatal mistake of believing that Zia-ul-Haq was 'in his pocket'. He thus failed to understand an iron law of politics in the third world: no general is ever 'in the pocket' of a civilian politician. The army as an institution is more powerful than any individual politician.

9. Though not everyone was displeased: some of the country's richest capitalists celebrated the event in lavish style at their palatial residences, and General Zia's ban on liquor was ignored with impunity.

10. Quoted in the *Daily Telegraph*, 18 October 1979.

11. *Pakistan: Human Rights Violations and the Decline of the Rule of Law*, Amnesty International, London, 1982.

12. Nubar Housepian, 'Pakistan in Crisis: An Interview with Eqbal Ahmed', *Race and Class*, London, 1980. In a series of extremely perceptive observations, Eqbal Ahmed pinpoints the contradictions confronting the ruling élite.

13. In 1953, Maulana Maududi was sentenced to death by a special court for inciting religious riots. The sentence was subsequently commuted.

14. *Kayhan International*, Teheran, 18 September 1977. In this interview Zia rejected any comparisons with Israel!

15. Lawrence Ziring, *Pakistan: The Enigma of Political Development*, Folkestone, 1980, p. 110.

16. Mustafa Khar's period of governorship of the key province of the Punjab was characterized by chicanery, grotesque misuse of the powers of patronage, large-scale corruption and several instances of women being abducted at the encouragement of Government House. Such acts were resented by large sections of the population (including many PPP supporters), but it was the Jamaat that made the real gains –

inside the army. 'Our sisters and daughters are no longer safe to walk the streets while Bhutto's *goonda* sits in Government House,' was a popular refrain amongst junior officers.

17. Memorandum of Rao A. Rashid Khan, Special Secretary, Prime Minister's Secretariat, 13 July 1976, reprinted as Annexure of the *White Paper on Conduct of the General Elections*, Government of Pakistan, Rawalpindi, 1978.

18. Interview with author, London, 1981.

19. Quoted in *Cambridge History of India*, vol. 6.

20. Editorial, *Financial Times*, London, 28 September 1979.

21. ibid., 15 January 1982.

22. Amnesty Report, op. cit.

23. Michael Löwy, *The Politics of Combined and Uneven Development*, London, 1981, contains the most useful recent account of this development.

24. Michael Löwy, 'Marxists and the National Question', *New Left Review*, no. 96, London, 1976.

25. Yu. V. Gankovsky, *The Peoples of Pakistan*, Academy of Sciences, USSR, English translation, Lahore, undated.

26. Perry Anderson, *Lineages of the Absolutist State*, London, 1974.

27. Ghaus Bux Bizenjo, interviewed in *Viewpoint*, Lahore, 3 February 1982. Selig S. Harrison, *In Afghanistan's Shadow: Baluch Nationalism and Soviet Temptations*, New York, 1982, remains the most comprehensive and up-to-date study on Baluchistan. It is vital reading for all those anxious to study the national dimension in South Asian politics. See review of the same in the *Guardian*, London, 26 February 1982: Tariq Ali, 'Is Baluchistan the Next to Blow?'

28. Quoted in Hasan Askari Rizvi, *The Military and Politics in Pakistan*, Lahore, 1976, p. 177.

29. 'N.C.', 'Passage Through Pakistan', *Mainstream*, New Delhi, 16 January 1982.

30. During a PPP conference in Karachi in 1973, a number of Sindhi peasant delegates assailed Bhutto, who was chairing the event. The PPP leader listened patiently as peasant leaders attacked the record of the régime and contrasted the promises made with what had been delivered. At the end Bhutto stood up and replied: 'Many of the points you've made are correct. We have proceeded slowly. But let *me* ask *you* one question. Who gave you the courage to stand up and confront the prime minister of this country as you have done? Who gave you a voice?' Patronizing, perhaps, but effective.

31. 'Theses on the Eastern Question', *Inprecor*, Moscow, vol. II, no. 118, 30 December 1922.

32. Fernando Claudin, *The Communist Movement: from Comintern to Cominform*, London, 1975, is a powerful indictment of Comintern policies by a former central leader of the Spanish Communist Party.

33. K. Damodaran, 'Memoirs of Indian Communism', *New Left Review*, no. 93. To be re-published in Tariq Ali (ed.), *What is Stalinism?*, London, forthcoming.

34. An extremely lucid and original critical survey of the Comintern's analysis of Indian nationalism is contained in Jairus Banaji, 'The Comintern and Indian Nationalism', *International*, vol. 3, no. 4, London, 1977.

35. In contrast, the United States had 500,000 soldiers in Vietnam at the peak of the war in the late sixties and seventies.

36. Bipan Chandra, 'Total Rectification', *Seminar*, New Delhi, June 1974.

37. *Pakistan Times*, Lahore, 29 March 1972.

38. Faiz Ahmed Faiz, 'A Few Days More', in *Poems by Faiz* (translated by Victor Kiernan), Oxford, 1971.

7. Between the Hammer and the Anvil: Geopolitics and the Super-Powers

1. Leon B. Poullada, *Reform and Revolution in Afghanistan: 1919–29*, Cornell, 1973, provides the most detailed and largely sympathetic account of the period. Poullada's book, however, is marred by a tendency to whitewash British involvement in the region. His view of the Soviet Union in the twenties is also distorted by seeing it as qualitatively no different from Tsarist Russia.

2. See Fred Halliday, 'Revolution in Afghanistan', *New Left Review*, no. 112, London, 1979.

3. Akbar S. Ahmed, *Social and Economic Change in the Tribal Areas*, Karachi, 1977.

4. Lawrence Lifschultz, 'Afghanistan, the Not So New Rebellion', *Far Eastern Economic Review*, 30 January 1981. This is the most complete account of the Bhutto régime's involvement in the affair. Apart from other facts, Lifschultz revealed that 5,000 right-wing opponents of the Daud régime were trained at secret camps. Razmak was undoubtedly one such centre.

5. This is not simply a left-wing view. It is accepted by US writers specializing in the region. For an insightful analysis, see Selig S. Harrison, 'The Shah, not the Kremlin, Touched Off the Afghan Coup', *Washington Post*, 13 May 1979. Also Louis Dupree, 'Afghanistan Under the Khalq', *Problems of Communism*, vol. 28, July–August 1979.

6. *Kabul Times*, 24 May 1979.

7. Halliday, op cit.

8. Leon Trotsky, *On China*, New York, 1976, pp. 400–401. A survey of Trotsky's ideas on the semi-colonial world is contained in Michael Löwy, *The Politics of Combined and Uneven Development*, London, 1981. Löwy, a Brazilian Marxist, describes the genesis of Trotsky's theory of permanent revolution, rebuts ultra-left interpretations of the same, and explores the evolution of the Yugoslav, Chinese, Cuban and Nicaraguan revolutions within its framework. Halliday, op. cit., cites numerous examples of Stalinization, including grotesque personality cults and indiscriminate repression.

9. Feroz Ahmed was editor of *Pakistan Forum*, a socialist Urdu-language monthly in Karachi, throughout the Bhutto period. His perceptive writings on the national question and US penetration of Pakistan were not matched by an equally critical approach to early PDPA propaganda on Afghanistan. In a subsequent interview with *Merip Reports* (July–August 1980) in the United States, Feroz Ahmed admitted: 'When I came back to Pakistan [after interviewing Amin in Kabul] I did not write about my real impressions, but I told my close friends.' He also described in graphic detail the failures of the PDPA after 1978, but appeared now to have transferred his support to the present rulers in Kabul.

10. Kuldip Nayar, *Report on Afghanistan*, New Delhi, 1981; Newell and Newell, *The Struggle for Afghanistan*, Cornell, 1981.

11. Selig S. Harrison, 'Did Moscow Fear an Afghan Tito?', *International Herald Tribune*, 16 January 1980.

12. Halliday, op. cit.

13. Ernest Mandel, 'Peaceful Co-Existence and World Revolution', in R. Blackburn (ed.), *Revolution and Class Struggle: Reader*, London, 1977. Also Fernando Claudin, op. cit.

14. *Pravda*, 28 June 1968.

15. Babrak Karmal's speech was released by the Soviet news agency Tass and published in the world press on 28 December 1979.

16. In Angola a victorious national liberation movement, the MPLA, was confronted by a South African military intervention. The Ethiopian case is less clear, but none the less aid was requested by an established government.

17. At the seventh plenum of the PDPA on 19 December 1981, Karmal reiterated his appeal to the Pukhtoon tribes in the name of *jihad* (holy war), Sunnah (Mohammed's precepts) and Islamic values. This attempt did not produce any results.

18. The fact that most of these reports are based on hearsay and unsubstantiated bazaar gossip can usually be gauged by phrases such as: 'A military source reported recently . . .', 'According to diplomats in New Delhi . . .', 'There is speculation . . .', etc.

19. Newell and Newell, op. cit., p. 140.

20. Lawrence Lifschultz, 'External Resistance, Internal Conflicts', *Far Eastern Economic Review*, 23 January 1981.

21. Thomas E. Ewing, *Between the Hammer and the Anvil? Chinese and Russian Policies in Outer Mongolia, 1911–1921*, Bloomington, 1980.

22. Fred Halliday, *Iran: Dictatorship and Development*, London, 1979, provides a useful recent account of Iran under the Shah.

23. The boss of Pakistan's Federal Intelligence Agency during the Bhutto years, Saghir Anwar, was trained by SAVAK. After the fall of Bhutto, Anwar helped to organize the intelligence services in Abu Dhabi. He is currently employed by the Bank of Credit and Commerce International, as the head of its travel agency.

24. Karl Marx, 'A Contribution to the Critique of Hegel's Philosophy of Right', in *Early Writings*, London, 1975, p. 244.

25. Mohammed Ja'afar and Azar Tabari, 'Iran: Islam and the Struggle for Socialism', *Khamsin*, no. 8, London, 1981. This is the most cogent and convincing essay on Iranian politics since February 1979.

26. ibid.

27. These moves marginalized the left and ended the brief period of press freedom. The only two left-wing papers allowed to publish were *Mardom* of the Tudeh Party and *Kargar*, the organ of a tiny Trotskyist sect. Both groups had politically prostrated themselves before the 'line of the Imam'.

28. Ahmed Ghotbi, *After Khomeini, Another Despotism?*, London, 1982. This contains an interesting and original polemic against the Tudeh.

29. The Non-Aligned Movement of today appears as a vindication of Marx's aphorism regarding history repeating itself on the second occasion as farce. How else can one describe a movement which embraces both Fidel Castro and General Zia-ul-Haq?

30. Robin Blackburn (ed.), *Explosion in a Subcontinent*, London, 1971, contains a transcript of Kissinger's remarks on 'tilting' towards Pakistan.

31. Selig S. Harrison, 'As He Courts Pakistan, Reagan is Alienating India', *International Herald Tribune*, 25 July 1981.

32. See K. Sarwar Lateef, *China and India: Economic Performance and Prospects*, Brighton, 1975, p. 33.

33. Lawrence Lifschultz, 'Ring Around the Gulf', *Far Eastern Economic Review*, 11 December 1981.

34. Selig S. Harrison, op. cit.

35. These remarks were made during an exclusive interview with Arnaud de Borchgrave, 'A Talk with Zia', *Newsweek*, 14 January 1980.

36. Mustafa Khar, 'Four Choices Facing Front-Line Pakistan', *The Economist*, 31 October 1981.

37. Quoted in *Sunday*, Calcutta, 1981.

38. On 7 March 1982, General Sawar Khan, a senior member of the ruling junta, visited the Al-Kharj military base near Riyadh, Saudi Arabia. He was received at the base by Pakistani officers, and reviewed a guard of honour containing many Pakistani soldiers. It is Pakistan which supplies the praetorian guard to defend the Saudi ruling family class. Some of the most oppressed and down-trodden sections of workers in Saudi Arabia are Pakistani immigrants. In the event of a popular revolt against the monarcho-confessional tyranny, we could well see Pakistani officers ordering Pakistani soldiers to fire on Pakistani workers thousands of miles from home!

39. Raymond Noat, 'Interview: Murad Khan, a Representative of the BPLF',

Pakistan Progressive, vol. 3, nos. 3, 4, New York, 1980. For an extract, see Appendix Two.

40. Hamid Baluch was hanged on the same day as Assistant Secretary of State Buckley arrived on an official visit to Pakistan.

41. A correspondent writing in *The Economist* on 6 June 1981 could not fail to notice the similarities between old and new: 'Watching General Zia reviewing his khaki soldiers and hussar-style army band, then withdrawing to a gloriously painted canopy, this correspondent could not but feel that, when Britain went, only the nationality of the man inside the uniform changed.'

42. *Poems by Faiz* (translated by Victor Kiernan), Karachi, 1973.

Index

Abbasi, Nazir, 196
Act of India (1935), 29–30, 31–2
Afghanistan: Bhutto's policy towards, 166–8; communism in, 168–72; Daud coup, 165–6; first attempts to modernize, 164–5; Iran and, 168; origins of Pakistan/Afghan conflict, 126–7; projected consequences of Soviet withdrawal, 179; resistance in, 176–8; Soviet intervention in, 172–6
Ahmed, Akbar S., 166–7
Ahmed, Feroz, 125, 130, 210–14
Ahmed, Mozaffer, 76
Ahmed, Sir Syed, 17–19
Ahsan, Admiral, 89–90
Akbar, 16
Al-Zulfiqar, 160
Ali, Chaudhri Mohammed, 49
Allahabadi, Akbar, 54
Amanullah, King, 26, 164–5
Amin, Hafizullah, 168, 170, 171, 172, 175
Amjad, Dr Rashid, 106–7
Aslam, C. R., 77
Ataturk, Kemal, 26, 183–4
Aurungzeb, 16
Awami League: Ayub and, 80; communists and, 58, 59; formation, 45; election campaign and victory, 84–7; political characteristics of, 89, 93–4; political evolution during civil war, 92; pro-American elements, 93; Suhrawardy and, 50
Azad, Maulana, 31
Azad Pakistan Party, 55, 56

Babar, 16
Baghdad Pact, 52, 189
Bahadur Shah Zafar, 17
Baluch, Hamid, 196
Baluch, Isman, 109, 110–11
Baluchistan: accession to Pakistan, 42; Bhutto and, 112–13, 114, 118–19, 121, 123, 143; formation of BPLF, 119–20; NAP in, 76, 87, 108, 114, 117; neglect by central government, 148; war in, 115–23; weakness of communists in, 53, 157
Baluchistan People's Liberation Front (BPLF), 119–21, 122, 195–6, 201, 205
Bangladesh, 95–6
Baraktullah, Mohammed, 26
Bashir, Col., 121
Ben Bella, Ahmed, 184
Bentinck, Lord, 22
Bhashani, Maulana, 45, 53, 76, 77, 80
Bhutto, Mumtaz, 78, 152
Bhutto, Murtaza, 160
Bhutto, Zulfiqar Ali: assumption of power, 99–101; and Baluchistan, 112–13, 114, 118–19, 121, 123, 143; and Bonapartism, 131; campaign against Six Points, 88–9; domestic politics, 107–15; and economy, 101–7; election campaign, 84; and establishment of PPP, 78; failure to transform PPP into genuine political party, 108–9; fall of, 128–32; foreign policy, 123–8; inadequacy of land reforms, 103–5; and Iran, 114; and Kashmir conflict, 74; and military

Bhutto Zulfiqar Ali – *contd*
assault on East Pakistan, 90, 91;
nationalization under, 105–6; and
problem of the army, 158; régime's
clashes with working class, 109–11;
repressive measures, 111; trial and
execution, 135–6, 137, 152
Birdwood, Field Marshal Sir W., 64–5
Birla, G. D., 32
Biswas, Tipu, 92
Bizenjo, Ghaus Bux, 76, 114, 115–16,
117, 149
Bogra, Mohammed Ali, 48
Bonapartism, 131
British: characteristics of British
Indian Army, 63–5; and creation of
state of Pakistan, 15; and formation
of Muslim party in India, 19; and
'Indian Mutiny', 17; modernizing
impact on India hoped for by Marx,
21; restriction of indigenous
industrialization, 23; role of army
and bureaucracy in maintaining
colonial rule, 63; self-image, 22;
stimulation and utilization of
religious divisions, 15–16; strategy in
India, 22–3; withdrawal, 39–40
Bugti, Akbar, 118

Caliphate question, 26
Causes of the Indian Mutiny, The (Sir
Syed Ahmed), 18
Central Treaty Organization
(CENTO), 52, 97, 189
Césaire, Aimé, 91
Chandra, Bipan, 32, 156
Cheema, Hafeezullah, 130
Chen Yi, Marshal, 75
Chiang Kai-shek, Gen., 154
China: Bhutto's policy towards, 126;
and civil war, 97–8; communist party
in, 154, 155; influence on Pakistani
Left, 126; relations with Pakistan,
73; support for Pakistan over
Kashmir, 74–5
Chou En-lai, 77, 97, 126

Comintern, 36, 153, 154, 155, 156
Communist Party in East Pakistan:
establishment of Youth League,
58–9; insurrection and
imprisonments, 57–8; links with
CPI, 57; and National Awami Party,
59; relative strength, 57; and
Sino-Soviet split, 76–7
Communist Party of India (CPI):
approach makes application of
Marxist politics impossible, 39;
growth of influence, 36; and 1939–45
war, 36–8; repression of, 35; strategic
misconceptions, 36
Communist Party of Pakistan (CPP):
dissolution, 56–7; foundation, 55–6;
involvement in Rawalpindi
Conspiracy Case, 56
Creagh, Gen. Sir O'Moore, 149
Curzon, Lord, 20, 143–4

Damodaran, K., 36
Dastidar, Sukhendu, 57, 76
Daud, Prince, 165–6, 167, 168
Dawn, 33, 76, 103, 111
Defence of Pakistan Regulations
(DPR), 110, 111, 112
Deoband, 18, 28
Dulles, John Foster, 48, 51
Dutt, R. Palme, 39, 156–7
Dyer, Gen., 15

East Bengal Communist Party
(EBCP), 92
East Pakistan, *see* Pakistan, East
East Pakistan Students Union
(EPSU), 58
Economist, The, 191
economy: Bhutto régime and, 101–7;
consequences of industrial growth,
71; economic indicators, 86;
exploitation of E. Pakistan, 46, 79–80;
growth of capitalism, 68–70, 71;
situation of new state, 43–4, 45–6
Engels, Friedrich, 21–2, 38
Eritrea, 203–4

Faiz, Faiz Ahmed, 161–2, 197
Far Eastern Economic Review, 177
Financial Times, The, 144
foreign policy: under Ayub, 71–6;
   Bhutto's, 123–8; of new state,
   50–53; *see also under* Afghanistan;
   China; India; United States of
   America
Free Press Journal, 35
Frontier Guardian, 111
Fukuyama, Francis, 190

Gandhi, Indira, 94, 124, 129, 130, 163
Gandhi, Mohandas: and Act of India,
   32; and agitation on Caliphate
   question, 26; economic nationalism,
   23; and Jinnah, 27; and Moplah
   uprising, 25; and 1946 strikes, 35;
   political style, 20–21
Gankovsky, Y. V., 147
Ghaddafi, Muammar al, 127
Ghosh, Ajoy, 58
Gracey, Gen. Sir Douglas, 158
Gromyko, Andrei, 173–4

Habib, Irfan, 22
Haig, Alexander, 192–3
Haji, Kunna Amed, 24
Halliday, Fred, 179
Haq, Abdul, 92
Haq, Dr Mahbubul, 70, 159
Harijan, 35
Harrison, Selig S., 114, 119
Hindu, The, 24
Hindu Mahasabha, 21
Hinduism: Hindu communalism, 21;
   Hindu–Muslim riots, 31, 34, 40;
   Indian National Congress and,
   20–21; and Moplah revolt, 24
Ho Chi Minh, 154–5
Hunter, W. W., 28–9
Hyat, Sir Sikander, 54, 55

Ibrahim, Mirza, 56, 77
Iftikhar-ud-Din, Mian, 49, 54, 55, 56,
   67, 76

Imroze, 56
India: British stimulation and
   utilization of religious divisions, 15–
   16; current attitudes towards
   Pakistan, 191–2; first general
   elections, 32–3; formation of Indian
   National Congress, 19; growth of
   Islam in, 16; Mughal state, 16–17;
   naval mutiny, 34, 35; Pakistan's
   foreign policy and, 124; revolt of
   1857, 17; US relations with, 189–90;
   weakness of communism in, 153–7;
   see also Communist Party of India;
   Indian National Congress
Indian National Congress: and Act of
   India, 32; and Caliphate question,
   26; campaign of civil disobedience,
   27; composition of, 22, 23; and first
   general elections, 32–3; formation of,
   19; and Hinduism, 20–21; and
   Moplah revolt, 23–4; Nehru report,
   31; and 1939–45 war, 33; political
   approach, 23
Iqbal, 30–31
Iran: Afghan policy, 167–8; armed
   forces in, 187–8; Islamic take-over,
   182–3; repression by the theocracy,
   185–6; revolution in, 163, 181–2;
   Shah of, 113–14, 120, 122, 126–7,
   160, 167
Islam: growth in India, 16; the
   'Islamic bomb', 127, 128; Islamic
   take-over in Iran, 182–3; rival
   interpretations of, 28; Shi'a sect, 183,
   184; Zia's utilization of, 139–42; *see
   also* Muslim League; Muslims; *ulema*
Islamic Government (Khomeini), 184

Jahanzeb, Gen., 119
Jalib, Habib, 76, 197
Jamaat-i-Islami, 28, 92, 127, 139–42,
   196
Jinnah, Fatima, 73
Jinnah, Mohammed Ali: and demands
   for establishment of Pakistan, 33, 34;
   failure to create party organization,

Jinnah Mohammed Ali – *contd*
150–51; and independent Pakistan, 41,
42–3; and language question, 44–5;
and naval strike, 35; and Nehru
report, 31; and partitioning of
provinces, 39; political style and
tactics, 27

Kabul Times, 169
Karmal, Babrak, 168, 169, 171, 172,
175, 176
Kashmir, 71–2, 74
Kasuri, Ahmed Raza, 135
Kennedy, John F., 72
Khan, Maj. Gen. Akbar, 56
Khan, Air Marshal Asghar, 152
Khan, Gen. Ayub: character, 66; and
Convention Muslim League, 73; and
coup of 1958, 62; and dissolution of
Constituent Assembly, 48; fall of, 80,
82; foreign relations, 71–6; and
USA, 51
Khan, Bawar, 109
Khan, Gen. Fazal Muqeem, 100, 101
Khan of Kalat, the, 115
Khan, Khan Abdul Ghaffar, 166
Khan, Khan Abdul Qayyum, 113
Khan, Liaquat Ali, 41, 43, 45, 51
Khan, Mairaj Mohammed, 78
Khan, M. S., 35
Khan, Murad, 195, 200–209
Khan, Nauroz, 116–17
Khan, Gen. Tikka, 90, 91, 96, 99–100,
123
Khan, Wali, 76, 113, 115, 166
Khan, Gen. Yahya, 81, 83, 89, 90, 96,
97, 98, 100
Khar, Mustafa, 78, 140, 191, 192
Khomeini, Ayatollah, 182, 184, 186,
187, 188
Khyber, Mir Akbar, 168
Kissinger, Henry, 96, 127–8
Krishak Samik party, 59
Kurdish movement, 204–5

Lawrence, John, 15

Lenin, V. I., 26, 36, 38
Lifschultz, Lawrence, 177, 191
Löwy, Michael, 147
Loyal Mohammedans of India (Sir
Syed Ahmed), 18
Lumumba, Patrice, 73

MacMunn, Sir George, 63
Maddison, Angus, 22, 63
Mansur, Ferozedin 'Dada', 56
Mao Tse-tung, 77, 154
Marri, Khair Baksh, 76, 114, 118
Martial Races of India, The
(MacMunn), 63
Marx, Karl, 21–2, 38, 147, 182
Maududi, Abul-Ala, 28, 139
Maududi, Maulana, 127
Mayo, Lord, 29
Mazdoor-Kissan Party (MKP), 113
Mengal, Asadullah, 121
Mengal, Ataullah, 76, 114, 116, 117–
18, 121, 122–3, 143
Menon, Narayan, 25
military/bureaucratic régimes, *see
under* Khan, Gen Ayub; Khan, Gen.
Yahya; Zia ul-Haq, Gen.
Minto, Lord, 19–20
Mirza, Iskander, 47, 49–50, 51, 63
Mohammed, Ghulam, 48, 49
Mohieddine, Khalid, 66
Moorer, Admiral Thomas, 190
Moplah revolt, 23–6
Morrison, Sir Theodore, 27
Mountbatten, Lord, 39
Mughal state: basis of rule, 16;
disintegration of, 16–17
Muslim Brotherhood, 66
Muslim League: alternatives available
to through electoral politics, 30–31;
composition, 29, 30; domination by
landlords, 43–4; and E. Pakistan, 45;
failure to become reliable political
party, 151; fear of free elections,
47–8; and first general elections, 32–3
foundation, 19–20; and independent
Pakistan, 41, 42, 43; and Indian

National Congress, 27; Maududi and, 28; and 1939–45 war, 33; Pakistani Left and, 55; and partitioning of provinces, 39–40

Muslims: agitation on Caliphate question, 26; and Bolshevism, 26; held responsible for Indian rebellion of 1857, 17; Hindu–Muslim riots, 31, 34, 40; hostility to British in India, 17, 18; Hunter Report and, 28–9; linguistic and social differences between Indian Muslims, 28; Moplah revolt, 23–6; political alternatives, 29–31; *see also* Islam; Muslim League; *ulema*

Nasser, Gamal Abdel, 52–3, 66, 184, 189

National Awami Party (NAP), 59, 76, 77–8, 87, 108, 114–15

Nawaz, Ahmed, 118

Nehru, Jawaharlal, 21, 32, 34, 51, 53, 72, 189; Nehru report, 31

New York Daily Tribune, 21

New York Times, 99, 113

Nixon, Richard M., 189

North-West Frontier Province (NWFP): Bhutto and, 112–13; NAP in, 76, 87, 108; weakness of communists in, 53, 157

Outlook, 111, 115

Pakistan: and Afghanistan, 180–81; centralism in, 146; characteristics of Pakistan army, 65–7; civil war, 91–6; consequences of industrial growth, 71; contradictions inherent in, 145–6; coup of 1958, 62, 67; demands for establishment of, 33–4; East/West economic indicators, 86; East/West educational disparities, 87; economic situation of new state, 43–4, 45–6; election-rigging, 73–4; first elections, 46–7; foreign policy of new state, 50–53; as 'front line state', 163;

government by the civil service, 48–9: growth of capitalism, 68–70, 71; Land Reform Commission, 67–8; language question, 44–5; the Left in, 53–61; Left in 1960s, decline of, 76–80; Left, problems of, 153–8; 'nationalities question', 146–50; and nuclear weapons, 127–8, 193; partitioning of the provinces, 39; political complications after independence, 41–3, 44; political discrimination against minority provinces, 149; political parties in, 150–53; survival of, issues involved in, 158–62, 194–7; terrorism in, 159–60; Yahya régime, 83–5; *see also* Baluchistan; Communist Party of Pakistan; economy; foreign policy; North-West Frontier Province; Pakistan, East; Pakistan People's Party; Punjab; Sind; *for events and policies under specific régimes, see* Bhutto, Zulfiqar Ali; Khan, Gen. Ayub; Zia-ul-Haq, Gen.

Pakistan, East: birth of Bangladesh, 95–6; economic exploitation of, 46, 79–80; economic indicators, 86; educational disparities cf. West, 87; Indian intervention in, 94–5; military assault on, 90–91; Rehman's election campaign, 84–7; Six-Point Programme for regional autonomy, 79–80; West Pakistan's refusal to consider concessions, 88–9; *see also* Awami League; Communist Party in East Pakistan; Rehman, Sheikh Mujibur

Pakistan National Alliance (PNA), 129–30

Pakistan People's Party: Bhutto's failure to transform into genuine political party, 108–9; and the economy, 101–7; election campaign, 84; establishment of, 78–9; failure to challenge army in 1971, 98; lack of organization since Bhutto's death,

Pakistan People's Party – *contd*
151–2; and local elections under Zia,
137; and 1977 election campaign,
128–30; repressive measures, 111
Pakistan Times, 49, 56, 68, 76
Palejo, Rasul Baksh, 137
Palestine question, 205–8
Papanek, Gustav, 69
People's Democratic Party of
Afghanistan (PDPA), 165, 168–71,
172, 175, 176, 179, 195
Pirzada, Hafiz, 152
Pol Pot, 174
Pravda, 177
Pritam, Amrita, 40
Punjab: dominant position of, 148;
mass chauvinism, 98; military
recruitment in, 65; NAP in, 76; PPP
in, 84, 107–8; partitioning of, 39;
radicals and the BPLF, 121–2;
reasons for weakness of communists
in, 53–5, 157; weakness of political
parties in, 152
Punjab Punch, 111
Puzanov, Alexander, 172

Qasuri, Ahmed Raza, 78

Rahim, J. A., 78, 108–9
Rahu, Fazil, 137
Ranadive, B. T., 57
Rashid, Rao, 142–3
Rashtriya Swayamsevak Sangh
(RSS), 21
Reagan, Ronald, 163, 175, 192–3
Rehman, Asad, 122
Rehman, I. A., 104
Rehman, Masihur, 77
Rehman, Sheikh Mujibur:
anti-communist campaign, 59; and
birth of Bangladesh, 95–6; and
Democratic Action Committee,
81–2; election campaign and victory,
84–7; Six-Point Programme, 79–80

Saadat, Anwar el, 66
Salem, Gamal, 66

Salim, Ahmed, 197
SAVAK, 168, 182
Sayed, G. M., 44
Shah of Iran, 113–14, 120, 122, 126–
7, 160, 167
Shah, Warith, 40
Shaukat, Sardar, 77
Shirokov, G. K., 23
Sikander, Arbab, 196
Sind: election rigging in, 210–14;
Muslim League in, 42; nationalist
movement in, 148; PPP in, 84, 103,
108, 151; peasant conference in, 137–
8; police attack on peasants in, 60;
weakness of communists in, 53, 157
Singh, Moni, 57, 76
Sino-Soviet rift, 76–8
Soho, Ismail, 130
South East Asia Defence
Organization (SEATO), 52, 97, 189
Soviet Union: intervention in
Afghanistan, 172–6; nature of
foreign policy, 173–4; projected
consequences of withdrawal from
Afghanistan, 179
Stalin, J. V., 36, 38, 58
Strategic Review, 190
Suhrawardy, H. S., 45, 48, 50, 53

Talpur, Mir Ghulam Ali, 68
Taraki, Noor Mohammed, 168, 169,
171
Tebhaga movement, 57
Tehrik-u-Istiqlal, 152
Toaha, Mohammed, 92
Trotsky, L., 26, 36, 123–4, 131, 160, 170
Turkey, 26

ulema: and Caliphate question, 26;
opposed by Sir Syed Ahmed, 17–18;
opposition to British in India, 17, 18;
and the Muslim League, 30
United States of America: Ayub's
relations with, 72–3, 75; Bhutto's
relations with, 126, 127–8; current
aims of military strategists, 190–91;

defeat in Vietnam, 174; involvement with Pakistan armed forces prior to Zia's coup, 134; military and economic aid to new state, 51–2; nature of foreign policy, 173; and Pakistani civil war, 96, 98; relations with India, 189–90; and situation in Iran and the Gulf, 194; support for military junta since Afghanistan intervention, 189–90
United States Military Assistance Advisory Group (USMAAG), 66–7
Urdu Digest, 111

Vietnam, 154
Viewpoint, 104
Von Vorys, Karl, 82

Washington Post, 99

Yepishev, Gen. Alexei, 172
Yogakshemam, 25

Zaheer, Sajjad, 55–6
Zahir Shah, King, 165, 166
Zia-ul Haq, Gen.: under Bhutto, 123; banning of 'political activity', 137–8; consolidation of rule, 138; diminution of civil service power, 143–4; local elections under, 137; political characteristics, 136; promise of elections, 133, 134, 135, 136; repressive measures, 138–9; seizure of power, 131, 133–5; utilization of Islam, 139–42
Zindagi, 111

Find out more about Penguin Books

We publish the largest range of titles of any English language paperback publisher. As well as novels, crime and science fiction, humour, biography and large-format illustrated books, Penguin series include *Pelican Books* (on the arts, sciences and current affairs), *Penguin Reference Books*, *Penguin Classics*, *Penguin Modern Classics*, *Penguin English Library* and *Penguin Handbooks* (on subjects from cookery and gardening to sport), as well as *Puffin Books* for children. Other series cover a wide variety of interests from poetry to crosswords, and there are also several newly formed series – *King Penguin*, *Penguin American Library*, *Penguin Diaries and Letters* and *Penguin Travel Library*.

We are an international publishing house, but for copyright reasons not every Penguin title is available in every country. To find out more about the Penguins available in your country please write to our U.K. office – Dept EP, Penguin Books Ltd, Harmondsworth, Middlesex UB7 0DA – unless you live in one of the following areas:

In the U.S.A.: Dept DG, Penguin Books, 299 Murray Hill Parkway, East Rutherford, New Jersey 07073.

In Canada: Penguin Books Canada Ltd, 2801 John Street, Markham, Ontario L3R 1B4.

In Australia: Marketing Department, Penguin Books Australia Ltd, P.O. Box 257, Ringwood, Victoria 3134.

In New Zealand: Marketing Department, Penguin Books (N.Z.) Ltd, P.O. Box 4019, Auckland 10.

In India: Penguin Overseas Ltd, 706 Eros Apartments, 56 Nehru Place, New Delhi 110019.